RACE WITH THE WIND

HOW AIR RACING ADVANCED AVIATION

BIRCH MATTHEWS

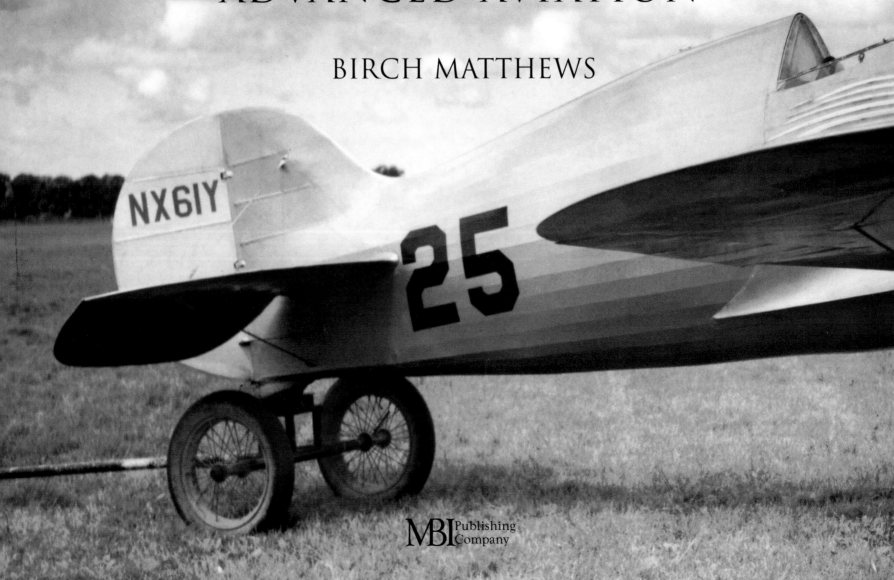

MBI Publishing Company

First published in 2001 by MBI Publishing Company, 729 Prospect Avenue, PO Box 1, Osceola, WI 54020-0001 USA

MBI Publishing Company books are also available at discounts in bulk quantity for industrial or sales-promotional use. For details write to Special Sales Manager at Motorbooks International Wholesalers & Distributors, 729 Prospect Avenue, PO Box 1, Osceola, WI 54020-0001 USA.

Library of Congress Cataloging-in-Publication Data Available
ISBN 0-7603-0729-6

Edited by Mike Haenggi
Designed by Katie Sonmor

Printed in Hong Kong

On the Front Cover: One of the most famous racing planes of all time was the Granville brothers Gee Bee Model R-1. With the very able hands of James H. Doolittle guiding this barrel-shaped racer around the pylon course, the R-1 captured the 1932 Thompson Trophy Race with relative ease. Pictured here is a Gee Bee R-2 replica. *John Garrett*

On the Back Cover: *Top:* Curtiss designs fared well in Schneider races. Shown here is the Curtiss R3C-2. Its unencumbered lines are apparent. Wing surface radiators on both the upper and lower flying surfaces cooled the Curtiss V-1400 engine. Note that the tail skid remains on the airplane, even though it has been equipped with pontoons.

Bottom: A dramatic race scene graced the cover of the program for the 1933 American Air Races held in Chicago. A speeding aircraft followed closely by a competitor swoops around the pylon to take the checkered flag and victory.

On the Frontispiece:
Curtiss developed a series of racing planes for both the Army and the Navy that were truly advanced. Pilot Bert Acosta, shown here with the 1921 Pulitzer Trophy, stands in front of Navy CR-1 racer. He actually won the race, held in Omaha, Nebraska, in the sister ship, CR-2. *Peter M. Bowers collection*

On the Title Page:
Roscoe Turner's Wedell-Williams Model 44 racer was upgraded with a more powerful Pratt & Whitney Hornet radial engine in 1934. To keep the frontal area of the large diameter Hornet to a minimum, the cowling incorporated "bulges" for the engine rocker arm housings. *Emil Strasser photo via Gerry Liang collection*

Contents

List of Figures

Acknowledgments

Any work of this nature is completed only with the kind assistance and encouragement of others. For this reason I am particularly indebted to the four individuals who contributed photographic material used to illustrate this book. Pete Bowers and John Garrett once again opened their massive photographic collections for my benefit. Gerry Liang, who inherited the late Emil Strasser's fine collection of race plane photographs, supplied numerous pictures of 1930s air racers. I only regret that Emil is not here to view the finished product. Hal Andrews, an old friend, graciously provided several key photographs that otherwise would not have been available to me.

This book consists of more than a series of illustrations, however. It was developed using a wide variety of research materials. Perhaps no person has a more extensive library of race-related memorabilia and documentation than John Garrett. As he has in the past, John again allowed me the privilege of researching his files. David Lednicer of Analytical Methods, Incorporated, supplied several key technical papers and pointed me in the direction of many more, especially with respect to airfoils. His frequent guidance in a number of technical matters was indispensable.

To the best of my knowledge, developing performance estimates for 1930s era airplanes has never been utilized as a research tool to assess the historical significance of various designs. What began as a somewhat vague concept in my mind was brought to reality by the very able assistance of Professor John D. Anderson, Jr., of the University of Maryland, and Professor Hubert Smith (Skip) from Pennsylvania State University. I appreciate not only their knowledgeable assistance and reference material, but their patience in guiding me through this process. Two other individuals, Daniel Whitney and David Lednicer, were extremely accommodating while helping me resolve technical issues involving aircraft engines, liquid cooling systems, and cooling drag considerations.

Walt Jefferies, one of the best aviation artists in the business, graciously responded to my call for assistance with art illustrations of classic airplanes from the 1930s. I am very appreciative of his artistic talents and willingness to support this effort. I am also grateful to aviation and racing historian Don Berliner. His fine book entitled *Victory Over the Wind* repeatedly proved an invaluable resource. The Menasco Manufacturing story was developed from a previous newsletter article I wrote some time ago. Author and engine historian Larry Rinek provided valuable information and peer review at that time, and so I thank him once again.

—Birch Matthews
Palos Verdes Peninsula

Chapter 1

Speed Merchants

The dawn speeds a man on his journey,
and speeds him too in his work.

Hesiod (Greek poet) c. 700 B.C.

The modern airplane design results from a complex weave of science and engineering involving many technical disciplines such as aerodynamics, materials, and chemistry. Each discipline can be shown to have a lengthy and time honored background. The history of aerodynamics, for instance, traces to antiquity and some of the great minds of that time: Aristotle, Archimedes, da Vinci.

The evolution of aeronautics may be viewed from a variety of technical perspectives, each with its own historical pedigree. Consider the advancement of material sciences. Airframe materials of construction for the early aviation pioneers were basically limited to wood, wire, and cloth. Development of aluminum alloys and fabrication techniques provided later designers with greater freedom to innovate. Modern titanium alloys and carbon composite materials provide even wider design horizons today.

One may similarly view advancements in aircraft design and performance by assessing improvements in propulsion. The aircraft piston engine began with the Wrights' anemic four-cylinder 12-horsepower water-cooled engine. By the end of World War II, liquid-cooled engines could generate 2,000 horsepower. Air-cooled radial engines were even more powerful, exemplified by the 3,000 horsepower Pratt & Whitney R-4360 first tested in 1941. Compared to the Wright brother's powerplant, this monstrous engine was 250 times more powerful. It took less than four decades to achieve this remarkable increase. What made this awesome aircraft engine development possible? It was facilitated by a number of factors: refinements in metallurgy and metal alloy composition; supercharger development based on a better understanding of internal aerodynamic flow; advances in engine cooling; and last but hardly least, significant progress in fuel technology.

One of the most famous racing planes of all time was the Granville brothers Gee Bee Model R-1. With the very able hands of James H. Doolittle guiding this barrel-shaped racer around the pylon course, the R-1 captured the 1932 Thompson Trophy Race with relative ease. Doolittle also established the landplane speed record of 294.418 miles per hour in this airplane. John Garrett collection

Recounting the underlying factors of aeronautical progress is a complex task. More easily discernible, however, are the results of this fascinating blend of technologies. Aircraft performance improved steadily, and at times rapidly, yielding greater range, more payload, higher altitudes, and greater speed. Although each of these attributes is important and worthy of study, this historical narrative is primarily concerned with speed.

Speed or velocity is the mathematical quotient derived from measures of distance and time. The terms or units assigned to velocity—feet per second, miles per hour, knots (nautical miles per hour), kilometers per hour, and Mach number—are applied as a matter of convention and convenience.[1] It is a fundamental quality describing every type of aircraft. More precisely, there are several defining aircraft speeds of compelling interest: maximum (at sea level and at altitude), climbing, landing, cruising, and terminal (diving) velocity. The relative importance assigned to each of these parameters depends upon the airplane mission. The most glamorous and frequently quoted number is maximum speed. Nowhere is high-speed performance more valued or sought after than in fighter and racing aircraft designs.[2]

Speed has always been an integral part of human history and particularly within the American culture. The "sport of kings" was wholeheartedly adopted in this country; fast horses were a component of fast mail delivery during the brief period of the romanticized Pony Express. Even our national pastime admires speed in pitching. A remarkably gifted baseball player named Leroy Paige (Satchel) once remarked: "Don't look back. Something may be gaining on you."[3] Although Satchel's forte was the grand old game (he was blessed with a rubber pitching arm), his quaint philosophical expression has merit. It was not a matter of the "devil take the hindmost." Quite the opposite, in fact. Paige spent his life confronting the future. The contemporary *Nemesis™* Formula One Air Racing Team expresses a similar message with the motto: "Chase the Dream, not the Competition."

Speed and air transportation go hand-in-hand. In the new millennium we think nothing of jetting across the continent in five hours—breakfast in Los Angeles, dinner in New York. Crossing the Atlantic is a four-hour jaunt by supersonic transport. Wagon

The pace of aeronautical progress has been exceedingly rapid. Aeroplanes, or flying machines as they were originally called, began as wooden structures and wings with thin airfoils. Only the wings were linen covered to provide the necessary lifting surfaces. Shown here is a Wright machine at Fort Myer, Virginia, on September 3, 1908. Wilbur Wright is at the wing tip in the foreground, while Orville Wright is standing between the landing skids with his back to the photographer. Peter M. Bowers collection

trains and sailing ships inched across these same obstacles in an earlier time. Journeys of yesteryear are merely trips of today, not terribly more significant than driving across town.

These startling advances dramatize the swift development of aircraft and engines. Spruce, wire, and linen construction materials have been successively replaced by aluminum, titanium, and graphite composites. Piston engines are being supplanted by turbine power. Fuel quality has traced a path from dreadful to superb. Aircraft landing speeds today exceed the maximum speeds of an earlier age. The transition has been so rapid we now often speak of Mach numbers rather than miles per hour, shock waves instead of shock chords. The lexicon of contemporary aeronautics would surely confound earlier generations.

SPEED RECORDS

Aircraft speeds advanced steadily, and at times dramatically, following the Wrights' first powered flight in December 1903. From that point until the beginning of World War II, a period of some 39 years, the world speed record increased on average well over 100 miles per hour every decade (Figure 1-1).

Consider that the Wright *Flyer* moved through the air at a majestic 7 miles per hour. Less than nine years later (February 1912), Jules Vedrines of France broke the 100-mile per hour barrier flying a Deperdussin monoplane. Equally impressive, the airplane also won the prestigious James Gordon Bennett Trophy Race that same year.

Armand Deperdussin was the financial angel behind the sinuous racers bearing his name; however, the genius responsible for the design was Louis Béchéreau, who perfected an elegant wooden fuselage of monocoque construction. With its cowled Gnôme rotary engine and generous propeller spinner, the Deperdussin was definitely state-of-the-art, and an aerodynamic harbinger of things to come. As for the wealthy Deperdussin, he earlier (1910) organized the Société pour les Appareils Deperdussin, more familiarly known as SPAD, a name that would soar to prominence during World War I. Deperdussin's personal fate was less kind, although equally deserving. He was arrested and convicted of swindling millions. As author Thomas G. Foxworth noted, "*le bon patron* received his [1913] Gordon Bennett victory congratulations in prison."[4]

During the pioneering years, France became the world center of aviation. Shown in this photograph is a 1911 French Blériot monoplane ready for takeoff. Note that a portion of the fuselage is covered with linen, an advancement compared to the earlier Wright machines. Wheels have replaced skids and the pilot sits in an upright position. As conventional as these features are now, they were novel in the early years. Peter M. Bowers collection

The world absolute speed record exceeded 200 miles per hour less than a decade after Vedrines broke the century mark. This time it was another Frenchman, distinguished Nieuport speed pilot Sadi Lecointe flying a Nieuport-Delage sesquiplane. Unlike the 1912 Deperdussin monoplane, the 1921 Nieuport-Delage was a well-streamlined biplane. (Single-wing craft did not become generally fashionable for several years to come.) The jump to 300 miles per hour occurred in 1928. Major Mario de Bernardi of Italy succeeded to this benchmark when he guided his Macchi M.52R to a speed of 318.624 miles per hour. In an amazingly short three-year period, Flight Lieutenant George Stainforth of Great Britain elevated the record to an unheard of 407.001 miles per hour on September 29, 1931. His aircraft was the elegant Supermarine S.6B. The last speed mark before World War II was established in 1939, when Germany's Flight Captain Fritz Wendel reached 469.224 miles per hour in a custom-built Messerschmitt Bf 209V-1.

In the 36 years between man's first powered flight and the beginning of World War II, the speed at which an airplane could move through the air increased an astounding 6,600 percent! This degree of improvement in such a brief time was truly remarkable, and historically was unparalleled.

BETWEEN WORLD WARS

The governing body for all aviation records is the International Aeronautics Federation (Fédération Aéronautic Internationale or FAI) founded in Paris during 1905.[5] This organization establishes the

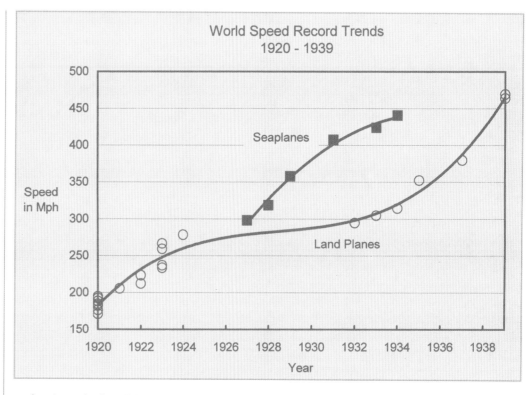

Seaplanes dominated the absolute speed record beginning in 1927 and extending through 1934. It was not until 1939, when Germany set two consecutive world speed marks, that seaplanes were finally overtaken by land-based airplanes. During the earlier years and before controllable-pitch propellers, seaplanes were used because water provided an essentially unlimited takeoff run. Beginning in about 1932, a separate land plane category was established. This graph shows the trends for both types of aircraft.

rules and sanctions new records. Until 1927, absolute speed records were held by land-based airplanes. With the advent of more and more powerful racing airplanes competing for the Schneider Trophy, seaplanes dominated the world of speed. There is no mystery to this phenomenon. Before controllable-pitch propellers these high-powered racers required long takeoff runs; the propeller pitch being optimized for high speed, not acceleration during takeoff. Most contemporary airports, if not all, lacked sufficient length to accommodate this requirement. So for a period of approximately seven years, the absolute speed record remained the exclusive domain of planes that could only take off and land on water.

A closer look at the progress of airplane maximum speed during the two decades between world wars is shown graphically in Figure 1-2. Two curves are presented, one for land-based planes and a second for seaplanes. For a period of several years (1927–1934) seaplane racers dominated the record books. No landplane could match, let alone exceed, the speeds set by seaplanes at that time. It was not until Flight Captains Hans Dietrle and Fritz Wendel successively broke the record in March and April 1939 that landplanes recaptured the absolute world speed record.

From 1920 through 1924, the absolute world speed record was set and broken no less than 15 times, rising from 171 miles per hour to 278 miles per hour. New landplane speed records languished for eight years as resources were poured into Schneider Trophy racers. In 1932, however, Jimmy Doolittle made a speed run of 294 miles per hour in

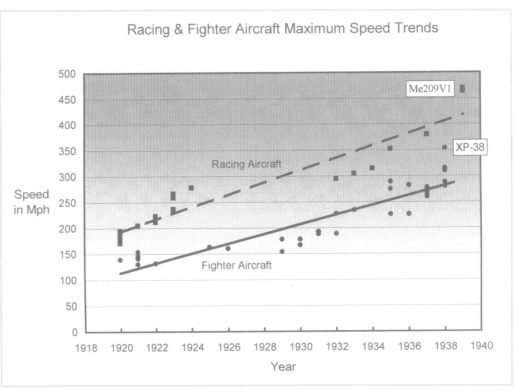

Racing aircraft were always faster than their military counterparts, the Navy fighter and Army pursuit planes. Both types of aircraft drew upon the same technology at any given point in time, so the gap in speeds between racer and fighter was reasonably constant as the trend lines in this chart illustrate. Fighter aircraft data points plotted in this graph represent sea level velocities, because absolute speed records established by racing planes of the time were made at or near this altitude. Note that the XP-38, for example, was capable of 400 miles per hour at about 20,000 feet. At sea level this historic fighter prototype was capable of only about 350 miles per hour.

World War I witnessed the introduction of airplanes to combat. This profile view of a Royal Aircraft Factory S.E.5 demonstrates the pronounced design advances, compared to prewar machines, that were made in just a few short years. Like most World War I aircraft, however, the S.E.5 retained thin airfoils in the wing design. It was mistakenly believed that thick airfoils possessed unacceptably high drag characteristics. Peter M. Bowers collection

Another World War I fighter of considerable fame was the SPAD XIII shown in this photograph. The importance of aerodynamic streamlining had yet to be fully appreciated by designers. The thin airfoils necessitated considerable external bracing. In addition, lift characteristics were such that a biplane configuration was required to generate sufficient lift to offset airplane gross weight. Peter M. Bowers collection

the famous Granville Brothers Gee Bee R-1 to grab the landplane record, now a separately recognized category. His record was broken four more times in the next five years as Jimmy Wedell, Raymond Delmotte (France), Howard Hughes and Hermann Wurster (Germany) all established new marks. The final world record prior to World War II was set by Fritz Wendel at a blistering speed of 469.224 miles per hour.[6]

COMPARISONS

With some appreciation for the progression in absolute speed for pure racing planes, it is reasonable to attempt a comparison with the similar advance of contemporary pursuit aircraft maximum speed. One way to make this comparison is to plot the trends of both racing and military pursuit (fighter) aircraft top speeds. Such a comparison is shown in Figure 1-3 for the 20-year period between world wars. The results are interesting but should be viewed with some caution.

The trend lines for both types of aircraft diverge slightly as a function of time. This is, in part, an artifact of the data. Race aircraft speeds represent sea level performance. To make the comparison, sea level performance was used or estimated for the military aircraft which exhibit better performance at altitude as advances in supercharging took place. Altitude was more important to military planners because the mission of pursuit aircraft was to intercept and attack invading bombers. Take the case of the Lockheed XP-38 which flew for the first time in early 1939. Its best performance was at 20,000 feet with a high speed of 413 miles per hour. At sea level the XP-38 had a speed of approximately 353 miles per hour. Similarly, the Bell XP-39 could attain 373 miles per hour at 15,000 feet, but only around 310 miles per hour on the deck. Nevertheless, America's three newest generations of pursuit aircraft were demonstrating increased performance. It was a tendency, indeed a requirement, that would continue.

That the maximum speed trend lines in Figure 1-3 for military and racing are roughly parallel is not surprising. The same aeronautical technology governed designers of both classes of aircraft. Racing aircraft, unencumbered by military necessities, were understandably faster. As shown in this illustration, the trend of internationally recognized speed records grew on average about 25 miles per hour per year during

Postwar military designs were little more than modest aerodynamic refinements of their predecessors. This early 1920s vintage Curtiss AT-5A (an advanced trainer), although powered with a 220-horsepower Wright J-5 engine, was quite similar in general configuration to a World War I fighter. The externally braced biplane arrangement was retained, showing little deference to the problem of parasite drag. One unseen improvement was the use of welded steel tube fuselage frames. Peter M. Bowers collection

the 1930s. A comparable number for fighter aircraft is around 20 miles per hour during the same period. The average (sea level) growth in speed difference between the two aircraft types accounts for the divergent trend. There was typically a little more than a 100-mile per hour differential between the two types, however.

Fighter aircraft sea level speeds in the 1935–1937 era hovered between 250 and 280 miles per hour, with better speeds at moderate altitudes. Emerging designs were targeted at much higher speeds with emphasis on performance at 20,000 feet. The XP-38 broke the 400-mile per hour barrier and this became a standard objective in future pursuit aircraft procurement. The very real prospect of war stimulated this desire for greater speed.

Comparing military combat and civil racing machines of that era is a reasonable though somewhat academic activity, due to the very different mission of each type. In a sense, air racing may be likened to aerial warfare. In each instance the aircraft are fast and maneuverable, the pace is physically as well as mentally demanding, and the element of risk is inherent. Here the simile ends, however. A racing pilot counts his purse at day's end. The combat pilot tallies a deadlier score.

THE AWAKENING

As might rationally be anticipated, race aircraft were consistently faster (Figure 1-3) than their military counterpart, the fighter or pursuit plane as they were then called. Public and pundit awareness of this actuality first surfaced during the 1929 National Air Races. The seed of this realization germinated when results were tallied for an unpretentious free-for-all (no restrictions) pylon race with the benign designation, "Event 26."[7] The winner was Douglas Davis of Atlanta, Georgia, flying a Travel Air *Mystery Ship*. Attention was suddenly drawn to the fact that in winning, Davis bested two competing military fighters, both biplanes, specially modified for the race. His victory margin was a scant 7 miles per hour (36.5 seconds) over the second-place finisher, Army Air Corps Lieutenant R. G. Breene in a Curtiss P-3A *Hawk*.[8] Nevertheless, criticism surfaced over a perceived deficiency in military aviation; a privately financed racing plane had proven to be faster than current Army and Navy pursuit aircraft. As Figure 1-3 illustrates, of course, pure race planes had always been faster than their military counterparts.

Doug Davis' 1929 victory in Event 26 coupled with the consistently higher speeds exhibited by racing aircraft compared to contemporary pursuit airplanes might indicate that the former manifestly contributed to the latter with respect to future fighter designs. Was air racing truly an aerial proving ground? More specifically, did racing contribute directly or indirectly to the design and development of World War II fighters? And if so, what was the nature of these contributions?

Certainly the grand and glorious races of the 1920s inspired new thinking. These were the renaissance days of the Schneider, Deutsch de la Meurthe, Pulitzer and Curtiss Marine trophy races. It was the beginning of serious aerodynamic drag reduction in airframe design, coupled with engine development aimed at increasing horsepower. In this country, sleek Curtiss and Verville racers dominated the early competition scene. Concurrently, Packard and Curtiss coaxed their liquid-cooled engine designs to greater and greater power levels. Government and industry participation was a common denominator behind these successful American and European racing programs.

The interest and emphasis various governments placed on the prestige associated with world absolute speed records and celebrated trophies ebbed and flowed with the passage of time. France led all countries, setting no less than 11

The Nieuport-Delage sesquiplane was a model of aerodynamic refinement in its day. Two airframes were built, one of which broke the world speed record and was the first airplane to exceed 200 miles per hour. This particular sesquiplane won the 1921 Coupe Deutsch race. Two Lamblin radiators, slung beneath the fuselage on the landing gear struts, provided cooling for the Hispano-Suiza Model 42 liquid-cooled engine. Peter M. Bowers collection

Biplanes represented the standard for Army fighters throughout the 1920s and into the early to mid-1930s. The Navy clung to this configuration even longer. Grumman biplanes were in service until the late 1930s. Shown here is the F3F-2 model. Bowing to advances in aerodynamic design, this squat Grumman fighter did incorporate retractable landing gear, a three-blade metal propeller, a full engine cowling, metal fuselage construction, and an enclosed cockpit. Judging from the antenna, it was also equipped with a radio. Peter M. Bowers collection

Supermarine designed some of the finest Schneider Trophy racers. This example is the Supermarine S.6 model (N247) shown being launched at Calshot, England. Flying Officer H.R.D. Waghorn won the 1929 Schneider event in this airplane with a speed of 328.63 miles per hour. Power for N247 was supplied by a Rolls-Royce "R" engine. John Garrett collection

records between 1920 and 1924 (Table 1-1). The great Curtiss racers of 1922–1923 captured the international speed record four times in a running battle with the speedy French Delage Sesquiplane design. In a shortsighted move, significant American funding for domestic military race plane design and construction evaporated after 1924, however. World dominance quickly reverted to Europe. The Schneider Trophy—augmented by a healthy dollop of nationalism—provided an impetus to vigorously pursue speed records in both Italy and England. Even after the trophy was permanently retired by England, Italy's fascist dictator, Benito Mussolini, envisioned bygone Roman glory through owning the world's speed record. Accordingly, the Italian high-speed flight group sought and gained the record. Pilot Francesco Agello tamed the Macchi-Castoldi MC.72 float plane long enough to break the record over Lake Garda on April 10, 1933, with a speed of 423.824 miles per hour. On October 23 of the following year, Agello raised the mark to an astonishing 440.678 miles per hour. His mark would stand for five years.

When the Travel Air Mystery Ship first appeared at the 1929 National Air Races in Cleveland, it instantly caught the eye of the press and race fans. Piloted by Doug Davis, the Mystery Ship handily won Event 26, predecessor of the famous Thompson Trophy Race. Davis bested both the Army and Navy entries in this contest. John Garrett collection

Germany belatedly entered the fray in 1939 with two consecutive absolute world speed records. The initial record was established on March 30, 1939. Hans Dieterle pushed a Heinkel He-100V-8 to 463.921 miles per hour. For the first time in many years, a land plane owned the record. Dieterle's ascendancy was short lived. Five days later, Fritz Wendel again broke the record. His mount was a Messerschmitt Me-209V-1. (Messerschmitt and Heinkel vied both for the prestigious speed record and, more importantly, for Luftwaffe fighter plane contracts that would follow.) In four separate passes on the prescribed course, Wendel inched ahead of his corporate rival by averaging 469.224 miles per hour. It was another propaganda windfall for the Third Reich.

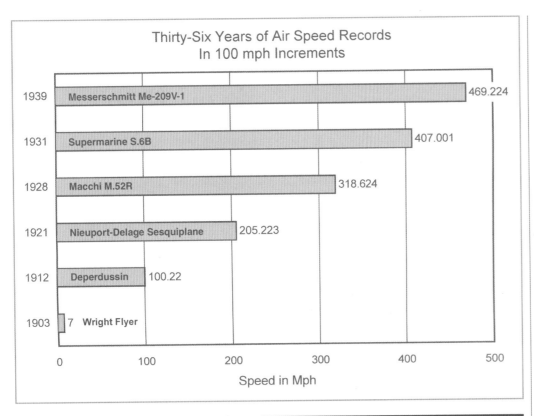

Thirty-Six Years of Air Speed Records
In 100 mph Increments

Year	Aircraft	Speed (Mph)
1939	Messerschmitt Me-209V-1	469.224
1931	Supermarine S.6B	407.001
1928	Macchi M.52R	318.624
1921	Nieuport-Delage Sesquiplane	205.223
1912	Deperdussin	100.22
1903	Wright Flyer	7

Speed in Mph

Aircraft speed advanced rapidly in the years following the Wright brothers' first powered flight. This chart illustrates the first airplane to reach or exceed each 100 miles per hour speed increment. It took only nine years to break the century mark. A few months before the outbreak of World War II in 1939, the Germans were closing in on the 500-mile per hour mark when they established a record of 469 miles per hour. The next record, 606 miles per hour, was set in November 1945 by the British in one of their Gloster Meteor IV jet-powered fighters. The piston engine was no longer king of speed.

Table 1-1

World Absolute Speed Records

Country	Period	Records
France	1920–1922	9
USA	1922–1923	4
France	1923–1924	2
Italy	1927–1928	2
England	1929–1931	2
Italy	1933–1934	2
Germany	1939	2

THE MILITARY TREND

American single-seat fighter airplanes in the years following World War I were modest extrapolations of wartime biplane designs. The Thomas–Morse MB-3 was the first-line Army Air Service fighter (nee pursuit) in 1921.[9] A squat compact biplane, the 12 cylinders of its water- cooled Hispano-Suiza Type H engine powered the MB-3 to a sea level maximum speed of 151 miles per hour.

With only a few daring experimental departures, the biplane motif continued as the standard within the Air Corps through 1933. The Navy clung steadfastly to biplanes for another four years.

The first truly modern cantilever low-wing monoplane fighter was a two-seat Army model derived from the fast commercial Lockheed DL-2 Sirius.[10] Known as the Detroit-Lockheed YP-24 (Wright Field Project No. XP-900), this airplane was a forerunner of the future. A 600-horsepower liquid-cooled Curtiss V-1570-23 engine drove the YP-24 with its retractable landing gear and enclosed cockpit to a top speed of 214.5 miles per hour at sea level. The YP-24 was a success. Unfortunately, Detroit Aircraft was not. It went bankrupt in late 1932 as the Great Depression deepened, dragging its Lockheed affiliate into receivership as well. The Army canceled its production order and eventually transferred the work in 1934 to Consolidated Aircraft Corporation in Buffalo, New York. Consolidated modified the design and put it into production (now designated the P-30/PB-2A). Part of the redesign included a turbosupercharged Curtiss V-1570, giving it excellent (for the time) performance at altitude.[11]

Boeing also developed a low-wing pursuit aircraft for the Air Corps in 1931. Not nearly as adventuresome as the Detroit XP-900 concept, the Boeing XP-936 project was still advanced compared to standard biplane fighters of that era. Boeing's design incorporated an air-cooled radial engine, retained the traditional open cockpit, a wire-braced wing, and a fixed landing gear arrangement. The latter, however, was generously faired and panted to minimize drag. Accepted by the Army, it became the Boeing P-26A when put into production.

By the end of that decade, and in spite of austere budgets, Army fighters progressed considerably from the days of the XP-900. The Curtiss P-40, a liquid-cooled engine derivative of the earlier radial air-cooled engine Curtiss P-36, had been ordered into production. The 350-mile per hour class P-40 would be the fighter backbone of Army aviation during the early part of World War II. Even more radical fighters were on the horizon, with the development of the Bell XP-39 and Lockheed XP-38, production variants of which (together with the P-40) saw combat during World War II. Fighter design did not stop with the closing of the decade. Spawned during 1940 were North American's P-51 Mustang and Republic's (formerly Seversky) P-47 Thunderbolt, both destined to play major roles in World War II.

In sharp contrast, the U.S. Navy sailed on with its sturdy barrel-chested Grumman F3F biplane fighters to the end of the 1930s; they were in production through May 1939. (War began in Europe

Germany posted the last pre-World War II absolute world speed record on April 26, 1939. This Messerschmitt Me 209V-1 raced through the timing traps at an average speed of 469.224 miles per hour, a piston engine record that remained unbroken for 30 years, until Darryl Greenamyer flew his Grumman F8F-2 Bearcat to an average speed record of 482.462 miles per hour on August 16, 1969. Peter M. Bowers collection

air-cooled radial engines, a dictum established in 1926. Out of this reliance grew two notable Navy fighters. Chance Vought won the 1938 Navy fighter competition with its famous gull-wing Corsair design. After a prolonged development session, the Corsair became one of two dominant Navy fighters during the conflict. The other, of course, was Grumman's F6F Hellcat, design of which was initiated in June 1941.

Of the seven Army and four Navy combat fighter types used in World War II, all were either in production or under development prior to December 7, 1941, when the Japanese attacked Pearl Harbor. These include the Lockheed P-38, Bell P-39, Curtiss P-40, Republic P-47, Northrop P-61 and Bell P-63 for the Army, and Brewster F2A, Grumman F4F, Vought F4U and Grumman F6F for the Navy. As Francis H. Dean (Diz) notes in his wonderful book on American fighter planes, over 100,000 of these machines were produced.[13] Were any of these designs facilitated or influenced by innovative American racing machines that preceded them?

four months later, when Germany attacked Poland.) Acknowledging the inevitable, however, Navy single-wing fighter development was inaugurated in 1937.[12] Two prewar designs were put into production: the Brewster F2A Buffalo and Grumman F4F Wildcat. The former was universally unsuited for combat against any contemporary first-line opponent. Fortunately, the F4F proved adequate until more advance carrier-based fighters could be put into service.

Unlike the Army Air Corps, which enthusiastically endorsed liquid-cooled engines for its fighter aircraft, Navy planners continued to rely solely on

As World War II approached, the United States was reequipping Army Air Corps fighter units with a new breed of aircraft. One of these was the Bell Airacobra. This particular variant is the YP-39 service test model on a test flight over Buffalo, New York. The Airacobra resulted from an Army type specification issued in early 1937. By the end of June 1941, only 77 Airacobras had been delivered to the Air Corps. Birch Matthews collection

The only other modern pursuit airplane available to the Air Corps at the beginning of World War II was the Curtiss P-40. An Allison-powered derivative of the Curtiss P-36, the P-40 was put into production earlier than the Bell P-39. Consequently, at the end of June 1941, some 350 P-40s had been received by the Air Corps. This particular airplane belonged to the 8th Pursuit Group, 35th Pursuit Squadron, based at Mitchell Field. Emil Strasser photo via Gerry Liang collection

THE CIVIL SECTOR

The mid-1920s marked the gradual beginning of a new era in aviation. Three events stimulated the change. Congress passed the Kelly Act in 1925, permitting private contractors to carry air mail. Within 12 months the Air Commerce Act was passed, establishing an Aeronautics Branch in the Commerce Department to regulate and promote civil aviation. The Army and Navy concurrently developed five-year plans for their respective air arms. These factors provided requirements and gave needed focus to an emerging industry.

Yet another impetus was the largesse of Daniel Guggenheim. The wealthy mining industrialist bestowed a series of endowments on seven educational institutes: New York University, California Institute of Technology, Stanford University, Georgia School (later Institute) of Technology, Massachusetts Institute of Technology, and the Universities of Michigan and Washington. These endowments created experimental facilities, and improved the education of formally trained aeronautical engineers. Six of the seven schools were oriented toward graduating engineers rather than scientists. The exception was Caltech, under the leadership of Robert Millikan, who induced Theodore von Kármán, formerly director of the Aachen Aerodynamics Institute in Germany, to join the faculty. The orientation at Caltech was scientific, while the other schools concentrated on engineering.

Science is a branch of knowledge or study dealing with a body of facts systematically arranged and showing the operation of general laws, frequently described mathematically. In contrast, engineering applies the laws and knowledge of scientific discovery to make practical devices.

Government and academic intervention tended to formalize the aircraft industry. Engineering disciplines, chiefly aerodynamics and stress analysis, began to play an increasingly important role as aircraft designs became more sophisticated. Industry and academe became closely intertwined. Aeronautical

The North American P-51 Mustang, originally designed and built for the British, was a second generation of evolving fighter designs. It featured improved aerodynamics, including a laminar flow wing section, as well as a low-drag engine cooling system. Seen here is the North American prototype identified as company Model NA 73X. North American Aviation, Birch Matthews collection

engineering graduates filled positions of leadership and management at major aircraft manufacturers as well as the Naval Aircraft Factory and the Army Air Corps Engineering Division at Wright Field. The gifted and intuitive designer-mechanics of an earlier era diminished in importance. Although the change was gradual in the beginning, it was an unstoppable consequence of industry maturation.

In contrast, with the dawn of the 1930s, new American racing airplane concepts reverted to the domain of individual "backyard" designers. This is not a denigration of the efforts of these innovative men. It is merely a statement of fact. Government financial support for racing projects in this country—

producing impressive victories in the prestigious Schneider and Pulitzer Races—simply evaporated. No other source adequately filled this vacuum. The aviation industry was struggling to overcome financial woes of the Depression. Sponsorship money was perennially scarce. No major aircraft manufacturer, with the single exception of Seversky, cared to invest long term in racing. Money was in short supply and the ever present possibility of bad publicity due to racing accidents was a strong consideration.

CLOSING THOUGHTS

With all the foregoing elements at play, is it still possible to assess what, if any, contributions

air racing may have made to aviation in general, and the evolution of fighter aircraft in particular? The answer is yes, although it will be necessary to establish a baseline and recount certain historical events. It is entirely feasible to consider a time line of aeronautical events and relate them to advancements in racing as well as fighter aircraft design. From a subjective viewpoint, it is also possible to comment about political and economic events that affected racing. And finally, one can evaluate the thoughts of contemporary commentators concerning the value of air racing. Hopefully from all of these perspectives some reasonable conclusions may be drawn.

Chapter 2

From the Old World to the New

For I dipped into the future, far as human eye could see, Saw the Vision of the world, and all the wonder that would be; Saw the heavens fill with commerce, argosies of magic sails, Pilots of the purple twilight, dropping down with costly bales . . .

Alfred, Lord Tennyson • *The Day Dream [1842]*

History, according to the *Random House Dictionary of the English Language*, is "the branch of knowledge dealing with past events." Each step in history is by definition a prelude to the future. William Shakespeare put this thought more elegantly in writing *The Tempest*: "What's past is prologue." Before delving into the aeronautical events and trends during a 20-year period between the two world conflicts of the twentieth century, a brief review of the pioneering years of flight should add a measure of perspective. What follows then is prologue, a baseline for chapters that follow.

Reciting a complete history of the pioneering years in aeronautics is not the intent. A credible state-of-the-art perspective can be gleaned by reviewing certain events. To show the rapid extent of aeronautical progress, it is necessary to examine the Wrights' historic first flight and a few characteristics of their famous 1903 *Flyer*.

Recording the first flight of the *Flyer* quite literally resided in the hands of a man named John Daniels. His name is but a footnote in history, yet he would provide visual evidence of what was about to take place. In his grasp was a pliable rubber bulb that, in turn, connected to a small rubber tube. The other end the tube was attached to a large tripod-mounted camera. A simple squeeze of the bulb sent a pressure pulse down the tube triggering a camera shutter. Overlaying this relatively simple apparatus was an awesome charge. It was Daniels' responsibility to rather precisely judge when to trip the shutter and thus record the first man-carrying powered airplane flight. Neither he nor the two determined brothers who designed and built the flying machine about to be tested were absolutely certain that this trial would be successful.

In spite of its fragile appearance, the Wrights demonstrated the feasibility of powered flight with this machine in December 1903. The airplane pictured here is a replica built in 1953 to commemorate the 50th anniversary of the first controlled powered flight in history. Unfortunately, this beautiful recreation was destroyed by fire on the night of February 22, 1978. Dustin Carter photo via John Garrett collection

If any of the handful of participants and witnesses that day were doubtful of the ultimate success of the Wrights' adventure, they did not include Wilbur and Orville. Their scientific approach toward the objective was backed by study, peer consultation, extensive wind tunnel testing, engine development and glider test flights to validate their design.

DECEMBER 17, 1903

At 10:35 A.M. on a gray overcast winter morning in December 1903, Orville Wright guided a frail looking wood and fabric-covered biplane as it

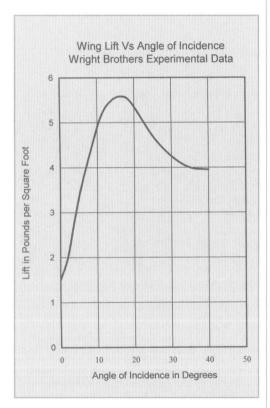

The Wrights experimented extensively, using their home-built wind tunnel. They gathered lift data for a number of airfoils before choosing a design for their Flyer. This figure illustrates the lift force in pounds for various angles of airfoil angle of attack. At or near a zero angle, this airfoil produced about 1.5 pounds of lift for each square foot of surface area. Knowing approximately how much their airplane would weigh, the Wrights were able to calculate the amount of wing surface required for flight.

This photograph of the Wright Flyer *is believed to have been taken as it rested on the sand dunes of Kitty Hawk on the Outer Banks of North Carolina. Prevailing winds together with a monorail launch system built by the Wrights got the* Flyer *airborne. More powerful engines and wheels on later models eventually permitted more conventional takeoffs.* John Garrett collection

gathered momentum down a launching rail. Wilbur Wright lay prone at the controls. Almost magically the craft lifted into a 27-mile per hour wind over a desolate sand-carpeted plain situated between Kitty Hawk and Big Kill Devil Hill on North Carolina's Outer Banks. Moments after liftoff, John Daniels reflexively squeezed the rubber bulb capturing the event for posterity. Wilbur's flight covered 120 feet, a trivial distance now, but a monumental achievement at the time. Ground speed was a very modest 7 miles per hour into the face of a relatively high wind velocity. Nonetheless, it was the first world airplane speed record.

The world watched and listened as astronaut Neil A. Armstrong stepped onto the moon surface 66 years later and said this was ". . . one small step for man, one giant leap for mankind."[1] The accomplishment of the Wright brothers was just as profound. The brief 120-foot powered flight was also a small step, but one signifying a previously unimaginable future.

The canard-style Wright *Flyer* was powered by a 201-cubic-inch water-cooled engine, whose four cylinders developed a modest 12 horsepower. Thrust was provided by two 8.5-foot propellers, which converted

engine shaft horsepower by means of chain drives. Lift was derived from two high-camber wings each spanning 40 feet and having chords of 6.5 feet. Empty weight of the *Flyer* was about 600 pounds, one-third of which was attributable to the engine. With pilot and a bit of fuel (0.4 gallon), it weighed approximately 750 pounds, giving it a wing loading of 0.7 pounds per square foot and a power loading of 62.5 pounds per horsepower.

Figure 2-2 is a plot of wind tunnel data showing lift versus airfoil angle of incidence measured by the Wright brothers for the airfoil used on their *Flyer*. At or near zero degrees angle of incidence, this airfoil generated about 1.5 pounds per square foot of lift. The wing surface area of the *Flyer* was 510 square feet. Thus the amount of lift that could be generated was 1.5 x 510 = 765 pounds, a figure consistent with the estimated gross weight of their vehicle. Regardless of how the Wright *Flyer* is characterized, however, only one is of paramount significance—it was the first powered airplane capable of sustained, controllable flight.

Early development of the airplane from conception to actuality was largely the province of private citizens and private capital, both here and in

The small biplane horizontal flying surfaces on the forward end of the Flyer *(on the left in this photograph) provided pitch control. Called "rudders," these flying surfaces were cable actuated by a lever in the pilot's hand. Vertical surfaces at the aft end of the machine were controllable and acted as rudders in the terminology of today. These devices, together with wing warping system, were controlled by movement of the pilot's hips for lateral and directional control. Dustin Carter photo via John Garrett collection*

The Flyer *suffered damage during a landing accident, as shown in this photograph taken on December 14, 1903. Note how the landing skids have dug into the sand. The pilot flew the machine from a prone position. Counter rotating propellers were employed and driven by chains affixed to the engine drive shaft. Harry Gann collection via John Garrett*

Europe. There were rare exceptions, of course. For example, Samuel P. Langley was funded both by the U.S. Army and the Smithsonian in his pioneering work. The fact remains, however, that few politicians or bureaucrats possessed sufficient vision to foresee commercial or military value in these awkward, dangerous, fragile and unreliable machines. After all, in the early 1900s only the courageous or foolhardy dared venture into the air.

Nevertheless, the airplane began to take form. From the box kite canard designs of the Wrights, heavier-than-air machines began evolving into a general format considered conventional today. Tractor engine designs gradually replaced pusher configurations. The monoplane was beginning to make an appearance, although biplanes would remain in vogue for years to come. Wheels replaced skids. Streamlining in rudimentary forms could be observed as open fuselage frameworks were eventually covered with fabric and sometimes a piece of sheet metal here and there. Although far from being paragons of reliability, more powerful engines were steadily materializing.

For years during the pioneering era of aeronautics, numerous designers sought to achieve absolute stability in their craft. If inherent equilibrium could be achieved, airplane safety would be greatly enhanced it was reasoned. Pilots could then turn their attention to navigation. The Wright brothers, to their everlasting credit, embarked on a different course. They recognized the need for positive control, and introduced the concept of wing warping for roll capability. This coupled with a canard elevator (it proved overly sensitive in the original *Flyer*) provided pitch authority. The Wrights patented their airplane design, including the wing warping mechanism.

When a young man from Hammondsport, New York, designed and built an airplane called the *Golden Flyer* during the spring of 1909, he incorporated mid-wing movable control surfaces—ailerons for lateral maneuvering. His name was Glenn H. Curtiss. Upon receiving news of the *Golden Flyer*, the Wrights took umbrage at what they perceived an infringement of their basic 1906 patent. Litigation soon followed and the issue dragged on in the courts for seven years. Only the exigencies of World War I produced a compromise in the interest of national security. Although wing warping and aileron deflection performed the

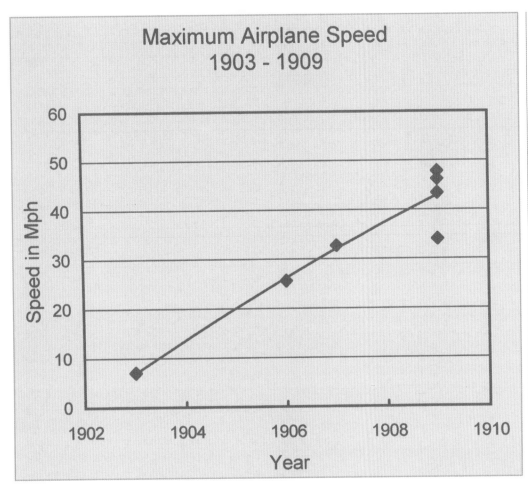

Maximum Airplane Speed
1903 - 1909

Airplane maximum speed advanced rapidly in the six years following the Wrights' famous powered flight, at 7 miles per hour. The average increase was about 7 miles per hour per year, as shown by the trend line in this plot. By the end of 1909, France's Louis established a world speed record of just under 48 miles per hour. At that time, France was the heart of aviation, a position it would retain through World War I.

same control function, the aileron was eminently more practical. Within a relatively short time it was universally adopted.

THE FIELD OF REIMS

Regardless of the more prosaic technical aspects of aerodynamics, stability and control, it can be said that aeronautical progress advanced with increasing momentum in the years following the Wrights' 1903 flight. Aircraft designers and pilots coaxed their mounts over longer distances, to higher altitudes and greater speeds. From December 1903 through the end of 1909, aircraft speed increased nearly seven-fold, as shown in Figure 2-2. The official world airplane speed record stood at 47.8 miles per hour at the end of this period.

Every form of locomotion in history has resulted in competitions of speed. It was inevitable that this competitive spirit would extend to the airways, once powered flight proved feasible. A scant six years after Kitty Hawk, the world's first air race was held near the historic town of Reims in northeastern France.[2] The origin of Reims dates to antiquity. Reims was the site of Durocotorum, the city of Remi, when France was part of a province (Gaul) belonging to the vast Roman Empire. The see of an archbishopric beginning in the eighth century, Reims played an exceptional role in French history. Its most notable landmark is the thirteenth century Reims Cathedral, considered one of the finest examples of Gothic architecture. As if to confirm its standing in French lore, Joan of Arc stood beside Charles VII in the cathedral as he was crowned King of France in 1492. With this heritage, it seems only fitting that the organizers selected Reims for the first air race.

Reims is located in the Province of Champagne, a picturesque land of vine-covered rolling hills forested with maple, elm and pine at higher elevations. The fertile region is famous for its sparkling wine, the creation of Dom Pérignon, a Benedictine monk who around 1700 discovered the unique double fermentation process, *méthode champenoise*, that gives this white wine its characteristic effervescence.

The race course was located 3 miles north of Reims on the plain of Béthany. Most of the contest sponsorship money came from regional champagne producers: Pommery, Möet et Chandon, Mercier, Mumm, Veuve, Cliquot, and Heidsieack-Monopole. It would not be hyperbole to suggest that champagne flowed like water during the course of the meet, and it was enjoyed by a grand ensemble of dignitaries and socialites from across Europe.

More than champagne and history drew people to Reims during the summer of 1909, however. It was excitement and the opportunity to see something most people had never witnessed: airplanes in flight. At that time, France was a hotbed of aeronautics—truly a world center of work in this new field. Experimentation was occurring in other nations as well—England, Germany, Italy, Austria, Russia and the United States. But in France these activities were embraced with characteristic French passion and enthusiasm. One *New York Times* writer in Paris described the fervor:

"This country is stark, raving mad on the subject of navigation of the air. Cabinet ministers, school boys, sedate matrons, boulevardiers, university professors, and sportsmen talk, think and dream of nothing else. The sidewalks are blocked by vendors demonstrating and selling toy flying machines. The kiosks are hung with journals, weeklies, and

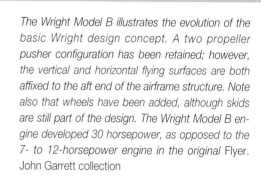

pamphlets devoted to the new interest. The windows are all occupied with the display of aeroplanes in varied situations. The post card craze has been revived beyond its previous magnitude through the enterprise of photographers with pictures of machines in flight. Hundreds of cinematography shows all over the city are thronged day and night by crowds eager to see representations of Blériot, Latham, and Farman in the air. The names of these and half a dozen other heroes of flight are the most renowned in France today."[3]

Arrangements for the Reims competition were made with an elegance and a *savoir-faire* at which the French excel. A railroad station was specially built to allow patrons direct access to the race course entrance some 300 meters away (984 feet). For those braving the trip by motor vehicle, a parking garage was erected. Once inside the grounds a covered grandstand and buffet restaurant awaited the more affluent. The open air restaurant allowed diners an unfettered view of activities both on the ground and in the air. Tables were covered with white linen, while guests were served by formally attired waiters. Less ostentatious but nonetheless serviceable viewing stands were provided for those of more modest means.

The Wright Model A was a two-place airplane shown here in flight. A notable change evident in this photograph is the position of the pilot and passenger, who are sitting upright, a more practical and comfortable arrangement than the prone position required in the Flyer. *The action of the figures on the ground suggest the horses were somewhat skeptical of this new flying creature about to overtake them. Note also the elegant carriages and formal attire of the spectators. John Garrett collection*

Another perspective of the Wright Model A in flight over Fort Myer, Virginia, on September 12, 1908. This picture provides an excellent view of the wing and "rudder" plan forms. Wing tip geometry is more accentuated than on the original Flyer. *Orville Wright was piloting the craft and his passenger was Army Major G.O. Squier. John Garrett collection*

Table 2-1

Grande Semaine d'Aviation de la Champagne Events & Prizes

Event	Prizes	Remarks
Grand Prix de la Champagne & de la Ville de Reims	1st 50,000 fr. 2nd 25,000 fr. 3rd 10,000 fr. 4th 5,000 fr. 5th 5,000 fr. 6th 5,000 fr.	Airplane race awarded to pilots covering the greatest distance without landing to refuel.
Grand Prix de Vitesse	1st 10,000 fr. 2nd 5,000 fr. 3rd 3,000 fr. 4th 2,000 fr.	Airplane speed race of three laps over a 10-kilometer course for a total of 30 kilometers (18.64 miles).
Prix des Passagers	1st 10,000 fr.	Passenger-carrying airplane race over 10-kilometer course (6.21 miles).
Prix de l'Altitude	1st 10,000 fr.	Airplane climb for maximum altitude.
Prix du Tour de Piste	1st 7,000 fr. 2nd 3,000 fr.	Airplane speed race of one lap over the 10-kilometer course (6.21 miles)
Prix des Aéronats	1st 10,000 fr.	Dirigible speed race of five laps over a 10-kilometer course for a total of 50 kilometers (31.07 miles)
Concours d'Atterrissage pour Ballons Sphériques	1st 1,000 fr. 2nd 500 fr. 3rd 300 fr. 4th 200 fr.	Balloon spot landing contest
Coupe d'Aviation Gordon – Bennett Cup 12,500 fr.	1st 25,000 fr.	Airplane speed race of two laps over a 10-kilometer course for a total of 20 kilometers (12.43 miles)
Éliminatoires Francaises	(no prize money)	Elimination trials for French entries in the Gordon Bennett Race

Source: Official 1909 program.

Seemingly no detail was overlooked. The plain on which the races would take place consisted largely of recently plowed fields, a decided disadvantage should a forced landing become necessary. Aesthetically, the grounds were landscaped with 1,200 transplanted pine trees. Each grandstand or tribune was surrounded by garden beds. The event was indeed quite *grande* in every respect.

The race course was rectangular in layout with pylons rising at each corner. The formal viewing facilities were located at the south end of the rectangle on one of the short legs of the course. Each long straightaway was 3,750 meters, while the shorter ends were 1,250 meters, yielding a total course length of 10,000 meters—10 kilometers.[4] Pilots and mechanics were provided with sheds in which to store and work on their airplanes. A special larger shed was constructed for dirigibles participating in the *Prix des Aéronats*.

Thus when it was announced there would be a *Grande Semaine d'Aviation de la Champagne*, preeminent builders and flyers were drawn like moths to a flame: Gabriel Voisin, Hubert Latham, Louis Blériot (who previously conquered the English Channel), Léon Delagrange, Paul Tissandier, Henri Farman, Louis Paulhan, and Eugène Lefebvre, were among the aviation celebrities in attendance (see Appendix A). Only one American arrived on the scene, and it was neither Orville or Wilbur Wright, as one might have justifiably anticipated. The brothers refused to participate. The lone representative was Glenn Hammond Curtiss, an up and coming flyer although certainly not at that time held in the same esteem as the Wrights.

An inquisitive and determined innovator, the lean 39-year old Curtiss first flew in 1908. He became involved in aviation in a somewhat circuitous way. Curtiss established a reputation in motorcycling—successfully designing and fabricating his own bikes and engines. A daring rider who was fully enthralled with the concept of speed, the future aeronaut set a world record of 137 miles per hour, riding his own creation on the hard sand surface of Ormond Beach, Florida. It was his facility with engines that attracted the attention of noted balloonist Thomas Baldwin, however. Their subsequent association brought Glenn Curtiss into the field of aviation, first with airships, then with airplanes. By 1909, Curtiss was designing and building flying machines of his own creation.

With the announcement of a great aviation meet to be held in France during the summer of 1909, Curtiss was belatedly urged to represent the Aeronautical Society of New York. It seems doubtful he needed a great deal of encouragement, though time was in short supply. By his own admission, Curtiss only began building his airplane in early July. Later, as he was about to sail for France on August 6, he told a *New York Times* reporter of his concern:

"I don't exactly like the manner in which I am, for I have had no opportunity to try out my new machine. I only knew definitely that I was to represent the Aero Club about four weeks ago, and it has been a rush to get the machine finished on time for shipment.

The Army took an interest in "flying machines" and contracted with the Wright brothers in December 1907 for a single example of their design for experimentation by the Signal Corps. The government author of the single page of specifications thought it worthwhile to require that the flying machine "be supported entirely by the reaction of the atmosphere and having no gas bag" for partial support. Seen here is the Wright Model C, powered by a 50-horsepower engine. John Garrett collection

30-kilometer Coupe d'Aviation Gordon Bennett race. He would also try his hand at the Tour Prix du Tour de Piste, a 10-kilometer, one-lap speed dash around the Reims course. Others could challenge for the altitude, distance and load-carrying events. Curtiss was intent upon preserving his airplane and engine. Although this caused some disgruntlement among the French press and other contestants, Curtiss reasoned that he did not have a spare airplane as did Latham, Blériot and Leblanc. One mishap and he was out of the competition. His conservative strategy was well founded, for there were numerous accidents and mechanical problems among the contestants. During one flight, Curtiss observed "his fallen rivals strewn around the course."[8]

Glenn Curtiss never lost his focus. He astounded many by capturing the Gordon Bennett aviation cup, edging out Louis Blériot by the nar-

Aviation contests took hold with the American public in 1910, based largely on the success and interest generated by the 1909 Reims meeting. The first American air race took place in Southern California at Domínguez Hills Rancho. By October that same year, for the price of $1, one could also attend the aviation meet at New York's Belmont Park, where many would see their first airplane. John Garrett collection

A Wright Model EX with a 30-horsepower engine is seen in this photograph. Wheels coupled with skids are part of the design, as are aft-mounted vertical and horizontal flying surfaces. This picture shows the modified controls adopted by the Wrights, consisting of a steering wheel mounted on a control column. Somehow the fuselage framework has a sturdier appearance when compared to earlier Wright airplanes. Their designs were slowly evolving as they gained experience. John Garrett collection

Unfortunately, it has not been guaranteed for delivery at Rheims (sic) before August 19, and that will give me but a few days for trials."[5]

Curtiss' strategy for the looming competition was straightforward. He built a light airframe and equipped it with a powerful engine, an approach endlessly imitated to this day. The product of his labors—only the second original Curtiss design—was simply named the Reims *Racer*. (His first design was called the *Gold Bug* or *Golden Flyer*.) Power was supplied by a

water-cooled V-8 engine also fashioned by Curtiss. It reportedly developed around 50 horsepower.[6] Empty weight of the finished craft is thought to have been around 400 pounds, while gross weight (including pilot and fuel) was stated as just under 550 pounds.[7]

Glenn Curtiss need not have fretted over the short amount of time for preparation. His airplane arrived at Reims in time for assembly and test. Choosing a conservative campaign, Curtiss elected to compete for the premier speed contest, the

rowest of margins. The differential was a mere 5.6 seconds, as Curtiss posted a winning speed of 47.07 miles per hour. Blériot's speed was 46.08 miles per hour. The lone American had bested the pride of France in an untried machine. Horatio Alger could not have done better.

STATE-OF-THE-ART

The physical characteristics of the 1906 Curtiss' Reims *Racer* and the original Wright *Flyer* provide a

Glenn Curtiss was the only American to arrive in France for the Grande Semaine d' Aviation de la Champagne *aerial competition at Reims in 1909. The intrepid flyer used what has become a time-honored tradition of building a lightweight airframe and powering it with a new and larger engine. The formula worked, and Curtiss departed France with the Coupe d'Aviation Gordon Bennett Trophy, much to the disappointment of many Frenchmen.* Peter M. Bowers collection

Curtiss sits in his Reims Racer as his crew prepares to start the engine. The photograph was taken at Reims. Hangars for the contestants and their airplanes may be seen to the rear of the airplane on the right. A small part of the elegant grandstands erected for the event are seen to the left of the plane. Peter M. Bowers collection

snapshot in time of the advancements made in just six short years. During the minuscule amount of time the original Wright airplane was actually in the air during its maiden flight, its ground speed was less than 10 miles per hour against a strong headwind. In still air the *Flyer* would have been faster, probably with a top speed approaching 25 or 30 miles per hour. Curtiss flew a rectangular course of 12.43 miles (20 kilometers) at Reims and was clocked at 47 miles per hour. Without the necessity of making pylon turns—flying more than 20 kilometers in the process—Curtiss would

have surely exceeded 50 miles per hour. We can generally say, therefore, that the Reims *Racer* was about twice as fast as the 1903 *Flyer*. We thus have a measure of progress, at least in terms of maximum speed.

The reasons why Curtiss' airplane was significantly faster than the Wright machine are straightforward. His airplane was lighter than the *Flyer* by about 200 pounds. It was also smaller, with a modest reduction in drag. Most important, Curtiss had the luxury of a more powerful and more reliable engine. It produced four times more

horsepower than what was available to the Wrights six years earlier.

It should be noted there were at least two engines sporting 60 horsepower at the Reims affair. But Curtiss was an engine man at heart, and his engine developed 50 *reliable* horsepower. This coupled with good pilotage and a relatively light airplane won the day. The Hammondsport "aeroplanist" returned to the United States with the most prestigious trophy of the meet.[9] He may have departed for Europe with a modicum of recognition, but he returned from the continent enjoying full-fledged fame.

THE HILLS OF DOMÍNGUEZ

Emboldened by the popularity and financial success of the Reims affair, a group of well-to-do Southern Californians, under the auspices of the Merchants and Manufacturers Association, determined to sponsor the very first air race on American soil. They were endowed with great enthusiasm, but also a measure of naiveté. That they would undertake this adventure at the beginning of 1910 is even more remarkable, considering that no powered flight had yet occurred west of the Rocky Mountains.

In stark contrast to the lush green vineyards of Béthany plain, the first air race in the United States occurred above a semiarid, almost totally barren field in Southern California. A 20,000-seat grandstand was erected, together with tents for the participants. The site was the Domínguez Ranch, part of a large (originally over 75,000 acres) Spanish land grant issued to Juan José Domínguez 126 years earlier. The grant was known as Rancho San Pedro and included all or part of the present day California cities of Redondo Beach, Gardena, Torrance, Compton, Wilmington, and Carson.[10]

From a practical point of view, Domínguez was well situated for an aviation competition. It was close to major population centers (Los Angeles and Long Beach), yet consisted of largely undeveloped land used primarily for raising cattle. A rail line ran near the area, allowing aircraft to be shipped to the races. A modest network of roads facilitated access by automobiles and horse-drawn wagons. The most desirable attribute, however, was the mild Southern California climate. Beyond those endowments, however, Domínguez offered far fewer amenities than the inaugural air race at Reims some four months earlier.

Table 2-2

Grande Semaine d'Aviation de la Champagne (1909 Reims Air Race) Schedule of Results

Event	Place	Pilot	Speed or Result
Grand Prix de la Champagne	1	Henri Farman	180.2 kilometers (112.0 miles)
	2	Compte De Lambert	154.65 kilometers (96.0 miles)
	3	Louis Paulhan	130.0 kilometers (80.8 miles)
	4	Compte De Lambert	116 kilometers (72.1 miles)
	5	Louis Paulhan	70 kilometers (43.5 miles)
	6	Glenn Curtiss	30 kilometers (18.6 miles)
	7	Eugène Lefebvre	21 kilometers (13.0 miles)
Grand Prix de Vitesse	1	Glenn Curtiss	25:49.4 - 43.31 mph
	2	Hubert Latham	26:33.2 - 42.12 mph
	3	Paul Tissandier	28:59.2 - 38.58 mph
	4	Eugène Lefebvre	29:00.0 - 38.57 mph
	5	Compte De Lambert	29:02.0 - 38.52 mph
	6	Hubert Latham	29:11.4 - 38.31 mph
	7	Louis Paulhan	32:49.8 - 34.07 mph
	8	Étienne Bunau-Varilla	42:25.8 - 26.36 mph
	9	Roger Sommer	70:33.0 - 15.85 mph
Prix des Passagers	1	Henri Farman	1 lap with two passengers in 10:39–17.49 mph
	2	Eugène Lefebrve	1 lap, with one passenger in 9:52.8–18.86 mph
			1 lap with one passenger in 11:20.8–16.42 mph
Prix de l' Altitude	1	Hubert Latham	155 meters (508.53 feet)
	2	Henri Farman	110 meters (360.89 feet)
	3	Louis Paulhan	90 meters (295.27 feet)
	4	Henri Rougier	55 meters (180.45 feet)
Prix du Tour de Piste	1	Louis Blériot	7:47.8 - 23.89 mph
	2	Glenn Curtiss	7:48.4 - 23.86 mph
	3	Hubert Latham (#29)	8:20.6 - 22.33 mph
	4	Hubert Latham (#13)	8:32.6 - 21.81 mph
	5	Eugène Lefebvre	8:58.8 - 20.75 mph
	6	Henri Farman	9:06.4 - 20.46 mph
	7	Paul Tissandier	9:26.2 - 19.74 mph
	8	Compte De Lambert	9:33.4 - 19.49 mph
	9	Alfred LeBlanc	9:50.8 - 18.92 mph
	10	Ferdinand Ferber	9:56.8 - 18.73 mph
	11	Roger Sommer	10:25.0 - 17.88 mph
	12	Étienne Bunau-Varilla	10:42.6 - 17.39 mph
	13	Louis Paulhan	10:50.0 - 17.20 mph
	14	Léon Delagrange	11:03.6 - 16.84 mph
	15	Georges Cockburn	11:23.6 - 16.35 mph
Prix des Aéronats	1		Dirigible Col. Renard at 1:14:14 - 25.11 mph
	2	Count de la Vaulx	Dirigible Zodiac at 1:25:1 - 21.68 mph

Continued next page

Notification of the planned Domínguez event and application for an Aero Club of America license was received via telegram at club headquarters in New York during late December 1909.[11] Details of the event were sparse. No program or schedule information was included nor were any conditions associated with the events mentioned, a condition which immediately alarmed Aero Club officials. A squabble quickly developed. The Aero Club was the umbrella governing body for all local United States aero clubs. It was also the arbiter of aviation records in consonance with the Fédération Aéronautique Internationale.[12]

Two issues immediately raised serious concerns in New York about the legitimacy of the planned meet. One was philosophical involving ultimate control, while the other bordered on healthy skepticism. With regard to the latter, a total purse subscription of $80,000 was claimed. This was a huge amount of money in 1910. More specifically, $30,000 was set aside for special achievements. Two of these awards were virtually unattainable. For instance, a grand prize of $10,000 was to be given to the "spherical balloon" pilot who could travel from Los Angeles to the Atlantic coast. The practicality of such a feat in 1910 apparently did not concern the promoters. Similarly, another $10,000 prize would be awarded to the dirigible airship pilot making a flight from Los Angeles to San Francisco. This too was a Herculean task. And finally, a third prize of the same amount was to be awarded to the pilot breaking all of the existing world records for speed, endurance, distance and altitude. The Domínguez sponsors defined this as meaning the contestant had to make a series of flights resulting in a speed of 50 miles per hour; remaining aloft 4 1/2 hours; traveling a distance of least 120 miles; and, ascending to a height of

Table 2-2

Event	Place	Pilot	Result
Concours d'Atterrissage pour Ballons Sphériques	1	Unknown	Unknown
	2		
	3		
	4		
Prix des Mechaniciens[(1)]	1	Étienne Bunau-Varilla	100 kilometers (62.1 miles)
	2	Henri Rougier	90 kilometers (55.9 miles)
Coupe d'Aviation	1	Glenn Curtiss	15:50.6 - 47.07 mph
Gordon –Bennett	2	Louis Blériot	15:56.2 - 46.80 mph
	3	Hubert Latham	17:32.0 - 42.54 mph
	4	Eugène Lefebrve	20:47.6. - 35.87 mph
Éliminatoires Francaises	1	Eugène Lefebrve	Completed 1 lap, 8:55.8 - 20.86 mph
	2	Louis Blériot	Completed less than 1 lap, but qualified
	3	Hubert Latham	Selected by committee

(1) This event was added during the races as a means of giving recognition to the mechanics who assisted the pilots in preparing and maintaining the aircraft. A portion of the prize money was awarded to each mechanic of the winning airplanes.

Sources: Various including the New York Times.

Table 2-3

Comparison of Wright *Flyer* & Curtiss Reims *Racer*

	Wright *Flyer*	Reims *Racer*
Year	**1903**	**1909**
Theoretical Speed	Ç 25 - 30 mph	Ç 50+ mph
Demonstrated Speed	Ç 10 mph	47.08 mph
Length	21.1 ft	31.1 ft
Wing Span	40.3 ft	30.0 ft
Wing Chord	6.5 ft	4.5 ft
Wing Area	510 ft^2	270 ft^2
Wing Loading	1.47 lb/ft^2	2.04 lb/ft^2
Lateral Control	Wing warping	Ailerons
Empty Weight	605 lb	Ç 400 lb
Gross Weight	Ç 750 lb	œ 550 lb
Engine Power	12 hp @ 1,090 rpm	50 hp
Power Loading	62.5 lb/hp	11 lb/hp
Displacement	201.1 cu in	
No. of Cylinders	4 (In line)	8 (V-8)
Engine Cooling	Water	Water
Engine Weight	200+ lb	

Sources: Don Berliner, Victory Over the Wind, 1983, p. 7.
Harry Combs, Kill Devil Hill, 1979, p. 221.

the sponsoring Merchants and Manufacturers Association and the Aero Club involved pilot licenses. At that time, the Aero Club of America (not the federal government) granted pilot licenses. Many individual experimenters did not have one, and the club banned competition between those who did and those who did not. (The Domínguez sponsors received 45 entries for the airplane events alone, most of whom did not possess a license.) Association spokesman Dick Ferris rebelled. "This contradicts the precepts of the Aero club of America in that all interests be for the advancement of aviation and devoid of commercial profit."[15] Obviously licenses and aero club membership were not granted free of charge. Ferris went on to note this requirement would preclude many from participating simply because they had not been able to join a local club or the national organization. Telltale signs of hypocrisy did not end there. In spite of all the high-minded altruistic talk emanating from New York, Ferris went on to state:

"The Aero Club of America demands that none of its members shall participate in a commercial exhibition, and that all flights made by them must be made for the true advancement of aviation, and yet Glenn H. Curtiss, a member of that club, and other entrants, members of affiliated clubs, have demanded guarantees as a condition of flying. The fact is, that when we wired Mr. Curtiss and members of [other] aero clubs . . . asking whether they could participate in our meeting, they replied demanding guarantees ranging from $3,000 to $10,000 each."[16]

So much for altruism versus the profit motive. Ferris and his associates eventually capitulated, however. Glenn Curtiss, who rose to prominence with

Glenn Curtiss, after winning the Gordon Bennett Trophy at the 1909 Reims contest, entered the Domínguez meet of January 1910. This was the first air race ever held in America. Curtiss' performance was not as spectacular as his accomplishment at Reims, but he still walked away with $6,000 in prize money. This was a tidy sum in 1910. John Garrett collection

Domínguez may not have achieved the lofty social acclaim and status accorded the Reims contest with its prestigious Gordon Bennett Trophy, but it did gain recognition as the first American air race, something that may have irritated some East Coast afficionados. The race was well attended both by participants and fans. As expected, teams Paulhan and Curtiss garnered most of the prizes. In fact, Paulhan became the darling of the press. His frequent and often daring exhibitions (some would say reckless) made him the unquestioned favorite of the crowd.

his recent Reims victory, received a $10,000 guarantee up front, as did the French contingent led by Louis Paulhan. In the latter instance, the guarantee was $25,000. To insure success Ferris needed such star attractions. The French were preeminent in aeronautics and Curtiss was a homegrown hero. Although Paulhan had not won at Reims, he did place in the top four events. In contrast to Curtiss' taciturn character, Paulhan was dashing and charismatic and sure to garner headlines. An accommodation was eventually reached, and a sanctioning license granted, but not without conditions.

The Aero Club's overriding influence on the Domínguez affair is readily illustrated. Club rules prevailed and only licensed pilots were allowed to compete. From the list of 45 airplane entries, the number dwindled to 11. Certainly there were other reasons why some of these people could not participate including an embarrassing inability to get their mounts airborne. In spite of this, the licensing factor was significant and ruled out a number of western entries. The second factor involved prize allocations and magnitudes. Courtlandt Bishop dictated what these would be as shown in Table 2-5. Absent, lest anyone profit overly much, were the three $10,000 grand awards mentioned previously. The special "appearance guarantees" to Curtiss and the French syndicate remained untouched, however. Lastly, Bishop was appointed chairman of the judges committee.

Regardless of disagreements or misunderstandings between the sponsors and the Aero Club—long-distance communications in that era were relatively primitive—the Domínguez meeting was successful and popular. Each day of the contest running from January 10 through January 20 drew crowds in excess of 20,000 spectators to the field. Certainly there were even more outside the grounds.

GRANDE SEMAINE D'AVIATION DE LA CHAMPAGNE

REIMS
DU 3 AU 10 JUILLET
1910
250 000 FRANCS DE PRIX
EPREUVES FRANÇAISES DE LA COUPE GORDON BENNETT

The very first air race took place outside Reims, France, during 1909, only six years after the Wright brothers' epic flight at Kitty Hawk, North Carolina. The 1909 contest was a huge success, drawing spectators from nearly all walks of life. The grand event was repeated in 1910, offering 210,000 francs in prize money. John Garrett collection

One of Glenn Curtiss' more important contributions to aeronautics was the use of what became known as ailerons. He opted for controllable surfaces mounted between the upper and lower wings, in place of wing warping as pioneered by the Wrights. Although these devices would eventually be incorporated as integral parts of the wing surfaces, the basic Curtiss approach was more practical than wing warping. John Garrett collection

Table 2-4

1910 Domínguez Aviation Meet Participants

Race No.	Pilot	Aircraft
Airplanes		
1	Louis Paulhan	Farman Biplane
2	Louis Paulhan	Blériot Monoplane
3	Didier Masson	Blériot Monoplane
4	Charles Miscarol	Blériot Monoplane
5	Charles K. Hamilton	Curtiss Biplane
6	Glenn H. Curtiss	Curtiss Biplane
7	J. C. Klassen	California Monoplane
8	Roy Knabenshue	Wright Biplane (modified)
9	Charles F. Willard	Curtiss Biplane
10	H. W. Gill	Gill-Dash
11	Clifford B. Harmon	Curtiss Biplane
Dirigibles		
1	Roy Knabenshue	5,500 Cu Ft
2	Lincoln Beachy	5,500 Cu Ft
3	Lt. Beck	20,000 Cu Ft
Balloons		
1	Roy Knabenshue	The Dick Ferris
2	George B. Harrison	City of Los Angeles
3	Clifford B. Harmon	City of New York
4	Frank J. Kanne	City of Peoria
5	J. C. Mars	City of Oakland
6	Charles D. Colby	Co. A, Signal Corps, Cal. Nat. Guard
7	A. C. Pillsbury	The Fairy

Source: Official program

Table 2-5

1910 Domínguez Aviation Meet Awards

Best Speed for 10 Laps	$3,000
	$2,000
	$500
Highest Altitude	$3,000
	$2,000
	$500
Endurance	$3,000
	$2,000
	$500
Best Flight With Passenger	$1,000
	$500
Slowest Lap	$500
Quickest Start	$250
Shortest Takeoff Distance	$250

Source: New York Times, January 13, 1910, p. 1.

THE END OF INNOCENCE

For the next four years, the airplane (or aeroplane as it was often referred to during the pioneering years) remained the province of the wealthy and venturesome. Governments were slow to recognize any true value in aviation. Granted, it was difficult to envision useful military or commercial applications for these frail early craft, in most cases barely able to lift one person aloft. Nevertheless the U.S. Army Signal Corps issued a one page specification on December 23, 1907, for "a heavier-than-air flying machine."[17] The Army's specification was tailored around a proposal the Wrights had tendered shortly before Thanksgiving that same year. Although there was surprising competition, only the Wrights met all qualifications. They delivered one example of their Wright Model A design in 1908. From this humble beginning evolved the mightiest air force in the world. Coincidentally, delivery of the Wright airplane also marked the beginning of a parallel evolution of military and racing aircraft, about which, more later.

Roy Knabenshue of Toledo, Ohio, entered a dirigible in the 1910 Domínguez meet. He is shown here bringing the ungainly looking craft in for a landing. From a historic perspective, it is unfortunate that the site of the first United States air race has been converted into a large industrial park. Security First National Bank Historical Collection via John Garrett

In the period between 1908 and August 1914, when World War I began, the airplane advanced rapidly. Landing skids gave way to wheels. Engines became more powerful, allowing greater payloads. The tractor configuration largely replaced the pusher. The aileron was conceived and quickly substituted for the Wright Brothers concept of wing warping. One aspect of these early aircraft designs remained relatively constant, however. This was the thin airfoil characteristic of virtually all wing structures.

THE SCIENTIFIC PROCESS

Aeronautical science, like the fragile craft at Reims and Domínguez, was in its infancy when the these extravaganzas took place. Nevertheless, serious minds were at work. One of them was that of 41-year-old Frederick William Lanchester in England. Belatedly recognized for his contributions, Lanchester published his book, *Aerodynamics,* in London during 1907. Lanchester visualized a circulatory flow around a body producing lift. He also foresaw the generation of drag-producing wing tip vortices. In Germany, meanwhile, mathematician Wilhelm Kutta was developing a mathematical expression for lift. Kutta, whose work was first published in 1902, was unaware of Lanchester's work. (The age of instant communication and systematic dissemination of scientific discovery remained in the distant future.) Yet another seminal work was presented in 1904 by Ludwig Prandtl at the Third International Mathematical Congress in Heidelberg. Prandtl, who was born in Bavaria in 1874, contributed the boundary layer concept to the growing body of aerodynamic theory.

In spite of some remarkable advances in understanding fundamental aerodynamic precepts, one design criterion persisted for years. This was the use of very thin wing airfoil sections. Thin airfoils posed several disadvantages to the designer. With the materials available in those years for airframe construction—largely wood—wings had to be structurally braced by external struts and wires. This was conveniently done using multiple wings with external bracing. Using more than one wing also provided adequate lift in an era when thin airfoil sections had relatively poor lift to drag ratios. The penalty was increased drag and decreased aircraft performance. Equally important, thin wing sections precluded using the structure for any subsidiary purpose such as

This 1910 photograph of a Curtiss airplane flown by pilot J. J. Ward provides an excellent view of the wing design. Typical of the pioneering years of aviation, a very thin high camber airfoil was employed. Also note the tricycle landing gear and a complete absence of any skids, as employed by the Wrights. Today almost all aircraft use a tricycle landing gear. Peter M. Bowers collection

fuel storage, baggage, armament, and stowing retractable landing gear. Thin wing sections limited the evolution of practical aircraft design.

Why did this occur? Why did pioneers such as the Wrights, Blériot, Langley and a host of others constrict their designs by utilizing thin airfoils? Author John Anderson, Jr. explains what happened in his excellent book, *A History of Aerodynamics*:

"Early wind-tunnel tests, including those of the Wright brothers, comparing thin and thick airfoils had shown that thick airfoils led to higher drag, but those early tests involved only low Reynolds numbers, and the data were misleading. Modern studies of low [Reynolds number] flows over thick airfoils clearly show high drag coefficients and low lift coefficients . . ." for very thin airfoil sections.[18]

The Reynolds number to which Anderson refers is a mathematical parameter used to describe the flow of a fluid, in this instance air in a wind tunnel.[19] Below a threshold Reynolds number, the flow is always laminar. Conversely, above a higher (upper critical) Reynolds value, the air flow is and remains turbulent. In between is a regime of transition.

The problem was that early wind tunnels had very low wind velocities compared to the speed at

which an aircraft moves through the air. Variations between wind tunnel and flight Reynolds numbers could easily be a factor of 20 to 30 or more, flight numbers being higher. A bias against thick airfoils in the early years at very low wind tunnel Reynolds numbers was due to the "creation of a laminar-separation bubble near the [wing test section] leading edge . . ."[20] If these bubbles broke down, a very large flow separation ensued, producing a significant drag increase. This phenomenon does not occur at higher Reynolds numbers (in tunnel tests or in flight). It remained for German experimentalists during World War I to show that thicker, rather than thinner, airfoil sections had more beneficial lift and drag relationships. These newer sections appeared as the Göttingen numbered series of airfoils. As Anderson points out, this contributed to the excellent performance of the 1917 Fokker D-VII, which incorporated a much thicker airfoil than its British and French foes.

Although definite inroads were being made in the science of aerodynamics, it is important to note that aircraft were largely the product of skilled craftsmen using empirical knowledge. The integration of scientific findings into design considerations would not occur for some time.

Chapter 3

The Roaring Twenties

. . . something should be said as to the general status and general usefulness of the high-speed airplane. Is it merely a vehicle of sport, a man-carrying projectile devoid of practical utility, or is it rather a valuable accessory in the progress toward the improvement of those airplanes designed for a definite task in commerce or in war?

Edward P. Warner • *Professor of Aeronautics*
Massachusetts Institute of Technology

The pace of pioneering aeronautical development quickened with the passage of time. European experimental work with cantilever wing monoplanes was initiated in 1910 by Junkers at Aachen Technische Hochscule, and by Levavasseur of Antoinette. Junkers investigated stressed skin construction the following year, wherein the skin covering a structure such as a wing or fuselage bears some or all of the load.[1]

The field of pure scientific research was becoming accepted and respectable in the academic world as well. The German University of Göttingen was rapidly gaining recognition as a center for aerodynamic research in the relatively close-knit European scientific community. The National Physical Laboratory in England and the French Aerodynamical Laboratory in Paris were also conducting investigations in the field. That same year, the Massachusetts Institute of Technology began teaching courses in aeronautical engineering. Little did any of these institutions realize that the quiescent methodical academic environment would become more turbulent in the months ahead.

Barbara Tuchman used a fitting title for her classic history of World War I, *The Guns of August*. The guns did indeed roar across Europe in 1914.[2] It would prove a bloody conflict. It would also introduce the airplane as an offensive instrument of war. The fighter aircraft was born, and names like Spad and Fokker became symbols as war in the sky spread over Europe.

Another area of dawning interest was the concept of a retractable landing gear. This was first reduced to practice, albeit somewhat primitively, with the German Wiencziers monoplane during 1911. It did not find acceptance. Others would pursue the idea. As author Thomas G. Foxworth notes, "Walter Brierley of the British Varioplane Company patented a retractable-gear scheme in 1914 . . ."[3] In the United States, Princeton student Charles Hampton Grant, an avid airplane modeler, laid out a fighter airplane design in 1917 with what he termed a "collapsible gear." This rather unfortunate choice of words never became popular, most likely due to the unintended connotation.

The SPAD XIII (Société pour Aviation et les Dérivés) was one of the better aircraft of World War I. American ace Captain Eddie Rickenbacker poses beside his airplane in this photograph. The SPAD design was not very aerodynamically clean, but it performed well enough with its 235-horsepower Hispano engine. Top speed was 135 miles per hour. Peter M. Bowers collection

Contemporary designers were aware that fixed landing gear was a nontrivial source of drag. The practicality of retractable gear remained illusive for several reasons, however. Perhaps the most important concern was one of reliability. What if the gear retracted but wouldn't extend? The result would be disconcerting if not downright perilous for a trusting pilot. Not far behind reliability concerns were those of added complexity, weight and cost. Distrust of retractable landing gears lingered for many, many years. Even the remarkably advanced transports culminating in the Douglas DC-3 of the early 1930s did not have fully retractable landing gears. In the retracted position, a goodly part of the wheel was still exposed to the slipstream. If the gear would not extend the pilot was comforted in knowing that he could still put the airplane down without undue damage, because the wheels were exposed and could still rotate.

POST-WORLD WAR I

One particularly interesting project occurred at the beginning of the decade. This was the Dayton-Wright

From an aerodynamic perspective the Fokker D-VII was a significant step forward. Fokker engineers incorporated a thick airfoil section and a comparatively high aspect ratio wing setup, probably influenced by the work of Germany's Ludwig Prandtl. The D-VII proved to be a formidable adversary. Prandtl developed the boundary layer theory, thus forming one of the building blocks of modern aerodynamics. Peter M. Bowers collection

The Royal Aircraft Factory S.E.5A was perhaps typical of World War I fighter designs. Like so many of its contemporaries, the S.E.5A relied upon a thin airfoil section, and little attention was devoted to streamlining. The flat radiator core serving the Hispano liquid-cooled engine is but one indication of this fact. It reportedly had a top speed of 121 miles per hour. Peter M. Bowers collection

Model RB-1 racing monoplane of 1920. Built specifically for entry in the 1920 James Gordon Bennett Aviation Cup competition, the Dayton-Wright design was literally quite revolutionary in concept. Not only did it incorporate a retractable landing gear, but also a 21-foot, 2-inch span, variable-camber cantilever wing. The entire airframe was made as aerodynamically clean as possible, marred only by a flat-faced radiator for the liquid-cooled six-cylinder Hall Scott engine.

The complexity of the variable-camber wing proved to be the undoing of the Dayton-Wright racer. Pilot Howard M. Rinehart took off from the Villesauvage Aerodrome, Éstampes airfield at 2:14 P.M. on the afternoon of September 28, 1920, for his three-lap run at the Bennett Cup. A broken cable resulting in a jammed leading edge slat forced his return to the field before completing even one lap. The innovative and forward looking Dayton-Wright racer was out of the race almost before it started.

RACING EVOLUTION

The character of air racing changed following World War I for two significant reasons. One rather

The Douglas DC-3 became immensely popular with the air lines during the 1930s. One of its features was a retractable landing gear. The wheels rotated aft into the engine nacelle, a common design approach in this era. This 1948 photograph illustrates details of the gear extended for a landing by this DC-3A belonging to Southwest Airways, as it goes over the fence at San Francisco's airport. Bill Larkins photo via Peter M. Bowers collection

obvious factor was the rapid aeronautical advancement spawned by the exigencies of war. Equally important, if not more so, was industry and government involvement in air racing. This equated to more available funding. The epitome of this coupling could be seen in the Pulitzer and Schneider Trophy Races.

The concept of an international competition involving seaplanes devolved from the imagination of Jacques P. Schneider. Born near Paris into a wealthy family, Schneider could indulge his taste for adventure by racing hydroplane boats, and later through ballooning and piloting heavier-than-air machines during the pioneering years of flight. Trained as an engineer, Schneider's pragmatic mind led him to conclude that seaplanes were the wave of the future. He based this deduction on the fact that almost three-quarters of the earth surface is covered by water. Water offered unlimited takeoff distances for large heavy aircraft. From his perspective, this was highly desirable. (He did not foresee dynamic advances in technology that within 20 years would render his philosophy obsolete). Schneider consequently announced in 1912 the establishment of a Coupe d'Aviation Maritime Jacques Schneider. The

first competition was held the following year off the coast of Monaco. It was repeated in 1914—mere months before the outbreak of World War I. Competition resumed in 1919 amid inept management planning and execution. The contest committee ultimately declared the contest void. Matters improved after that and nine more races were held until Great Britain permanently retired the cup after her third victory in 1931.

The Schneider aircraft are technologically interesting, although the fact that this is true is not without a touch of irony. Jacques Schneider envisioned the contest would be an impetus toward developing fast dependable seaplanes. More than that, he hoped it would foster viable designs possessing commercial value. Author Derek James notes that Schneider took pains to establish contest rules aimed at "producing not simply high-speed racing 'freaks' but practical aircraft that were capable of operation from the open sea, were reliable and had good range."[74] It was not to be.

The first few contests may have been consistent with Schneider's goal. It did not take long before winning the cup became a matter of urgent national prestige, especially among European nations, where

historical animosities smoldered just below the political surface. Winning meant having the fastest airplane. Range and reliability requirements existed only for the length of the race, a matter of 20 miles or less. The racers consequently became single-point designs, focused exclusively on high speed at sea level.

In a real sense capturing the Schneider Trophy also became synonymous with setting the absolute world's speed record for a decade or so. Several Schneider class racers were used or intended for this purpose. Added to the compromising of Schneider's desires, technological evolution of the Schneider racers proved more beneficial to military applications and almost not at all to commercial endeavors.

In the context of new high-speed airplanes, the circumstances surrounding the Schneider event represented an unparalleled environment. Money was made available to design, build and test new racing planes, new engines, new fuels. Compared to any other era, the resources available to support air racing were lavish. Schneider racing produced some exotic aircraft. Equally important, if not more so, liquid-cooled engines were developed to an amazing state, especially in Great Britain.

Table 3-1

Winning Aircraft of the Schneider Trophy Races

Year	Aircraft	Engine	Pilot	Country	Speed (Mph)
1913	Deperdussin	160 hp Gnome	Maurice Prévost	France	45.75
1914	Tabloid	100 hp Gnome Monosoupape	Howard Pixton	Great Britain	86.78
1919	Contest declared void				
1920	Savoia S.12	550 hp Ansaldo 4E	Luigi Bologna	Italy	107.224
1921	Macchi M.7	250 hp Isotta-Fraschini	G. de Briganti	Italy	117.859
1922	Supermarine Sea Lion II	450 hp Napier Lion	Henri Biard	Great Britain	145.721
1923	Curtiss CR-3	465 hp Curtiss D-12	David Rittenhouse	United States	177.374
1925	Curtiss R3C-2	565 hp Curtiss V-1400	James Doolittle	United States	232.562
1926	Macchi M.39	800 hp Fiat AS.2	Mario de Bernardi	Italy	246.496
1927	Supermarine S.5	875 hp Napier Lion VIIB	S.N. Webster	Great Britain	281.655
1929	Supermarine S.6	1,900 Rolls-Royce R	H.R.D. Waghorn	Great Britain	328.629
1931	Supermarine S.6B	2,300 Rolls-Royce R	John Boothman	Great Britain	340.08

Sources: Official results; Derek N. James, *Schneider Trophy Aircraft–1913–1931*; Robert S. Hirsch, *Schneider Trophy Racers*.

THE CURTISS DESIGNS

The evolution from practical seaplane to ultimate speed in the Schneider began in 1923 with the inaugural appearance of American entries in the competition. What would ultimately be a triumphant performance in the Schneider was preceded by two years worth of racing experience by such companies as Curtiss, Thomas-Morse, Verville, and Wright. It was Curtiss Aeroplane & Motor Company, however, that would rise to the top.

The U.S. Navy commissioned Curtiss to build two biplane racing aircraft for the 1921 Pulitzer Trophy competition. Designated CR-1 (Curtiss Racing), both machines were powered by Curtiss-designed CD-12 water-cooled engines. Dimensionally identical, the fuselages utilized wooden monocoque construction, complemented by a close-fitting engine cowling. The result was an aerodynamically clean configuration marred only by two bulky Lamblin "lobster pot" radiators of French design, employed to remove waste heat from the engine cooling water. The radiators were mounted between the fixed landing gear struts, giving the appearance of being an afterthought. In fact, there was really no other practical place to mount them.

The CR racers were not raced by Navy flyers in the 1921 Pulitzer, the Navy having withdrawn

This in-flight picture of an American Airlines Douglas DST (Douglas Sleeper Transport) illustrates the retractable landing gear in a full up position. Like a number of such early landing gear designs, the wheels of the Douglas transport were exposed to the slipstream. In the event the gear would not lower, the aircraft theoretically could still make a comparatively safe landing. This configuration was used on a number of 1930s era racers as well. Peter M. Bowers collection

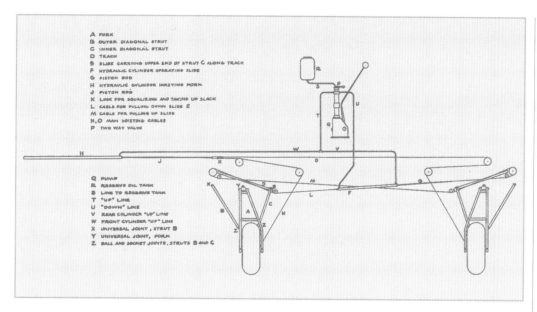

A — FORK
B — OUTER DIAGONAL STRUT
C — INNER DIAGONAL STRUT
D — TRACK
E — SLIDE CARRYING UPPER END OF STRUT C ALONG TRACK
F — HYDRAULIC CYLINDER OPERATING SLIDE
G — PISTON ROD
H — HYDRAULIC CYLINDER HOISTING FORK
J — PISTON ROD
K — LINK FOR EQUALIZING AND TAKING UP SLACK
L — CABLE FOR PULLING DOWN SLIDE E
M — CABLE FOR PULLING UP SLIDE
N, O — MAIN HOISTING CABLES
P — TWO WAY VALVE

Q — PUMP
R — RESERVE OIL TANK
S — LINE TO RESERVE TANK
T — "UP" LINE
U — "DOWN" LINE
V — REAR CYLINDER "UP" LINE
W — FRONT CYLINDER "UP" LINE
X — UNIVERSAL JOINT, STRUT B
Y — UNIVERSAL JOINT, FORK
Z — BALL AND SOCKET JOINTS, STRUTS B AND C

The concept of retractable landing gear is believed to have originated in 1911 with the German Wiencziers monoplane. It was not until the early 1930s that practical applications began to appear. One of the early applications was designed by Lockheed Aircraft in 1931 and used on it low-wing Orion and Altair models. The operating system for the Lockheed gear is shown in this illustration. A hydraulic hand-operated pump in the cockpit actuated a hydraulic cylinder. A cable and pulley arrangement connected the hydraulic cylinder to the landing gear. Gravity aided in lowering the gear. It would be several years before power-assisted retractable landing gears became common.

from the event. Curtiss obtained permission to enter the Pulitzer with one of the two racers (Navy Serial Number A-6081), however. Flown by Curtiss test pilot Bert Acosta, the nimble CR-1 won the race handily with an average speed of 176.75 miles per hour.

A year later, the Navy was back in Pulitzer competition with several airplanes including both CR racers (A-6080 and A-6081). Both airplanes underwent modest aerodynamic cleanup. A major change, however, was made in the cooling system. The two Lamblin radiators were replaced by wing surface (skin) radiators. Curtiss records indicate these changes resulted in the aircraft nomenclature being changed to CR-2.[5] Noting the 1921 performance of the Navy CR-1 racer, the Army jumped into the fray for 1922 with orders for no less than nine aircraft, two of which were the R-6 design built by Curtiss. Similar in overall appearance, the R-6 design was a bit more advanced and managed to capture first and second place in the Pulitzer. The Navy had to settle for third and fourth. For Curtiss, it was a clean sweep.

Schneider contest VII was hosted in 1923 by Great Britain at Cowes on the Isle of Wight. The American contingent from the U.S. Navy arrived a month early with a small fleet of aircraft, including two Curtiss CR-3 racers equipped with twin floats. The CR-3, an extrapolation of the CR-2 design, was nonetheless quite similar in appearance. Like the CR-2 the CR-3 utilized surface radiators on the wing for engine cooling. Pontoons were added to the airframe and the vertical tail surface area was increased almost 25 percent (from 11.78 square feet to 14.7 square feet). A high compression Curtiss D-12 engine provided an additional 50 horsepower delivered to a Curtiss Reed metal propeller. The combination was a

This photograph of the Dayton-Wright RB-1 racer illustrates its novel and advanced aerodynamic features. The aircraft was built specifically for the 1920 James Gordon Bennett Aviation Cup competition. The variable camber wing also featured cantilever construction which was very rare. The landing gear retracted into the fuselage in a fashion later emulated by Grumman. Pilot Howard Rinehart is standing on the cantilever wing. Peter M. Bowers collection

Table 3-2

Curtiss Racers (Land-Based)

Model	CR-1	CR-2	R-6	R2C-1	R3C-1
Year Built	1921	1922	1922	1923	1925
Length	21 ft 3/8 in	21 ft 3/8 in	18 ft 11 in	19 ft 8-1/2 in	20 ft 0 in
Span (Upper)	22 ft 8 in	22 ft 8 in	19 ft 0 in	22 ft 0 in	22 ft 0 in
Span (Lower)	22 ft 8 in	22 ft 8 in	19 ft 0 in	22 ft 0 in	22 ft 0 in
Wing Area	168 ft^2	168 ft^2	133 ft^2	144.25 ft^2	144.0 ft^2
Airfoil	Sloane	Sloane	C-27	C-62	C-80
Empty Weight	1,728 lb	1,782	1,642 lb	1,677 lb	1,792 lb
Gross Weight	2,158 lb	2,212	2,110 lb	2,098 lb	2,181 lb
Engine	CD-12	CD-12	D-12 hi comp.	D-12A hi comp.	V-1400
Horsepower	410 hp	410 hp	460 hp	500 hp	600 hp
Cooling System	Lamblin	Surface radiators	Surface radiators	Surface radiators	Surface radiators
Max. Speed	185.3 mph	198.8 mph	224.4 mph	247.5 mph	263.9 mph

Source: Curtiss Aeroplane & Motor Co. characteristics sheets

Table 3-3

Curtiss Racers (Float Planes)

Model	CR-3	R2C-2	R3C-2	R3C-4
Year Built	1923	1924	1925	1927
Length	25 ft 3/8 in	22 ft 7 in	22 ft 8 in	22 ft 4 in
Span (Upper)	22 ft 8 in	22 ft 0 in	22 ft 0 in	20 ft 0 in
Span (Lower)	22 ft 8 in	ft - in	22 ft - 0 in	20 ft 0 in
Wing Area	168 ft^2	144.25 ft^2	144.0 ft^2	144.1 ft^2
Airfoil	Sloane	Curtiss C-62	Curtiss C-80	Curtiss C-80
Empty Weight	2,119 lb	2,036 lb	2,134.9 lb	2,344 lb
Gross Weight	2,747 lb	2,640 lb	2,738.4 lb	3,223 lb
Engine	D-12 hi comp.	D-12A	V-1400	V-1550 hp
Horsepower	460 hp	502 hp	600 hp	705 hp
Cooling System	Surface radiators	Surface radiators	Surface radiators	Surface radiators
Max. Speed	194.0 mph	226.9 mph	245.7 mph	255.0 mph

Source: Curtiss Aeroplane & Motor Co. characteristics sheets

nascent Army and Navy air services. What airplanes existed were of European origin although some were license-built by American companies.

The first indigenous design to equip squadrons of the Army Air Service was the Thomas-Morse MB-3 single-seat fighter, designed during 1918. Prototypes were delivered in 1919 and a production run of 50 aircraft initiated in 1920. A subsequent production order for 200 fighters (designated MB-3A) went to Boeing, which entered the lowest bid in an open competition.[6] Thomas-Morse, whose company ori-

gins dated to 1910, continued on the fringes of the aircraft business until 1929, when it was acquired by, and became a division of, Consolidated Aircraft Corporation. Five years later, in 1934, Consolidated discontinued the division, most likely when it moved from Buffalo, New York, to San Diego, California.

A squat, compact biplane, the MB-3A served as a first-line fighter for the Army Air Service from 1921 to 1926. Powered by a water-cooled 300-horsepower Wright H-3 engine, it exhibited markedly superior performance to the World War I vintage S.E.5A

imports from Great Britain, which the Service used until the MB-3 series arrived on the scene.

The Navy air arm, without aircraft carriers in World War I, was equipped with land-based aircraft and, of course, seaplanes. The first Navy aircraft specifically designed as a single-seat fighter was the Curtiss-built TS-1 (tractor, single-seat, first of its type). A rugged-looking conventional biplane, it could be equipped either with fixed landing gear or twin floats. Power was provided by an air-cooled Lawrence J-1 200-horsepower radial engine.[7]

Comparing the Boeing MB-3A and Curtiss TS-1 fighters with the contemporary Curtiss CR-1 race plane illustrates design variances based upon mission requirements between Army, Navy and race planes. There are marked differences between the contemporary Army MB-3A and Navy TS-1 fighters. The Boeing MB-3A had the highest gross weight of the two fighter designs, part of which may be attributed to its heavier and more powerful liquid-cooled 300-horsepower engine. This amount of power also gave it a top speed 12 percent greater than its Navy counterpart. A comparison of landing speeds shows the MB-3A at 55 miles per hour while the TS-1 could ease onto the pitching deck of an aircraft carrier at 48 miles per hour.

When the first U.S. Navy aircraft carrier was commissioned (christened the *Langley*, CV-1), a shipboard fighter was needed that could operate within the restrictions imposed by the vessel. The result was the Curtiss TS-1 (which, with some changes, subsequently became the Curtiss F4C-1). The TS-1 was over 600 pounds lighter than the Army MB-3A, and possessed only two-thirds as much horsepower. Design requirements for the TS-1 were different than for the Army fighter. For instance, the TS-1 had to take off and land on the *Langley*, whose deck was slightly more than 500 feet long. Once the new Navy fighter touched down it had to be arrested. Gross weight for the Navy plane was only 1,920 pounds, purposely low so that arresting forces

Alfred Verville designed this low-wing monoplane racer for the 1922 Pulitzer Race. Built by the Lawrence Sperry Aircraft Company for the Army, it was powered by a 340-horsepower Wright Hispano H-3 V-8 water-cooled engine. The Verville Sperry R-3 featured a full cantilever wing and retractable landing gear. John Garrett collection

The 1922 Verville Sperry R-3 used a NACA 81 airfoil. The thickness of this airfoil permitted the landing gear to be retracted inward and into the wing center section. A hand-operated mechanical retraction system was provided for the pilot. No landing gear fairings were employed, resulting in some air flow discontinuity with the wheels in the retracted position. John Garrett collection

A full rear view of the Dayton-Wright RB-1 reveals the actuating control mechanism for the variable camber wing. The tail section as well as the wing were fully cantilever in structure, a unique feature in 1920. Unfortunately, a jammed leading edge slat on the variable camber wing forced pilot Rinehart to withdraw from the Gordon Bennett Race on the third lap. Peter M. Bowers collection

were within airframe structural limits. Army pilots, by contrast, enjoyed the luxury of landing fields of much more generous proportions.

Curtiss' CR-1 racing design was basically unencumbered by military requirements of endurance, armament, time-to-climb and service ceiling. It essentially had only one requirement—maximum speed at sea level. Thus it was a single-point design, and quite successful at that. Curtiss records indicate the CR-1 had a high speed of 185 miles per hour.

Its landing speed was 69 miles per hour, rather high for that era, and perceived to be much too fast for a carrier approach and perhaps the skill levels of many military pilots touching down on dry land. The racer was only slightly heavier (238 pounds) than the TS-1, but it enjoyed a tremendous power-to-weight ratio advantage due to its 410-horsepower Curtiss CD-12 engine. Range estimates for the racer indicate it was rather minimal (something around 180 miles) due to its limited fuel capacity. This was of little concern. In fact, a large fuel load would have imposed a performance penalty.

Although the CR-1 was never converted into a fighter, it served more than one purpose. The airplane won the 1921 Pulitzer Race, thereby giving Curtiss well-deserved recognition. It set a standard and provided a basis for subsequent more advanced Curtiss racing designs. There seems little doubt that engineering knowledge and flight experience gained from the aerodynamically clean Curtiss racers was subsequently used to advantage in their long line of Curtiss *Hawk* fighters in the years that followed. This was undoubtedly the most important contribution of the Curtiss racing experiments.

The National Air Races became an institution during the two decades between world wars. This decal was prepared for the 1927 races held in Spokane, Washington. A feature of these early American air races was the long-distance racing between cities and across the country. The 1927 event included a New York to Spokane race. John Garrett collection

Other early racing endeavors during the 1919—1925 period also contributed to the general body of empirical knowledge. Eight Army projects plus one funded jointly by the Army and the Navy provided a design forum in the quest for greater aircraft speed. The degree of success of these projects varied, but nonetheless served to provide experience, especially with respect to designing aerodynamically clean airframes.

THE SCHNEIDER YEARS

Postwar Schneider Trophy races were important for the impact they had on several fronts: dramatic speeds, aerodynamic refinements, liquid-cooled

Table 3-4

Fighter – Racer Comparisons: 1921 - 1922

	Boeing MB-3A	Curtiss TS-1	Curtiss CR-1
Max. Speed	141 mph	125 mph	185 mph
Range	280 mi	482 mi	180 mi (Est.)
Landing Speed	55 mph	48 mph	69 mph
Wing Area	229 ft^2	228 ft^2	168 ft^2
Gross Weight	2,539 lb	1,920 lb	2,158 lb
Horsepower	300 hp	200 hp	410 hp

Note: Range estimate for CR-1 based upon: cruise power = 70 % of maximum, Bsfc = 0.55 lb-fuel/hp-hr, and cruise speed of 120 mph.

Sources: MB-3A & TS-1 from: Ray Wagner, *American Combat Planes*, 3rd edition, Doubleday & Company, Inc. CR-1 data from Curtiss Aeroplane & Motor Co. aircraft characteristics.

Table 3-5

Army Air Service Racing Projects

Designation	Year	Manufacturer	Engine	Remarks
R-1	1919	Verville	Packard 1A-2025	Former VCP-1[1]
R-2	1921	Thomas-Morse	Wright-Hispano H-2	Former MB-6
R-3	1922	Verville-Sperry	Wright H-3	Retractable gear
R-4	1922	Loening	Packard 1A-2025	
R-5	1922	Thomas-Morse	Packard 1A-2025	All-metal
R-6	1922	Curtiss	Curtiss D-12	
R-7	1922	Engineering Div.		Design canceled
R-8	1924	Curtiss/Navy	Curtiss D-12A	Former Navy R2C-1
R3C-1	1925	Curtiss	Curtiss V-1400	Joint Army-Navy project

Note: 1. The VCP-1 was the first postwar American pursuit. It was designed by Alfred Verville and V. L. Clark, and built by Air Service Engineering Division.

Source: James C. Fahey, *U.S. Army Aircraft, 1908–1946*, Ships & Aircraft Publishing, NY, 1946.

engine development, and innovative design. Conversely, there was a reluctance to depart from the biplane motif even though some monoplane racers competed before the war, notably the Moranne-Saulneir, Nieuport and Depredussin machines of 1913. It was not until the 1925 contest, hosted by the United States at Baltimore, Maryland, that designers dared to create monoplane Schneider racers, thereby setting a new (or renewed) trend for this event.

One was fashioned by noted British designer R. J. Mitchell. This was the Supermarine S.4 racer. It was unique in that it was not only a monoplane, but employed a cantilever wing and wing flaps as well. The finished result was an aerodynamically sleek midwing design. All three banks of the 650-horsepower Napier Lion VII direct-drive liquid-cooled engine were tightly cowled and well faired. Engine cooling was provided by two long but shallow Lamblin radiators, one mounted to the lower surface of each wing. The overall effect was esthetically pleasing and suggestive of high-speed potential, even when the plane was at rest.[8] Unfortunately, the S.4 met an untimely demise when it stalled into Chesapeake Bay during a navigability trial. The pilot, Henri Biard, believed that wing or aileron flutter caused him to lose control.[9,10]

The other monoplane racer at the 1925 contest was a product of Macchi's chief designer, Mario Castoldi. Designated Macchi M.33, this craft was a flying boat employing a shoulder-mounted wing with the engine strut-mounted above the fuselage. Although the engine (a Curtiss D-12A) was nicely cowled, its overhead location detracted from the otherwise well-streamlined airframe. (In choosing a flying boat configuration, the designer had little option but to place the engine overhead to obtain propeller clearance with the water.)

This Italian entry was flown by Giovanni de Briganti, who managed a third place finish with a speed of 168.44 miles per hour. Jimmy Doolittle won the race flying a Curtiss R3C-2, while Hubert Broad from Great Britain captured second place in a Gloster IIIA. There speeds were 232.562 and 199.17 miles per hour, respectively. The Macchi M.33, symbolically closer to Jacques Schneider's original vision, was clearly outclassed by the American and British entries. Indeed, had the other two Curtiss R3C-2 entries not retired from the race, the Macchi might well have come in fifth instead of third. In any event, Mario Castoldi's flying boat marked the last appearance of this design type in the Schneider races.

There were many extraordinary Schneider racer designs, some of which never reached the starting line. The Italians produced some of the most creative designs including: the world seaplane speed record-holding Macchi-Castoldi MC.72, powered by two tandem Fiat AS.6 engines with counterrotating propellers; the striking Piaggio-Pegna P.c.7, equipped with main and tail hydrofoils in place of floats; and Savoia Marchetti's S.65, featuring a push-pull engine setup. If imaginative creativity fairly describes the Italian efforts, design pragmatism captures the British approach to the Schneider contests toward the end of the 1920s.

SUPERMARINE'S FINEST

Supermarine's foray into custom high-speed racing designs began in 1925 when the ill-fated S.4 was conceived. Reginald J. Mitchell's next venture, the Supermarine S.5 powered by an 875-horsepower Napier Lion VIIB, reversed his fortunes completely. Victory for Great Britain was secured in the 1927 Schneider when Flight Lieutenant S. N. Webster sped around the 50-kilometer course at Venice, Italy, at an average speed of 281.655 miles per hour.

One of the earlier commercial applications of retractable landing gear appeared on the Lockheed Orion and Altair. The Altair shown here belonged to Sir Charles Kingsford Smith. Unlike many 1930 era designs in which the wheels rotated aft, the Lockheed concept brought the gear up into the wing root section, an approach that became common. Lockheed's gear retraction was a manually operated hydraulic system.

The S.5 configuration evolved from the S.4, and embodied numerous improvements. Mitchell notably avoided using a cantilever wing this time, relying instead on conventional wire bracing. This may seem a step backward, but concern over the possibility of flutter, a little understood phenomenon at the time, probably influenced the decision. The S.4 wing structure was suspect from the standpoint of stiffness. The externally braced S.5 wing was a prudent concession, and one that proved correct. The Supermarine design group was also conscious of gross weight, and a wire-braced wing could be built lighter than a cantilever wing. The downside was an incremental increase in aerodynamic drag.

The later S.6 and S.6B racers were further refinements of the basic S.4 arrangement. There is no secret to Mitchell's design formula. It was a straightforward two-prong approach consisting of reducing drag coupled with massive doses of horsepower. The former was important and the latter was imperative. During the five-year period of 1926–1931, the Mitchell-designed racers exhibited an overall speed increase of 77 percent, from 231 miles per hour to 407 miles per hour. Horsepower increased 3.4 times over the period to gain this speed increase, accompanied by a tight control on gross weight and concurrent emphasis on drag reduction. Three years later, the Italians raised the world speed record to just

Harry Crosby's sleek CR 4 racer was a more advanced design than many of its contemporaries in the late 1930s. Among other features, it incorporated retractable landing gear. In the retracted position the struts and wheels were fully enclosed within the inboard wing section. Note the piano hinge along the bottom edge of the gear fairing. This served as a hinge point to attach a small fairing to cover the lower portion of the wheel and tire when the gear was retracted. John Garrett collection

A full front picture of the Crosby racer under construction shows the landing gear partially retracted. At the upper end of each landing gear strut in proximity to the pivot point, part of the actuating gear drive may be seen. The overall design proved less than satisfactory and the box beam construction was subsequently replaced by a welded tube structure. Retraction was actuated by compressed carbon dioxide. John Garrett collection

Jacques Schneider's vision of a race to spur design of fast dependable seaplanes for commercial purposes must have seemed quite reasonable at first. The Supermarine Sea Lion I was a British entry in 1919 and possessed utility beyond air racing. It was powered by a 450-horsepower Napier Lion IA engine. John Garrett collection

Unlike the Sea Lion entry of earlier years, the Supermarine S.5 of 1927 was designed for a very singular purpose–all-out speed. Race Number 4, powered by an 875-horsepower Napier Lion Model VIIB engine, won the Schneider Trophy that year. Its winning speed was 281.656 miles per hour. John Garrett collection

under 441 miles per hour in a Macchi-Castoldi MC.72 float plane originally intended for the 1931 Schneider contest, but too late.[11] When the new world record was established in 1934, the twin Fiat AS.6 liquid-cooled engines powering the MC.72 were generating a combined 3,000 horsepower.

Had Great Britain elected in 1935 to challenge Italy for the world speed record, what might Mitchell and his design staff have done to push the speed limit beyond the 1934 record of 440 miles per hour by the required one percent? They might have followed the Italian's lead and placed two Rolls-Royce R engines in tandem to provide well over 4,000 horsepower. A stretched airframe would have been necessary for two reasons. Obviously the addition of a second engine would have lengthened the fuselage by several feet. Equally important, the extra wetted airframe area would have been needed for skin radiators to handle waste heat from the second engine. Considering that the S.6B was already festooned with surface radiators (for engine oil and coolant), it is improbable that any stretched airframe could have handled the additional cooling requirements without imposing unacceptable drag build-up.

Coincident with what might have been, Supermarine was engaged in developing a Type 224 gull-winged fighter prototype. This aircraft was powered

Supermarine Schneider Trophy Racers

Model	S.4	S.5	S.6	S.6B
Year	1926	1927	1929	1931
Overall Length	26 ft 7.75 in	24 ft 3.5 in	25 ft 10 in	28 ft 10 in
Wing Span	30 ft 7.5 in	26 ft 9 in	30 ft 0 in	30 ft 0 in
Wing Area	139 ft²	114 ft²	145 ft²	145 ft²
Aspect Ratio	6.75	6.28	6.20	6.20
Airfoil	RAF 30	RAF 30	RAF 27	RAF 27
Empty Weight	2,600 lb	2,680 lb	4,471 lb	4,590 lb
Gross Weight	3,191 lb	3,242 lb	5,771 lb	6,086 lb
Engine	Napier Lion VII	Napier Lion VIIA Napier Lion VIIB	Rolls-Royce R	Rolls-Royce R
Propeller Drive	Direct Drive	VIIA: Direct VIIB: Geared	Geared	Geared
Horsepower	680 hp	900 hp	1,900 hp	2,300 hp
Wing Loading	22.96	28.44	39.80	41.97
Power Loading	4.69	3.60	3.04	2.65
Fuel Capacity	45 gal	50 gal	106 gal	135 gal
Oil Capacity	5 gal	5 gal	10 gal	15 gal
Water Capacity	10 gal	15 gal	20 gal	25 gal
Max. Speed	231.4 mph	319.57 mph	357.7 mph	407.5 mph

Sources: Derek N. James, *Schneider Trophy Aircraft, 1913–1931,* and Supermarine Aircraft Since 1914 by C. F. Andrews and E. B. Morgan

The ultimate in British Schneider racers was the Supermarine S.6B design of 1931. Photographed during an engine test run, S.6B Number 7, S-1596, was the reserve aircraft for the 1931 Schneider contest. Powering the S.6B was the marvelous Rolls-Royce "R" engine, capable of developing 2,350 horsepower. A sister ship, S-1595, won the final Schneider race and retired the famous trophy to England's permanent possession. John Garrett collection

with a Rolls-Royce Kestrel IV (Goshawk) engine which utilized a steam cooling system. In conventional aircraft engine cooling, then using low-pressure systems, designers maintained the cooling water below boiling (approximately 180 degrees Fahrenheit) by passing heated water from the engine through a radiator. The Kestrel IV engine, conversely, took advantage of the additional thermal energy required to convert water from a heated liquid to steam.[12] The steam was subsequently condensed and returned to the liquid state. The Type 224 airframe incorporated steam condensers on the wing leading edge, a derivative of Mitchell's Schneider race plane design experience using surface radiators.

For a race plane designed for only short duration flights, Mitchell might have proceeded to the next logical step by eliminating the condenser portion of the system, and allowing the steam to vent overboard. Obviously flight time would be limited to the amount of water onboard, but for short duration record flights this was not an overly severe limitation. Indeed, Germany gained the final pre-World War II world speed record (469.224 miles per hour) with the Messerschmitt Me 209 V1 aircraft using evaporative cooling for the Daimler-Benz racing engine.

A Wright T-2 water-cooled V-12 engine powered this 1922 Navy racer. The aircraft was designed by Jerome Hunsaker and built by Wright. Identified as NW-1, the racer was flown in the 1922 Pulitzer contest, but forced out during the fourth lap with an oil leak. Note that the spreader bar and winglets outboard of the landing gear were built using an airfoil section for a bit of additional lift. John Garrett collection

Great Britain and Supermarine did not, however, turn their attention toward a new world speed record in 1935. By that time, R. J. Mitchell was intimately involved designing what would become the legendary Royal Air Force Spitfire. This remarkable fighter was *not* an extrapolation of his famous Schneider racing machines. Rather, it was a culmination of all of his knowledge and past experience. The Schneider projects, of course, were part of this accumulated education and Mitchell used it well. The

The 1922 Navy Wright NW-1 fuselage was a relatively clean design with a nicely cowled engine and small wing fillet. Two Lamblin radiators slung beneath the fuselage and a massive landing gear design detracted from what otherwise might have been a very advanced racer. Close examination of the nearby three-quarter right front view of this aircraft shows that two flying wires have been added to each wing, apparently to augment the large outboard landing gear struts. John Garrett collection

heritage of the Schneider designs may be seen in the aerodynamic cleanliness of the Spitfire. Beyond that, however, the Spitfire incorporated more recent design and fabrication technology: A fully cantilever wing replaced the wire braced wings of the S.5, S.6 and S.6B; a retractable landing gear was a design requirement from the beginning; an enclosed cockpit canopy replaced the windscreen and open cockpit configuration of the racers; and, surface radiators, impractical on a combat airplane, were replaced with tunnel radiator installations beneath the wing panels. Needless to say, the Spitfire had one very distinguishing feature the racers did not: eight .30-caliber machine guns.

The British Air Ministry fighter specification was translated by Mitchell into the Supermarine Type 300 prototype. Mitchell's fondness for symmetrical airfoils carried over from the Schneider days insofar as his response to the initial Air Ministry specification for a new fighter. His design used a root airfoil NACA 0018 (symmetrical about the chord) section tapering to an RAF 34 at the tip. When the prototype Spitfire emerged from its design cocoon, however, its wing was formed using the NACA 2213 root and NACA 2209.4 tip sections. These are cambered as opposed to symmetrical airfoils. In the four-digit NACA series of airfoils, the first digit indicates the maximum camber in terms of *hundredths* of the chord length. The second digit denotes the location of maximum camber given in *tenths* of the chord length. The final two digits define the maximum thickness of the section

The 1928 National Air Races held at Mines Field (now Los Angeles International Airport) featured a large aeronautical exposition as well. The nine-day program drew thousands of spectators, who roamed the exhibition tents and packed the grandstands. This year marked the introduction of Cliff Henderson to the position of managing director of the races. He continued in this role through 1939.
John Garrett collection

Left: *Curtiss developed a series of racing planes for both the Army and the Navy that were truly advanced. Pilot Bert Acosta, shown here with the 1921 Pulitzer Trophy, stands in front of Navy CR-1 racer. He actually won the race, held in Omaha, Nebraska, in the sister ship, CR-2. The Curtiss racers were very clean, compact designs with excellent attention to detail. Lamblin radiators, of French design, provided engine cooling. Peter M. Bowers collection*

For the 1922 racing season, Curtiss introduced wing surface radiators, thereby eliminating drag associated with the Lamblin units. This innovation became a standard for most racing aircraft competing in the Pulitzer and Schneider contests. Although not drag free, the surface radiators were a decided improvement over other forms of heat exchangers. Their use on pursuit airplanes proved impractical, due to the likelihood of battle damage. Peter M. Bowers collection

Curtiss designs fared equally well in Schneider races. Shown here is the Curtiss R3C-2. Its unencumbered lines are apparent. Wing surface radiators on both the upper and lower flying surfaces cooled the Curtiss V-1400 engine. Note that the tail skid remains on the airplane, even though it has been equipped with pontoons. A companion, R3C-2, flown by James H. Doolittle won the 1925 Schneider with an average speed of 232.753 miles per hour.

in hundredths of the chord length. (Reference in each instance is made to the chord leading edge.)

The Spitfire went on to acquit itself exceptionally well in defense of Great Britain. It was a versatile airframe as confirmed by the many variants produced. Its one shortcoming was limited range, for it was designed as a defensive weapon. Long-range bomber escort missions were a future necessity not envisioned in military requirements of the 1930s by any World War II combatant.

The Boeing MB-3A was the standard Army pursuit airplane from 1921 to 1926. It was powered by a 300 horsepower Wright H-3 water-cooled engine, which gave it better performance than the Royal Aircraft Factory S.E.5A which it replaced. Note the engine coolant radiator mounted on the side of the fuselage. This pursuit was also somewhat more aerodynamically advanced than the S.E.5A. Peter M. Bowers collection

Curtiss designed and built the first Navy aircraft designed as a fighter for carrier use. The Navy was about to receive its first carrier, the U.S.S. Langley. Powered by a 200-horsepower Lawrence J-1 air-cooled radial engine, the TS-1 was considerably lighter than its Army counterpart, the Boeing MB-3A. It had a slower high speed than the MB-3A, but landed at a lower speed too. This made it more desirable for carrier operations. Peter M. Bowers collection

chapter 4

The Marathon Racers

In what distant deeps or skies
Burnt the fire of thine eyes?
On what wings dare he aspire?
What the hand dare seize the fire?

William Blake • *The Tiger*

U p to this point, we have considered only maximum speed over a relatively short predefined straight-away, or pylon course of a specified number of laps. However, there was another type of racing that played a role in the development of the sport. These were the long-distance events, epitomized by the disastrous 1928 Dole Race, and the grueling 1934 MacRobertson contest. Did long-distance racing contribute to pursuit aircraft development? Not in any direct or tangible sense. Yet the experience gained and lessons learned formed a contribution, or at least a confirmation, to the overall body of aeronautical knowledge.

The inspiration for these events can be found in Charles Lindbergh's epic Atlantic crossing in 1927. Exceedingly popular during the late 1920s and throughout the 1930s, the potential contribution of these races is worthy of exploration. For instance, the Dole race saw the entry of the very first Lockheed Vega. This was a truly exceptional design and foreshadowed the future. That it was one of many entrants lost during this Transpacific race does not in the least diminish its prominence. In fact, the *Vega* and its derivative designs went on to dominate long-distance racing for several years thereafter.

THE DOLE RACE

James Drummond Dole became enchanted, as did so many others, with Lindbergh's absolutely breathtaking solo 1927 flight across the Atlantic from New York to Paris. Dole was then a 50-year-old pineapple grower on the island of Oahu, then part of the Territory of Hawaii. Dole's first pineapple plantation was established at Wahia (Oahu). A resident of Honolulu, he was in San Francisco on business when newspaper extra editions proclaimed Lindbergh's conquest of the Atlantic Ocean. Lindbergh's flight inspired Dole to plan and sponsor an air race across the Pacific.

The first Navy carrier was the U.S.S. Langley (CV-1). It was commissioned on March 20, 1922. This vessel was not designed from the keel up as an aircraft carrier. Rather, it was to be a collier and therefore had to be converted into a carrier. Note the absence of any structure on the carrier deck for control and command operations. The 65-foot-wide deck was 523 feet in length. Peter M. Bowers collection

As author Lesley Forden noted, Dole was "another of those Yankee businessmen who followed American missionaries to the Islands; those missionaries of whom a cynic has said, 'They went forth to do good, and did well.'"[1,2] Dole certainly did well. So well, in fact, that he was able to offer, on May 25, 1927, a total of $35,000 in prize money for a 2,400-mile air race westward across the Pacific from Oakland, California, to Honolulu, Hawaii. The first pilot to arrive would receive $25,000, thus equaling the prize Charles Lindbergh received for his Atlantic flight. In addition, Dole would award a second-place prize of $10,000.[3]

Jim Dole's grandiose vision of an air race across the Pacific, intended as a westward replication of Lindbergh's triumph earlier in the year, devolved into a disaster when the final human toll was tallied. Eight aircraft arrived at Oakland, California for the race. Four actually took off from the airfield. Only two ever arrived.

The Dole Race was a significant event not only due to the attendant carnage, but because expectations generally exceeded existing aeronautical capabilities. Celestial navigation coupled with dead reckoning was the basis for negotiating the long journey, a technique easily frustrated by unexpected cloud cover and storms. Radio-aided navigation (direction finding) was then in its infancy as was direct air-to-ground wireless communication. Pilots in the Dole Race were attempting to find a relatively small island chain in the vast often unpredictable Pacific. In contrast, Lindbergh was searching for a continent, and had navigation error intruded, he would still have located some portion of the Europe. The Pacific flight was eminently more difficult at that point in time.

VEGA: A NEW GENERATION

At least one irony emerged from the Dole Race involving the fledgling Lockheed Aircraft Company. One Dole Race entry lost without a trace during its flight over the Pacific was the prototype Lockheed *Vega*. Normally loss of a prototype aircraft would be a severe setback if not an outright calamity for the company that produced the design. Yet this was not the case. The Vega went on to become a highly successful trend-setting airplane design.

The product of Jack Northrop's innovative mind, the high-wing Vega, was designed and built during the spring of 1927. It featured a patented wooden monocoque fuselage originally conceived and demonstrated in 1918 at Santa Barbara, California, by the brothers Malcolm and Allan Loughead (nee Lockheed), John K. Northrop and Anthony Stadlman.[4] Vega fuselage surfaces were molded under pressure in two longitudinal halves.[5] The half-shells were built up from three transverse layers of glued spruce veneer. Completed shells were assembled to a series of wooden elliptical fuselage former rings.[6] The resulting fuselage was a smoothly contoured structure that contributed greatly to the aerodynamic excellence of the Vega design. It also proved extremely versatile facilitating three distinct general arrangements: the high wing Vega; the parasol wing Air Express; and, the low-wing Sirius, Altair, and Orion.

The first flight of the new Vega occurred on July 4, 1927, when test pilot Edward Antoine Bellande (Eddie) lifted the new machine off the ground at Rogers Airport in Los Angles. Power was supplied by a 9-cylinder, 200-horsepower Wright J-5C Whirlwind air-cooled engine, the same type of engine that served Charles Lindbergh so well. As

The winner of the 1927 Dole Race was George Goebel in a modified Travel Air 5000. Goebel crossed the Pacific from California to Hawaii, a distance of 2,437 miles, in 26 hours, 17 minutes and 33 seconds. His average speed was about 93 miles per hour. Compare the Travel Air with nearby photographs of the new Lockheed Vega, which represented a newer technology. John Garrett collection

Of the many aircraft entered in the infamous Dole Race, the most modern was a Lockheed Vega. Purchased by the Hearst newspaper family, the first Vega built was entered in the race. The molded wood fuselage and cantilever flying surfaces were the essence of streamlining in 1928. It was the fastest commercially built plane and a natural for long-distance air racing. Lockheed via Birch Matthews collection

Vega Serial Number 1 is seen here during an engine run up reportedly prior to its first flight on July 4, 1927, at Mines Field (Los Angeles International Airport). Although the first models did not have an engine cowling, note that a spinner and fairing around the engine crankcase served to blend with the fuselage and smooth air flow to some degree. John Garrett collection

author and historian Walter J. Boyne noted, the Dole Race announcement "had an immediate effect upon the Lockheed Aircraft Company, when William Randolph Hearst's son, George, agreed to buy a Vega for the bargain price of $12,000."[7] The basis of his statement is twofold. The Hearst family, through its newspaper chain, was extremely wealthy and influential. Associating the Hearst name with the first Vega added a luster sure to attract other sales prospects to the small Lockheed factory. Second and more important, when George Hearst took possession of the airplane, pilot Jack Frost, who was selected for the Dole contest, demonstrated its outstanding perfor-

mance with a dash between Oakland and Los Angeles in three hours and five minutes. There was no doubt it was the fastest commercial airplane then flying.

Designed by Northrop as a light general purpose commercial transport or personal chariot of the very wealthy, the new Vega could carry a pilot and four or five passengers. Hearst's airplane was modified specifically for the long over-water flight to Hawaii by the addition of fuel capacity and safety provisions, however. The extensive preparations were all in vain. Pilot John Frost and navigator Gordon Scott were lost without explanation somewhere in the vast Pacific Ocean.

THE NACA COWLING

The Lockheed Vega design format proved to be as versatile as it was fast. It was an elegant solution in the quest for aerodynamic efficiency. The fuselage, by virtue of its molded form, was smooth and streamlined. If anything marred its appearance, however, it was the exposed Wright air-cooled engine. This flaw was subsequently corrected with the addition of a full NACA engine cowling. It was installed on a Lockheed Air Express, a design derivative of the Vega, and quickly adapted to all of the wooden Lockheeds. This addition was not only esthetically pleasing, but improved performance and enhanced engine cooling uniformity.

The NACA cowling, so named because it was developed by the National Advisory Committee for Aeronautics at the Langley Memorial Aeronautical Laboratory, was experimentally demonstrated in 1928. Prior to that time, most if not all, radial air-cooled engines were exposed to the slipstream to ensure adequate cooling. (An exception was the rotary engine of World War I, which is discussed in Chapter 9.) The impetus for cowling radial engines was a widening realization that air-cooled powerplants were a source of significant aerodynamic drag.

The Navy Bureau of Aeronautics approached NACA during June 1926 requesting a program to develop a cowling to reduce drag while simultaneously yielding adequate cooling. The Navy was leaning heavily toward aircraft powered exclusively by air-cooled radials. Although the Navy urged NACA to investigate cowlings, response was bureaucratically slow.

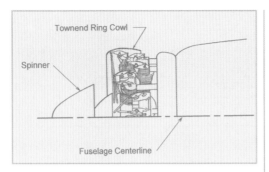

Cowlings for air-cooled radial engines represented a major advancement in aerodynamic cleanness. NACA work in this area quickly resulted in adoption of the cowling by most, if not all, airframe manufactures. Speed increases were noted with no additional power. Another type of cowl developed in proximity to the NACA work was the Townend ring. It served the same purpose as the NACA cowling, although the decrease in drag was significantly less. Several American aircraft utilized a Townend ring, including the Boeing P-26A.

During a meeting between NACA personnel and representatives of American aircraft companies, convened on May 24, 1927, (a year after the Navy's request) the idea of a cowling investigation surfaced again, this time at the urging of the manufacturers.[8] Shortly afterward the decision was made to proceed with an experimental program using the Langley Propeller Research Tunnel. The young engineer in charge of the tunnel, Fred Weick, was tasked with the responsibility. Coincidentally that same year, the Navy Bureau of Aeronautics "officially announced that in the future it would use nothing but air-cooled engines.[9] It was a pragmatic turn of events. Air-cooled radials had attractive horsepower-to-weight ratios, the engines were reliable, and maintenance and logistics were simplified, especially onboard ships where space was limited.

During the first half of 1928, Weick measured the drag of a Wright J-5 Whirlwind attached to a representative fuselage–it appeared remarkably similar to Lindbergh's *Spirit of St. Louis*.[10] With that information as a baseline, Weick proceeded to evaluate "several forms and degrees of cowling" on the same full scale mock-up in the 20-foot diameter Propeller Research Tunnel:

"The cowlings varied from the one extreme of an entirely exposed engine to the other in

The Vega became an instant success, due certainly to its excellent performance, and no doubt to its pleasing appearance as well. This profile of a Vega 5 shows the early approach to reducing drag due to the radial engine. The Wasp B cylinders are still exposed, but the remainder of the engine is nicely enclosed. Peter M. Bowers collection

NACA engineers addressed the problem of reducing drag produced by radial air-cooled engines installations. The seminal work was done in the NACA Langley Propeller Research Tunnel under the direction of Fred Weick. His wind tunnel work was entirely empirical, but it produced rather astounding results, confirmed through flight tests using the Curtiss AT-5A pictured here. Peter M. Bowers collection

which the engine was entirely enclosed. Cooling tests were made and each cowling modified if necessary until the engine cooled approximately as satisfactorily as when it was entirely exposed. Drag tests were then made with each form of cowling, and the effect of the cowling on the propulsive efficiency determined with a metal propeller."[11]

The results were astounding. A properly tailored full cowling could not only effect cooling comparable to a completely uncowled engine, but dramatically reduce aerodynamic drag. In his report describing the investigation, Weick concluded that with a cowling "which covers the entire engine and separates the cooling air from the general flow about the body, the reduction in drag is about *60 percent* (italics added) of the increase due to an uncowled engine."[12] This was heady stuff and the implications were significant. With no increase in horsepower, an airplane would be able to fly noticeably faster with a cowling installed. Conversely, a given cruising speed could be maintained using reduced engine power, thereby improving fuel economy.

Would flight test results be as dramatic as the wind tunnel findings? To answer this question, an Air Corps Curtiss AT-5A based at Langley was borrowed and modified to accept an NACA cowling. One of the

Upper left: Curtiss also evaluated full cowlings for its radial engine products. Shown here is a full cowl similar to the type developed by NACA. The aircraft is Curtiss XP-3A Number 1, mounting a Pratt & Whitney Wasp engine. Note the short exhaust stacks protruding from the cowling. This was not a feature replicated on other aircraft. The photograph was taken in May 1929. Peter M. Bowers collection

Ring cowls or Townend cowls were used on any number of aircraft including this Curtiss XF9C-1 Navy fighter. These cowlings essentially extended through the depth of the engine cylinder heads. Some pilots objected to cowlings when they first became fashionable, claiming that they obstructed forward vision. The short Townend-style cowl obviated this complaint to some extent, for the pilot still had a measure of visibility through the ring and between cylinders. Peter M. Bowers collection

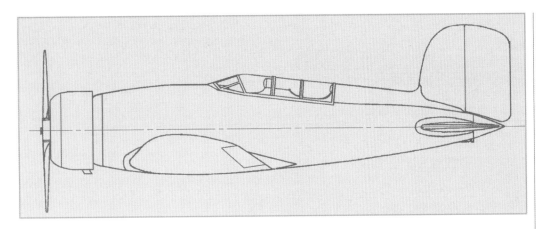

Wooden Lockheeds of the early 1930s were among the fastest commercially built airplanes in the world. This line drawing of a Lockheed Altair displays the clean lines inherent in the basic Lockheed airframe. Mating an Orion wing with retractable landing gear coupled with the two-place enclosed cockpit canopy was the basis for Kingsford Smith's intended MacRobertson entry. The sleek airframe concealed a massive fuel capacity of approximately 506 gallons.

ubiquitous single-seat Curtiss military designs of the period, the AT-5A was a compact no-nonsense airplane featuring a 220-horsepower Wright J5 engine. Although the wind tunnel cowl evaluation was done using a high-wing cabin monoplane mock-up, the AT-5A was a biplane. This was not particularly material, however. The flight test would demonstrate a relative drag reduction using the NACA cowling concept, and confirm that engine cooling was not impaired.

The initial flight test, after critical instruments were calibrated, was concerned with verifying AT-5A top speed in the as-built condition. A sea level run was made at wide open throttle with the engine turning 1,900 rpm. Measured speed was 118 miles per hour. With the engine cowled and again turning 1,900 rpm, the AT-5A sped over the course at 137 miles per hour, a 16 percent increase in maximum sea level speed with no increase in horsepower! To match the old top speed of 118 miles per hour required about 10 percent less horsepower.[13] Engine cooling proved quite adequate throughout the flight test program.

Weick's wind tunnel and confirming flight test program was of seminal importance. In addition to

The Curtiss XF9C-1 Sparrowhawk was an early attempt at the lightweight fighter concept. Developed against a 1930 Navy specification for a carrier-based airplane, the XF9C-1 did not prove to be a success, although it achieved a modicum of fame as a dirigible-based fighter. Like the Sparrowhawk, the Navy rigid airship program faded into history as did the XF9C-1. This photograph gives an excellent profile view of a typical Townend ring cowl. Peter M. Bowers collection

enhancing aircraft performance, the NACA cowling or its design derivatives became a standard feature on most air-cooled radial engine airplanes for the next 20 years. In recognition of this achievement, Weick and the NACA justifiably received the prestigious Collier Trophy in 1929, an award commemorating the most important advancement in aviation during the previous year.

The one drawback inherent in Weick's effort resided in the fact that it was entirely empirical. As author John Anderson, Jr., points out, "There was no accompanying aerodynamic analysis, for Weick's report had not a single equation . . ."[14] Lacking was any theoretical explanation of how and why the cowling worked, information useful to subsequent design efforts. It was a limitation that NACA would seek to correct as cowling and engine nacelle investigations continued over a decade or more. Particularly important were the contributions of Theodore Theodorsen, who took charge of the cowling program in 1935. Theodorsen was a Norwegian born and educated theoretician. His work was important in that it explored and explained the internal aerodynamics of the cooling air, such that a given design could be optimized with respect to internal engine cooling drag and external form drag.[15]

Radial engine cowlings were quickly adapted to commercial and military designs. Lockheed's Air Express is believed to be the first example of a commercial airplane to use the NACA cowl.[16, 17] It was rapidly applied to the Lockheed Vega, Altair, Sirius, and Orion designs with equally satisfying results. Never designed explicitly for air racing, the Vega nevertheless became a frequent contestant. Its reputation for speed was unmatched for two or three years after its introduction (see Table 4-1). That it emerged from the tragic residue of the Dole Race is even more remarkable, considering that only two aircraft reached Hawaii, Art Goebel in *Woolaroc*, a modified Travel Air 5000, and Martin Jensen in the Breese Monoplane named *Aloha*. In an ironic twist, and unlike the Lockheed Vega, both aircraft were quickly consigned to the dustbin of history.

THE MACROBERTSON RACE

The MacRobertson Race was the most ambitious aerial contest ever conducted. The race, from London, England, to Melbourne, Australia, was

Table 4-1

Lockheed Vega Characteristics

Model	Engine	Hp	Max Speed (Mph)	Max Speed With NACA Cowl (Mph)
Vega 1	Wright J5 Whirlwind	220	138	Not Used
Vega 2	Wright J6 Whirlwind	300	155	Not Used
Vega 2A	Wright J6 Whirlwind	300	160	Not Used
Vega 2D	P&W Wasp Jr.	300	162	Unknown
Vega 5	P&W Wasp B	420	165	175
Vega 5A	P&W Wasp B	450	165	175
Vega 5B	P&W Wasp C	420	165	180
Vega 5C	P&W Wasp C1	420	185	Included
Vega DL-1	P&W Wasp C1	420	178	Included
Vega DL-1B	P&W Wasp C1	420	178	Included

Notes: 1.) Horsepower ratings for Wasp engines taken from Pratt & Whitney data presented in source 3 below. 2.) Vega Models DL-1 and DL-1B indicate Detroit Aircraft Corporation-built aircraft with metal fuselages.

Sources: 1.) Richard Sanders Allen, *Revolution in the Sky*; 2.) Joseph P. Juptner, *U.S. Civil Aircraft Series*, Volumes 1,2 3; 3.) Pratt & Whitney Aircraft *Engine Models and Characteristics*, PWA-SD14.

This is one of five Curtiss P-3A pursuits taken on strength in late 1928 as service test models by the Army Air Corps. As the importance of drag reducing engine cowlings began to take hold, the Army added Townend rings to each of its service test P-3As. The ring cowls helped, but were not as efficient as full NACA cowlings. Peter M. Bowers collection

unprecedented and staggering in proportion, stretching over 11,300 miles, 19 countries and seven seas, all in 1934 no less!

The occasion of this extraordinary competition was a centennial anniversary celebration for the city of Melbourne. Prize money ($15,000 Australian) was guaranteed by wealthy Australian businessman Sir MacPherson Robertson. In return for this philanthropic gesture, he asked that the event be named the "MacRobertson Race," an abridgment of his given and family names. MacPherson Robertson was not entirely altruistic. MacRobertson was the name of his company, and the race was sure to garner a lot of publicity. Having nevertheless pledged so large a sum, it is readily understandable why the centennial directors and city fathers came to see the wisdom of granting his request.

The MacRobertson Race gained worldwide attention. Sixty-three entries were received by the British Royal Aero Club, chosen to organize the race for the Australian Centenary Council. It became a magnet attracting a host of aviation adventurers who might be roughly cataloged as verifiably famous, not-so-famous, and never-would-be-famous. In spite of the initial enthusiasm, only 20 entrants were actually on hand for the race start.

The selected route was a veritable travelogue through diverse cultures, ranging from the western civilization of Europe, the ancient societies of Persia, the mysterious cultures of the Orient, and culminating on the continent of Australia, a remote outpost of the British Empire. The route between Mildenhall Airfield and Melbourne was a tortuous, time-consuming southeasterly journey testing the limits of both man and machine.

This momentous contest was divided into two divisions. The first was the "Speed Division" based strictly on elapsed time from London takeoff to Melbourne landing. A "Handicap Division" was also established to attract as many entrants as possible, the promoters not unaware that few could afford specially built race aircraft in the middle of the Great Depression. Planes in this division were timed from takeoff to landing at each stop along the route, and judged on a handicap formula to establish the final standings. One important caveat was that to qualify for a final race standing, all entrants had to arrive in Melbourne no later than 16 days after the London start.

The aerodynamic importance of cowlings for air-cooled piston engines is almost intuitively obvious when viewing this photograph. Art Goebel poses in front of the Travel Air 5000, which he flew in the Dole Race. Engine cylinders, together with the heavy-handed exhaust collector ring, tended to cause significant flow disturbance around the nose of the aircraft. John Garrett collection

Lockheed chief engineer Jack Northrop quickly grasped the advantage of adding a full cowling to his Vega design. This particular airplane began life as a Wright J-5A Vega 1, but when equipped with a Pratt & Whitney R-985, it became a Vega 5. Note how close fitting the cowling is and how it readily conforms to the fuselage. Proper engine cooling was a matter of adjusting the pressure drop across the cowling (inlet plane to outlet annulus). Later cowling installations employed internal baffling around engine cylinders to more closely control the cooling air distribution. Birch Matthews collection

The Speed Division was won by two Englishmen, C. W. A. Scott and Campbell Black, flying a deHavilland 88 Comet built specifically for the race. Their elapsed time was 70 hours, 54 minutes, 18 seconds. A Dutch KLM Airline crew in a Douglas DC-2 captured the Handicap Division. The Dutch airliner was actually the second aircraft to arrive in Melbourne, about 10 hours behind the British Comet. Given the choice of second place in the Speed Division or first place in the Handicap portion of the race, the Dutch team elected the latter and was judged the winner based on their flying time of 76 hours, 38 minutes, 12 seconds. Crossing the finish line next were Americans Roscoe Turner and Clyde Pangborn in a Boeing 247D. Turner negotiated the course in 92 hours, 55 minutes, 45 seconds. When the Dutch elected to take the winning spot in the Handicap Division, Turner and Pangborn automatically moved up to second place in the speed race.

The MacRobertson Race attracted a wide variety of aircraft, ranging from transports like Douglas' DC-2 and Boeing's 247D, to small biplanes characterized by the diminutive deHavilland Moth. Many if not most were along for the sport and adventure of the contest. They were really not competitive. The degree of difficulty associated with planning for and winning this race is possibly best illustrated by the travails of one particular pilot who ultimately chose not to participate.

This story began in New York during the spring of 1934. On a warm spring day in June a trim athletic looking man strode into the St. Regis Hotel in New York City for a brief overnight stay. He had just come from Hartford, Connecticut, and conferences with Pratt & Whitney Aircraft representatives. His real destination, however, was the West Coast—more precisely the Lockheed Aircraft Corporation in the city of Burbank, California. To travel there, he would board a United Air Lines Boeing 247 airliner the following morning. He was someone in a hurry.

To the casual observer this individual might have been mistaken for a successful businessman or possibly a Hollywood actor; he was blessed with a genuinely photogenic smile punctuated by a Gallic nose, a firm jaw line and a furrowed brow. It was a combination producing a ruggedly handsome face crowned by short, unruly hair. His real occupation was neither industrialist nor actor, however. Rather, he was a celebrated Australian aviator. His name was Sir Charles E. Kingsford Smith, but he was known

The Boeing 247 was the first truly modern air transport. Introduced to the public in 1933, it featured all-metal construction, cantilever flying surfaces and retractable landing gear. Shown here is the first example powered by two Pratt & Whitney S1D1 Wasp engines. Note the use of Townend style ring cowls and the forward rake of the cockpit windows. One example would be used to advantage in the 1934 MacRobertson Race. Peter M. Bowers collection

more affectionately to his numerous friends as "Smithy." His haste that June day was engendered by the fact that the previous month he had purchased a sleek all-wood Lockheed monoplane. He was anxious to see his new mount.

Born in Hamilton, Queensland, Kingsford Smith served with the Royal Flying Corps during the Great War. After this terrible conflict, his love of flying turned to more peaceful pursuits. He began building an aviation career in 1919. His pioneering air transport efforts in Australia eventually led Kingsford Smith, accompanied by Charles T. P. Ulm, to become the first to fly across the Pacific Ocean from the United States to Australia. The year was 1928. The airplane the two men flew was a Fokker F-VII-3m trimotor christened *Southern Cross* after the heavenly constellation. It was a magnificent achievement, surely the equal of Charles Lindbergh's Atlantic crossing the year before. Kingsford Smith was equally determined to fly in the Mac-Robertson Race. His goal was to win.

Kingsford Smith was undisputedly Australia's most distinguished pilot. After he and Ulm traversed the Pacific, numerous other record flights followed: to England from Australia in record time; numerous flights in and around Australia. No one doubted that Kingsford Smith would be a formidable competitor in the MacRobertson Race, provided he could find a suitable aircraft. It was this mission that led the veteran flyer to Burbank, California, in the spring of 1934.

Race pilot Roscoe Turner and Clyde Pangborn entered a Boeing 247D in the MacRobertson. The D model had revised engine nacelles and full NACA cowlings producing a considerably cleaner power module. This helped boost cruise speed from 161 to 189 miles per hour, even though the Wasp S1H1-Gs were rated at the same power as the earlier S1D1 models on the original Boeing 247. Peter M. Bowers collection

Kingsford Smith evaluated other aircraft for the MacRobertson. His options were either unsuitable or unavailable, at least within his time and financial constraints. He finally turned to Lockheed, a company whose airplanes had acquired a well-deserved reputation for speed in long-distance racing during the early 1930s. The problem was that Kingsford Smith needed an airplane rather quickly. The race was scheduled for October 20, a scant six months away. Fortuitously, Lockheed officials offered a possible solution. They knew of an available Sirius Model 8A. Kingsford Smith's interest in this particular airplane quickly solidified. Lockheed was notified on May 9 that his deposit was "on the way from Fenchurch Export Corporation."[18] The company could begin modification work to convert the Sirius into an Altair.

Kingsford Smith's specifications to Lockheed were the essence of simplicity. He desired a two-place aircraft capable of cruising at 205 miles per hour, and sufficient fuel capacity to insure a 2,900-mile range. Meeting the second objective would prove easier said than done.

The need for a high cruise speed in a long-distance race is obvious. Perhaps less apparent at first glance is the need for a 2,900-mile range. Kingsford Smith's strategy becomes apparent if the MacRobertson route is examined, however. The minimum course distance was 11,300 miles along which were five mandatory stops (see Table 4-2). The first and longest leg was 2,530 miles from London to Bagdad. With the desired range and after expending fuel for takeoff and climb, he would still have a 10 percent reserve to cover en route contingencies.

FROM SIRIUS TO ALTAIR

The two-place Sirius was a four-year-old design with generously panted fixed landing gear and open cockpits. Modifications were required to make it more competitive, however. This was handily accomplished by converting the 175-mile per hour Sirius into the faster more powerful Altair configuration. The wooden aircraft manufacturing era at Lockheed was drawing to a close—only six such aircraft were built or modified during 1934. Lockheed was then concentrating on its new Model 10 Electra all-metal transport. Fortunately the capability to manufacture, repair and modify the wooden ships still existed within the company.

Converting a Sirius into an Altair was relatively easy. Primarily it involved substituting a Lockheed Orion wing, having a retractable landing gear in place of the Sirius fixed-gear flying surface. More generous fillets completed the wing-to-fuselage integration. In this particular conversion, landing flaps were also added. To complete the streamlining process and simultaneously provide a measure of crew comfort, a nicely faired cockpit canopy was added. A new Pratt & Whitney Wasp engine augmented by a controllable pitch propeller rounded out the conversion.

In addition, Lockheed issued factory orders for the installation of a larger oil tank (40 gallons), two small 16-gallon wing fuel tanks, a 110-gallon fuselage fuel tank, as well as a 2-gallon (drinking) water tank. This raised the total fuel load to about 242 gallons, not nearly enough to achieve the sought-after range of 2,900 miles; however, the resulting 5,800 pound gross weight was not excessive. In fact it was essentially the same as the Lockheed Orion Model 9D, which had already earned a Department of Commerce ATC—Approved Type Certificate.

THE ENGINE

The precise engine used in this airplane is a bit confusing at this late date. In his classic account of the great wooden Lockheeds, author Richard Sanders Allen states that it was a Wasp Model SE.[19] A contemporary piece of Lockheed correspondence, however, indicates it was to be an "H" model Wasp.[20] If true, the intended engine was a Wasp S1H1. Yet another reference indicates the Altair was equipped with a Wasp S1D1.[21] Lockheed factory work orders for the airplane shed a bit of light on the subject. The first orders issued for this work specified a *Wasp* Model SE. This was changed in a subsequent shop order to a *Wasp* S1D1. More

Roscoe Turner leased a United Air Lines 247D from October to December 1934 for the Mac-Robertson Race. Internal fuselage fuel tanks provided 869 additional gallons of gasoline, giving the Boeing a total capacity of 1,142 gallons for the race. Fuel filler ports were on top of the fuselage. Peter M. Bowers collection

authoritative and what should be the final answer is found in the Australian certificate of airworthiness issued on September 26, 1934, listing the engine as a *Wasp* Model SE.[22]

THE DILEMMA

MacRobertson rules required every entry to be licensed and certifiably airworthy. Therefore, the fuel capacity envisioned by Kingsford Smith had serious implications. Consider that with an 80 percent power setting to maintain a 205-mile per hour cruise speed, the big Pratt & Whitney Wasp engine would consume something like 35 gallons of gasoline every hour. With a 242-gallon capacity, the airplane had a range of approximately 1,400 miles. To sustain this speed for up to 2,900 miles, which is what Kingsford Smith desperately wanted, an additional 254 gallons

of fuel would have to be crammed into the Altair. Accommodating this fuel volume while simultaneously retaining an acceptable center of gravity condition may have been dicey, but perhaps feasible. The real problem was the added weight this fuel increment imposed—some 1,524 pounds. Gross weight shot up to 7,500 pounds, a whopping 29 percent increase. Moreover, no previous Altair had flown at this gross weight, and none had previously employed landing flaps.

The Australian flyer was advised that obtaining Department of Commerce approval and U.S. civil registration would take time and a new stress analysis on the wing. Quite possibly the wing structure would have to be strengthened. Government concurrence with the stress analysis would then be followed by a flight demonstration.[23] This would take both time and money, commodities in short supply, especially the former.

THE TEMPORARY RESOLUTION

What transpired next is a mixture of fact mingled with deduction. As will be shown, it is a fact that Kingsford Smith elected to forego licensing the aircraft in the United States. It is also known that he was confident in his ability to register the Altair once he was back in Australia. Available Lockheed records confirm that tankage providing a total fuel capacity of 242 gallons was installed as planned. Thus the gross weight would have been consistent with the existing Orion 9D wing stress analysis. It is difficult to imagine that Lockheed would consider reconfiguring Kingsford Smith's airplane for a substantially higher gross weight without insisting on formal certification. To do otherwise would have exposed the company to unacceptable liability.

Modification work on Kingsford Smith's airplane was completed in June. The fuselage was painted "Consolidated Blue" with silver trim. The wings were all silver. It was then sent completely assembled on the deck of the S.S. *Mariposa* from Los Angeles to Sydney, Australia, arriving on July 17, 1934. Originally named *Anzac*, the Altair was hastily renamed *Lady Southern Cross*.[24]

The Altair as built had a fuel capacity of 242 gallons. Kingsford Smith intended to add more capacity once the aircraft was in Australia. Modifying the aircraft further, however, proved to be a problem. The

situation is best summarized in the words of Lockheed President Robert E. Gross:

"At the time Sir Charles Kingsford Smith broached the subject of this plane to us, we pointed out to him that the particular airplane he wanted did not carry an Approved Type Certificate or, indeed, any license from our Department of Commerce. We even went so far as to tell him that in our opinion it could not receive an ATC. The gas load he wished to carry . . . meant that the plane would gross up around 7,500 pounds. This is almost 2,000 pounds over our standard ATC load of 5,800 pounds on the Orion.

"In spite of all our protestations along this line, Sir Charles wanted the airplane and represented to us that he had influence in Australia that could not refuse him an entry ticket. After all, his backer was supposed to be either the backer of the race itself, or somebody very close to him, and Sir Charles said that if he could not get an airplane in the race, nobody could."[25]

THE MISCALCULATION

Ten days after the aircraft arrived in Australia, it was registered and assigned license VH-USB. The vital certificate of airworthiness was not granted at the same time, however, due to the gross weight that would result from the additional fuel Kingsford Smith wanted to carry. In spite of his earlier optimism at Lockheed, Kingsford Smith found that the Australian government was not inclined to give him *carte blanche* with respect to the safety and operating characteristics of a foreign aircraft design. In quiet desperation he cabled Lockheed for help.[26]

Bob Gross was "perturbed over the fact that Kingsford Smith knew [there was no certification] when he bought the plane and [was now] trying to get us to mend his fences."[27] Nonetheless, Gross decided to help. From Lockheed's perspective, the 7,500-pound gross weight Kingsford Smith wanted to impose on the airframe might diminish stress analysis safety factors to unacceptably low or nonexistent value. Therefore, a wing analysis was performed to determine the maximum allowable load. Unfortunately the results of this analysis are lost in time; however, it is known that Kingsford Smith succeeded in having additional fuel capacity installed, bringing the total gross takeoff weight up to 6,700 pounds. An Australian certificate of airworthiness was finally granted at this gross weight on September 26, 1934.[28]

Table 4-2

Gross Weight Estimates
Kingsford Smith Lockheed Altair 8D

	As Built Pounds	As Modified Pounds	Remarks
Empty Weight	3,675	3,675	
Useful Load, Fixed			
Radio		46	Added in Aus.
Australian-built Fuel Tanks & Equip.		58	Estimated
Useful Load, Expendable			
Crew Weight	340	340	
Water, 2-Gal Tank	17	17	
Wing Tank Fuel, Two 16-Gal Tanks	192	192	
Fuselage Fuel, 210-Gal Tank	1,260	1,260	
Added Fuselage Fuel, 12-Gal Tank		72	Added in Aus.*
Added Under Seat Fuel, 20-Gal Tanks		120	Added in Aus.*
Added Wing Fuel, Two 60-Gal Tanks		720	Added in Aus.*
Oil, 40-Gal Tank	300	180	To 24 gallons
Miscellaneous	20	20	
Gross Weight	5,804	6,700	

* Estimated weights. Note that all fuel volumes represent U.S. gallons. To convert to Imperial gallons, multiply by 0.8327.
Sources: Lockheed data and Australian Certificate of Airworthiness.

How did Kingsford Smith finally obtain his Australian certificate of airworthiness? Only speculation is possible this long after the event, though the following scenario seems likely. The airframe and its components were designed to withstand some maximum expected load during normal aircraft operation. This is referred to as the *limit load*. No structural deformation is permitted under limit load conditions. The maximum load the airframe can support is defined as the *ultimate load*. And finally, the ratio of ultimate load to limit load is termed the *factor of safety*. This ratio is often 1.5, although it can vary, depending upon the structural component and aircraft mission. Should stress analysis (and test) indicate that a given structure or component will withstand somewhat more than the ultimate load, then a positive *margin of safety* exists.[30]

With these definitions in mind, Lockheed's special stress analysis results almost certainly indicated a permissible maximum gross weight of 6,700 pounds. This may be said with confidence for two reasons. First, Kingsford Smith solicited Lockheed input in his quest for an Australian airworthiness

Turner and Pangborn flew their Boeing 247D to second place behind the specially built deHavilland Comet in the MacRobertson Race Speed Division, with a total elapsed time of 92 hours, 55 minutes, 45 seconds. Their average speed was about 122 miles per hour. Following the race, the Boeing was returned to United Air Lines. Turner's race registration of NR-257Y was changed to NC-13369 when United took possession. Peter M. Bowers collection

The 6,700 pound gross allowed by the Australian authorities granting the certificate of airworthiness represented a 900-pound increase relative to the as-built gross weight. It was virtually all additional fuel weight (see Table 4-2).[29] Note that this was still considerably short of the 7,500 pounds that Kingsford Smith originally wanted. In the as-built configuration at Lockheed, the Altair was shipped with a fuel tank capacity of 375 gallons. When modifications were completed in Australia, this capacity increased to an estimated 394 gallons. At 7,500 pounds, fuel capacity would have approached 500 gallons.

The second airplane to finish the MacRobertson was a Douglas DC-2 belonging to the Dutch KLM airline. Christened Uiver and under the command of K. D. Parmentier and J. J. Moll, the DC-2 carried three paying passengers as well as mail during the race. Parmentier and Moll averaged slightly over 125 miles per hour. Parmentier elected to take first place in the Handicap Division, allowing Turner to move up to second place in the Speed Division. Peter M. Bowers collection

certificate. The company would not want to risk its reputation nor endanger the Altair crew. Second, Australian authorities had to rely on a Lockheed recommendation for there was really no alternate engineering basis upon which to make a determination under the time constraint. Lockheed most likely took advantage of any existing positive margin of safety and then, if necessary, suggested a small reduction in the factor of safety (for example, reducing this criterion from 1.5 to 1.4). As no evidence exists that structural reinforcement was undertaken in Australia, these are really the only two options available that would allow gross weight to be increased.[31]

During this period of suspended animation as Kingsford Smith struggled to certify the Altair, rumors began to circulate that he didn't really want to fly in the MacRobertson. The onslaught of malicious gossip angered Smithy: "If my critics think I am frightened, they can accompany me in the race!"[32] The uncertainty of Smithy's entry in the race played on through September. Finally on October 8, the U.S. Department of Commerce issued a Group 2 certificate for the airplane, apparently at the increased gross weight. This information was cabled to Australia. In the interim, the indefatigable flyer encountered a mechanical problem. While preparing for the journey to England, inspection revealed cracks in the engine cowling. This was at the end of September. The aircraft was grounded in Sydney for repairs.

Over the next few days, Kingsford Smith's participation in the big race oscillated between extremes. One day the prospect appeared hopeless while the next it seemed at least possible. Race rules required all aircraft to be in England at Mildenhall Airdrome no later than October 14. Kingsford Smith's participation appeared doomed. There was now insufficient time to make the long journey from Australia to England before the deadline. On October 2, Smithy announced his withdrawal from the race.[33] He "expressed bitter disappointment that he had been forced to withdraw because of delays in repairing the engine [cowling] of his plane. Two more days will be necessary to finish the work, making his departure impossible before Saturday, allowing only eight days to reach Mildenhall by the 14th."[34] Royal Aero Club officials in London then notified him that arrival at Mildenhall after October 14 "would not necessarily" disqualify him. Their equivocal pronouncement gave Kingsford Smith pause to briefly reconsider, but in the end he withdrew.

THE ASSESSMENT

Virtually all accounts of Kingsford Smith's withdrawal from the MacRobertson allude to the cowling problem. On closer inspection, there appears to have been not one, but three reasons for his withdrawal: the unexpected cowling problem; certification delay, leaving precious little time to arrive in Great Britain; and a fundamental lack of aircraft range. Cowling defects, although serious, should not have caused a major delay. More critical was lack of any certification until shortly before the race. Kingsford Smith withdrew on October 2. Department of Commerce certification occurred eight days later. His inability to obtain certification at a gross weight approaching 7,500 pounds thus placed a decided limit on range for the aircraft. Kingsford Smith sought a range of 2,900 miles at a cruising speed of 205 miles per hour, and this was not to be.

To fully comprehend why range was so critical, it is first necessary to understand how the race was organized, and then appreciate the major competition. There were two race divisions. One was pure speed—the first entry to arrive at the finish line (after five mandatory stops) won the race. The other section was a handicap race wherein a speed for each airplane was predetermined, taking into account gross weight, payload, maximum sea level horsepower and wing surface area.[35] The aircraft that exceeded this speed by the greatest margin would win the handicap division. Only flight time was counted in the handicap race, not elapsed time. Although

One famous flyer who did not participate in the MacRobertson was Sir Charles Kingsford Smith. Delays in obtaining an Australian certificate of airworthiness for his Lockheed Altair were blamed. This, together with a cracked engine cowling, eventually forced Kingsford Smith to withdraw from the spectacular race. In spite of esthetically pleasing lines and several modern aerodynamic features, the Altair represented older technology. Peter M. Bowers collection

this race was no less demanding, it was considerably less prestigious in the eyes of the press. This perception was reinforced by prize money allocation: A$12,000 and A$3,000 [Australian dollars] for the speed and handicap divisions, respectively. There is little doubt Kingsford Smith intended to run in the more glamorous and financially rewarding speed contest.

When Sir Charles Kingsford Smith selected an American-built aircraft for the race, a storm of criticism erupted. He was accused of being un-British and disrespectful of the "Mother Country." Author Terry Gwynn-Jones described Kingsford Smith's reaction to the furor: "I tried to obtain a British plane for this race—tried damn hard and couldn't,' he angrily answered his critics, pointing out that the only aircraft he had been offered was too slow and had insufficient range. 'By using such an aircraft I would be condemning myself to a loser's position. Why should I have to do that?' Smithy demanded."[36]

Ironically, even with the Altair, he was not very competitive. It was not the fastest aircraft in the race. Its cruising speed was about 200–205 miles an hour. The top competition was faster in the form of three de Havilland D.H.88 Comets, specifically designed and built for the MacRobertson. They could cruise at 220 miles per hour for an impressive 2,900 miles! This was sufficient to fly without refueling from London to Bagdad, the longest leg of the entire speed division race, and still have a comfortable fuel reserve.

Altair range limitations are quite evident as shown in Table 4-3. The Australian certificate of airworthiness permitted a maximum gross weight of 6,700 pounds of which 2,365 pounds (394 gallons) was gasoline. Assuming a cruising speed of 205 miles per hour the Altair would have had a range of around 2,300 miles, not enough to fly nonstop between all of the mandatory landing spots on the route. As a consequence, the Altair would have to make three additional refueling stops along the way. The Comets could fly at a

higher cruise speed and their range permitted the minimum five mandatory stops. Kingsford Smith was at a decided disadvantage.

Perhaps feeling dispirited by events that kept him out of the MacRobertson Race, Smithy vowed to fly across the Pacific in the Altair—now named *Lady Southern Cross*. By doing this he would "justify the faith of his backers and . . . return his machine to the United States for sale."[37] His departure date from Australia was October 21, 1934, one day after the launch of the MacRobertson racers from Mildenhall. Australia's most famous aviator would be out of the country when the racers crossed the finish line.

THE LAST LONG FLIGHT

Kingsford Smith's flight across the Pacific via Fiji, Hawaii and San Francisco was successful, more so than any subsequent attempts to sell the airplane. By mid-November, 1934, the Altair was back in Burbank for maintenance. In January, Lockheed test

Table 4-3

MacRobertson Race Routing
Estimated Refueling Stops Required for Kingsford-Smith *Altair*
394-Gallon Fuel Capacity

City	Speed Division Miles	Handicap Division Miles	Refueling Stops for Altair	Miles Between Refueling	Remarks
London, England		0			Start
Marseilles, France		629			Approved landing place
Rome, Italy		385	Rome	1,014	Approved landing place
Athens, Greece		652			Approved landing place
Aleppo, Syria		758			Approved landing place
Baghdad, Iraq	2,530	447	Baghdad	1,205	**Mandatory stop**
Bushire, Iran (Persia)		486			Approved landing place
Jask		484			Approved landing place
Karachi, Pakistan		586	Karachi	1,556	Approved landing place
Jodhpur, India		381			Approved landing place
Allahabad, India	2,300	542	Allahabad	923	**Mandatory stop**
Calcutta, India		462			Approved landing place
Rangoon, Burma		640			Approved landing place
Bangkok, Thailand		362	Bangkok	1,464	Approved landing place
Alor Star, Malaya		529			Approved landing place
Singapore	2,210	412	Singapore	941	**Mandatory stop**
Batavia, Dutch East Indies		571			Approved landing place
Rambang		602			Approved landing place
Koepang, Timor		495			Approved landing place
Darwin, Australia	2,084	510	Darwin	2,178	**Mandatory stop**
Newcastle Waters, Australia		381			Approved landing place
Cloncurry, Australia		517			Approved landing place
Charleville, Australia	1,389	538	Charleville	1,463	**Mandatory stop**
Narromine, Australia		418			Approved landing place
Melbourne, Australia	787	426	Melbourne	844	**Finish**
Total Miles	11,300	12,213	8 Fuel Stops	11,561	

pilot Marshall Headle flew the Altair to Union Air Terminal, where the airplane was put into storage.

In the summer of 1935, *Lady Southern Cross* was taken out of hibernation for one last glamorous adventure: an attempted record flight from England to Australia. At Kingsford Smith's orders the Wasp engine was overhauled and the plane made ready for the ocean journey to England.

On Saturday, September 21, 1935, "Sir Charles Kingsford Smith, Australian flier, sailed on the Cunard White Star liner Britannic . . . for what he hoped would be his last long flight."[38] His copilot for this final adventure was John Thomas Pethybridge (Tommy). If he succeeded in posting a new speed mark from England to Australia, it would amount to a vindication of sorts for missing the MacRobertson Race.

Kingsford Smith finally got away on November 6. All went well at first. The flyers reached Athens in eight hours, and then proceeded to Baghdad and Allahabad. After refueling and with the sun setting across the northern India landscape, Kingsford Smith guided the airplane into a darkening sky. This time his destination was Singapore, with an expected dawn arrival on November 9. This leg of the trip carried Smithy over Calcutta and Akyab, Burma. The last reported sighting of the Altair was 2:25 A.M. (local time) over the Bay of Bengal, south of Akyab. But by sunrise in Singapore there was no sign of the Altair. Within a short time it was apparent the two flyers were down somewhere.

A massive hunt began immediately, but failed to locate the missing pilots in the ensuing days. Contemporary newspaper stories tell of a monsoon raging over the Indian Ocean at the time of the flight. It was speculated that Sir Charles ran into this foul weather and crashed into the ocean. No trace of either Sir Charles Kingsford Smith or John Thomas Pethybridge was ever found. With the disappearance of the Altair and its pilots, a bright chapter in Australian aviation passed into history. Prophetically, this was truly Kingsford Smith's "last long flight," . . . and *with melting wax and loosened strings sunk hapless Icarus on unfaithful wings.* The Altair and its crew vanished into the sea.

By 1934–1935, the fabulous wooden Lockheeds, in spite of their brisk speed and aesthetically appealing lines, represented the technology of yesterday. On the drawing boards and in the air were much more advanced designs, possessing greater speed and better performance at altitude. The pace of development in the field of aviation was unrelenting.

chapter 5

The Crucial Years

And blood in torrents pour
In vain—always in vain
For war breeds war again.

John Davidson • *War Song*

The terrible chaos brought on by the 1914–1918 World War was superseded by a largely peaceful and prosperous period during the ensuing decade. In rather stark contrast, the 1930s were marked by a prolonged and severe economic depression. Both decades left indelible marks on the American landscape. The field of aeronautics was alternately stimulated and battered by the contrasting financial environments of these two decades. Nonetheless, this 20-year period marked breathtaking advances in theoretical and applied technology. Underlying this phenomenon, however, was the burgeoning postwar German economic and political turmoil. It was a harbinger of future strife tied to the outcome of the Great War. In the prophetic words of Scottish poet and playwright John Davison . . . *war breeds war again*.

In the decade leading up to World War II, aviation sustained a buoyant advance—from a technological if not always a commercial perspective. The industry remained tiny compared to more mature industries, yet its advances were heretofore unparalleled. The use of metal airframe construction, retractable landing gears, flush riveted surfaces, enclosed cockpits, superior fuels, and more powerful engines all became commonplace. (This period also saw the quiet birth of the aircraft turbine engine, a profound invention that would dramatically revolutionize air transport.)

America began to emerge, albeit slowly, as a world leader in aeronautics. It is somewhat ironic that during an era when this country began developing and producing the finest air transports, heavy bombers, air-cooled radial engines, high octane fuels and the like, it still lagged behind Great Britain, Germany and Japan in pursuit aircraft performance. This incongruity is most often attributed to existing Air Corps doctrine, in which strategic bombing was heavily emphasized. Author Phillip S. Meilinger makes an argument that design decisions regarding the application of new technology were responsible for this deplorable state of affairs.[1]

In spite of the definite race plane design trend toward low-wing monoplanes, the American military clung to the biplane configuration for its fighters. Boeing received an order for nine P-12 pursuits during November 1928. It was the beginning of a series of these sturdy biplanes, which ran through May 1932 when the last one was delivered. Shown here is a P-12E, counterpart to the Navy F4B-3 model. Over 100 P-12Es were produced, the most of any P-12 variant made for the Army. Peter M. Bowers collection

In part, so this argument goes, the pursuit airplane was underappreciated by the military. Coupled with this was an unwillingness on the part of industry to risk investing substantially in new and potentially attractive pursuit designs for lack of an adequate market. There was no commercial marketplace for pursuit airplanes, and foreign sales of arms and equipment was strictly regulated. In contrast, there was a definable market for new commercial airliners. This type of aircraft was more akin to bombers and, added to the prevailing Air Corps emphasis on strategic bombing, posed a less risky investment of universally limited capital resources. If this perspective is correct, it is also highly understandable during a prolonged period of economic distress, one based on sound business decisions.

Nineteen twenty-nine was a defining year in a number of respects. First and foremost, it marked the beginning of the Great Depression, an austere time that left its imprint on virtually every aspect of human endeavor. Certainly the nascent aircraft industry was hit very hard by the barren economic times then just starting. Survival, not growth, became a badge of success. Business failures littered the American landscape. The aphorism suggesting that a pilot stood a greater risk of starvation than of meeting his fate in an airplane accident seemed only a modest exaggeration.

This same year saw Great Britain capture the world speed record when Squadron Leader A. H. Orlebar flew a Supermarine S.6 to a speed of 357.723 miles per hour. It was the first time Britain gained the record, and Orlebar's speed represented a 12.3 percent increase over the previous mark owned by Major Mario de Bernardi of Italy.

The 1929 National Air Races in Cleveland delineated another significant first. A southern gentleman from Atlanta, Georgia, named Douglas Davis, sped to victory in a previously unheralded pylon contest simply identified as Event 26 on the race program. The spoils of this victory included a cash prize of $750 together with a silver loving cup valued at $25 provided by the sponsor, Thompson Products, Incorporated. It was the genesis of perhaps the most prestigious pylon racing event in history: the Thompson Trophy Race.

Davis flew a low-wing monoplane dubbed the Travel Air *Mystery Ship* in Event 26. This was a

The Schneider Trophy Race produced the fastest airplanes in the world. In 1929, Great Britain's Supermarine S.6 won the contest at a speed of just under 329 miles per hour. Not long after the Schneider victory, the S.6 broke the world speed record with an average velocity of 357.7 miles per hour. Compare this with the Travel Air *Mystery Ship* winning speed of 195 miles per hour in Event 26 (predecessor of the Thompson Trophy Race) in the 1929 National Air Races. The S.6 engine output was almost five times greater than that produced by the Travel Air powerplant. John Garrett collection

free-for-all race. In contemporary terms it would be cataloged an Unlimited Class event. Davis' winning speed was 194.9 miles per hour, although he may well have averaged over 200 miles per hour.[2] In the process he bested entries from both the Army and the Navy. Second place was taken by Lieutenant R. G. Breene in an Air Corps Curtiss XP-3A Hawk biplane specially modified for the race. Roscoe Turner placed third with a Lockheed Vega (163.44 miles per hour) followed by Navy Commander J. J. Clark in a modified Curtiss F6C-3 at a slow speed of 153.38 miles per hour. Table 5-1 gives comparative characteristics of the Travel Air, Army, and Navy entries in this race.

Davis' victory raised eyebrows. For first time a civilian airplane out-sped a military entry in a pylon race. That the Travel Air *Mystery Ship* was four percent faster than the Army XP-3A was really not the issue. Rather, the situation illustrated a fundamental deficiency in military pursuit development. Consider that Boeing and Curtiss biplane fighters were still being ordered and taken on strength by the Army and Navy during the 1930s. The Boeing P-12E and P-12F deliveries were ongoing during 1931 and 1932. A similar process was occurring on the East Coast with Curtiss. Its P-6 series fighters were taken on strength during the same period. Although perhaps the pinnacle of World War I period designs, these open cockpit, fixed landing gear, externally braced pursuits were nonetheless relics of a bygone time.

In startling contrast, the Army Air Corps proceeded with development of the Martin B-10 bomber, a significant and innovative step forward. Indeed, the B-10 was so advanced that Glenn Martin received the 1932 Collier Trophy award. Of all-metal semimonocoque construction employing a cantilever wing and retractable landing gear, the primary production version was the B-10B introduced

Table 5-1

1929 Thompson Race Aircraft Characteristics

	Travel Air Mystery Ship	Army Curtiss XP-3A	Navy Curtiss F6C-3
Year Built	1929	19281	19271
Serial Number		28-189	A-7144
Wingspan, Ft - In	29 - 2	31 - 6	31 - 6
Wing Area, Ft2	120	252	252
Empty Weight, Lb	1,475	2,107	1,980
Gross Weight, Lb	1,940	2,788	2,785
Maximum S/L Speed, Mph	235	1712	155
Race Speed, Mph	194.90	186.84	153.38
Engine	Wright	P&W R-1340-3	Curtiss D-12
Horsepower	425	410	400

Notes: 1. Modified in 1929 for the National Air Races.
2. This is the maximum speed of the military version. As modified for the 1929 National Air Races, the XP-3A was considerably faster

Table 5-2

Comparison of Contemporary American Bomber and Pursuit Aircraft

Type	Martin B-10B	Boeing P-12E	Curtiss P-6E
Year of Prototype	1932	1928	1931
Year Entering Service	1935	1931	1932
Maximum Speed, Mph	213	189	193
Rated Altitude, Ft	10,000	7,000	Sea Level
Cruising Speed, Mph	193	160	167

Source: Ray Wagner, *American Combat Planes.*

during 1934. It featured an enclosed cockpit for the pilot and gunners, and was faster than any pursuit in the Air Corps inventory (see Table 5-2). It was also the beginning of a period producing great strides in aeronautical technology: metal construction, more powerful engines, better fuels.

A disturbing victory by the Travel Air *Mystery Ship* may in part have caused Army Air Corps planners to reassess pursuit plane development. Certainly the sensational performance of Martin's B-10 bomber in 1932 brought into sharp focus the disparity between contemporary American pursuit and bomber performance. Martin's evolutionary XB-907 (prototype B-10 bomber) exhibited a high speed of just under 200 miles per hour aided in no small part by retractable landing gear and attention to streamlining. Subsequent versions exceeded the 200-mile per hour barrier—the B-10B production variant being the swiftest at 213 miles per hour—coupled with service ceilings in excess of 20,000 feet. Range was in the vicinity of 600 miles for the Martin bombers.

Existing first-line pursuits, in contrast, could not match this performance. Curtiss' P-12C, biplane pursuit delivered in quantity during 1930, could muster a top speed of only 178 miles per hour, hardly enough to chase down an "attacking" B-10 formation two years later except under ideal circumstances. Even the esthetically pleasing Curtiss P-6E, perhaps the epitome of biplane fighter design, could deliver only 198 miles per hour at sea level, and less at the altitudes where it would have to contend with evolving bomber designs.

The Travel Air Mystery Ship *was a sensation when it appeared before the 1929 National Air Race crowd at the Cleveland Municipal Airport. The racer took full advantage of the new NACA cowling. It was relatively small, compact, light weight and well streamlined for its day. Doug Davis won Event No. 26 with relative ease as he out-sped two military rivals. This profile drawing was one of several produced by the late Jack Abbott. John Garrett collection*

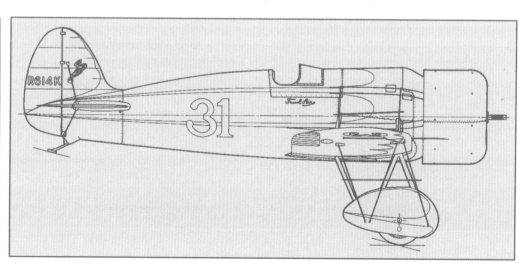

Sea Level Speed Trends for Pursuit & Racing Aircraft
1929 - 1934

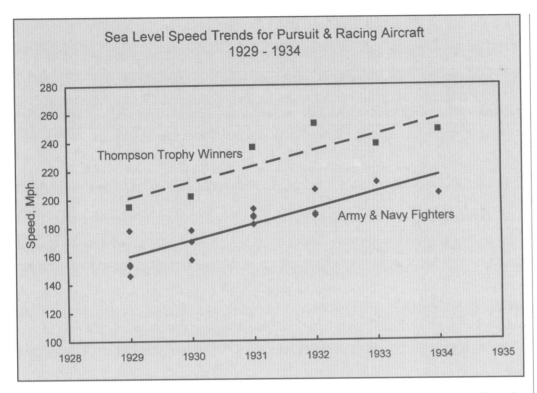

Thompson Trophy Winners

Army & Navy Fighters

Both Thompson Trophy racers and contemporary American military fighters demonstrated steady if not dramatic speed increases during the 1930s. The Thompson airplanes were about 40 miles per hour faster, based on the chart linear trend lines. That the two trend lines are basically parallel may be attributed to the fact that both classes of aircraft drew upon the same evolving technology.

The single exception to this rather forlorn situation was the Lockheed XP-900 (nee YP-24) pursuit of late 1931. Powered by a turbosupercharged Curtiss V-1570-23 engine, the short-lived two-seat Lockheed design provided a glimpse of the future. Patterned after the commercial low-wing Lockheed Sirius DL-2, the XP-900 demonstrated a top speed of 214 miles per hour, while its turbocharged engine permitted a

In past years, the National Air Races were held in various cities across the country on a rotating basis. Cleveland hosted the event in 1929. Cliff Henderson eventually negotiated a long-term arrangement in 1931 for use of the Cleveland Municipal Airport as a quasi-permanent site for the races. With the exception of 1933 and 1936, when the races were held in Los Angeles, the Cleveland continued to host the program. John Garrett collection

The Travel Air Mystery Ship caused quite a stir when it appeared at the 1929 National Air Races. It had a straightaway sea level top speed of around 235 miles per hour. Although a very clean design, it still relied on an externally braced wing, using both struts and wires. In this respect, it was not quite as advanced as Lockheed's basic 1927 Vega design. Beech Aircraft via John Garrett collection

service ceiling of over 26,000 feet.[3] Like the B-10, the XP-900 utilized retractable landing gear. Its fuselage was all-metal construction, but the design retained what was essentially a wooden Sirius wing. Delivered in September 1931, the prototype airplane proved generally superior in performance to any existing Army or Navy pursuit. Unfortunately, the prototype YP-24, whose designation was changed from XP-900 upon acceptance by the Air Corps, crashed shortly thereafter.[4] Detroit Aircraft Corporation descended into bankruptcy, and Lockheed, which was a division of the corporation, suffered the same fate.

The Detroit-Lockheed pursuit nonetheless may be considered an ancestor of modern fighter aircraft design. It clearly demonstrated the performance benefits accrued through use of aerodynamic refinements and supercharged engines. It was not without deficiencies, however. The fact that it was a two-place pursuit was one impractical aspect, insofar as what would be needed for most fighter applications in World War II. The wooden Sirius wing was not a step forward, but a financial expedient for a company about to go out of business. In spite of this, the design combined sufficient attributes to afford it recognition as a glimpse of a new era.

Navy fighters of this same period stubbornly adhered to the formula of a biplane powered by an air-cooled radial engine. An apparent reticence toward adopting monoplane arrangements with sleek liquid-cooled engines may appear backward today, but there were ample reasons at the time. Perhaps foremost was a lack of funding. Military budgets were austere during the Great Depression. The Navy had invested considerable money in the air-cooled radial and it only made sense to exploit this investment.

There were more pragmatic considerations as well. Navy aircraft carriers posed special constraints. Carrier decks were short, compared to the landing fields available to the Air Corps. Biplanes typically exhibited lower landing speeds than their monoplane counterparts. This was a critical consideration. Further, once on the carrier deck, compact biplane fighters presented a smaller footprint, thus allowing more planes to be stored on the flight deck as well as below. Conversely, monoplanes tended to be heavier and larger, and they landed at higher speeds. Money for a new generation of larger aircraft carriers was not in the fiscal cards at the turn of the decade.

U.S. Navy Aircraft Carriers Prior to December 7, 1941

Name	Commission Date	Flight Deck Size
CV 1 Langley	March 20, 1922	523 ft x 65 ft
CV 3 Lexington	December 14, 1927	866 ft x 106 ft
CV 2 Saratoga	November 16, 1927	866 ft x 106 ft
CV 4 Ranger	June 4, 1934	709 ft x 86 ft
CV 5 Yorktown	September 30, 1937	802 ft x 86 ft
CV 6 Enterprise	May 12, 1938	802 ft x 86 ft
CV 7 Wasp	April 25, 1940	727 ft x 93 ft
CV 8 Hornet	October 20, 1941	802 ft x 86 ft

Sources: U.S. Navy, *Dictionary of American Naval Fighting Ships.* See also Norman Friedman, *U.S. Aircraft Carriers.*

Table 5-3

The Travel Air Mystery Ship *was powered by a Wright J-6-9 Whirlwind. Its full cowling was patterned after the designs developed by NACA a year or two earlier. It is difficult to estimate how aerodynamically efficient the cowl may have been due to the rather large gap between the fuselage and the aft end of the cowl. Ideally, air flow leaving the cowl should merge with the external air mass at the same velocity to avoid discontinuity.* Beech Aircraft via John Garrett collection

Consider that the first Navy aircraft carrier, the U.S.S. *Langley*, was not commissioned until March 1922. Even then, it was a conversion of an existing Navy collier, the *Jupiter*. Almost six years elapsed before two more carriers joined the fleet. These were the U.S.S. *Saratoga* and *Lexington*, commissioned in late 1927. Like the *Langley*, these vessels were converted to carriers from partially completed battle cruisers. (Five more carriers would join the fleet before the Pearl Harbor attack as shown in Table 5-3).

In addition to the foregoing arguments, it can also be said from a Navy perspective that monoplanes were faster than biplanes, but not sufficiently so as to recommend their use on existing carriers. This can be seen from the data in Table 5-4, which presents maximum speed and landing speed for several Army

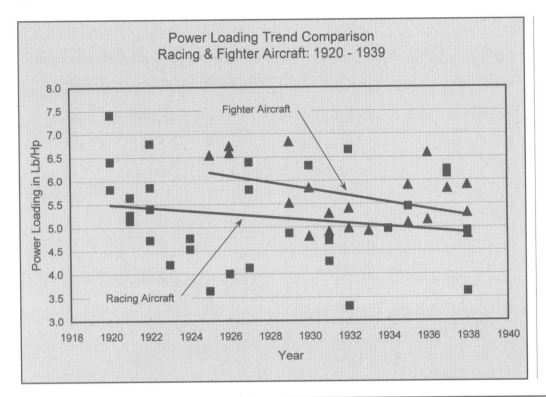

Power Loading Trend Comparison
Racing & Fighter Aircraft: 1920 - 1939

Refinements in aerodynamic streamlining were responsible in some measure for speed increases in the 20 years leading up to World War II. Brute horsepower, however, was equally the basis of higher speeds, if not more so. One parameter used to assess designs is power loading; namely, gross weight divided by rated horsepower. There is a great deal of scatter in the data; however, linear trend lines indicate both racers and fighter aircraft power loadings were decreasing. Fighter or pursuit power loading factors were diminishing at a greater rate than their counterparts as more powerful engines were readily available to the military. The aircraft were not getting any lighter. Rather, engine horsepower was measurably increasing.

Wing loading trends, that is gross weight divided by wing area, increased during the two decades between world wars. Interestingly, trends for racing and pursuit airplanes were essentially parallel during this period. Wing loading determines minimum speed, and thus stall and landing speeds. Greater wing loadings became acceptable in part because pilots learned to cope with higher landing speeds. More important, lift-increasing devices, such as slats and landing flaps, came into use, thus reducing landing speed to acceptable levels.

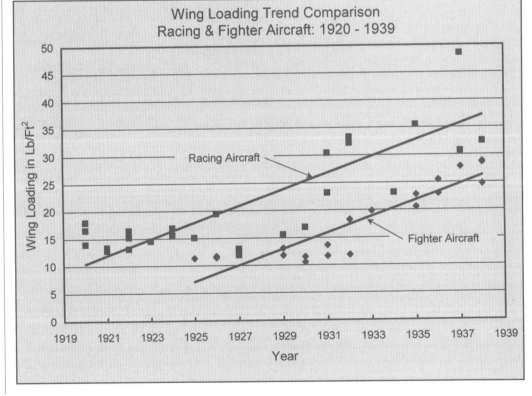

Wing Loading Trend Comparison
Racing & Fighter Aircraft: 1920 - 1939

One reason the late 1920s and early 1930s are looked upon as the "golden age" is the colorful markings applied to Army Air Corps pursuit airplanes. This series of three Curtiss P-6E Hawk profiles from the 1932–1933 era depict examples from the 17th and 94th Pursuit Squadrons, 1st Pursuit Group. Walt Jefferies artwork

The Army entry in Event 26 of the 1929 races was a specially prepared XP-3A The engine was reportedly a Pratt & Whitney Wasp R-1340-3 developing 450 horsepower. In addition to a propeller spinner and engine cowl, the racer incorporated fairings blending the cowl circular cross-section into the flat-sided fuselage geometry. A final touch was a sweeping low profile windscreen. The modified but dated biplane design was, however, no match for the new Travel Air racer. Peter M. Bowers collection

monoplane and Navy biplane fighters. Two aircraft in Table 5-4 make an interesting comparison: Boeing's P-26A monoplane flown by the Air Corps, and the Navy F4B-4 biplane. Each airplane was produced in quantity and used extensively by the respective air services. A prototype of the P-26 flew in early 1932. An early prototype of what became the F4B-4 first took to the air in mid-1928. The prototype of the F4B series (Boeing Model 83) metamorphosed to a workhorse Navy fighter by adopting a metal fuselage construction, and a drag-reducing ring cowl surrounding a Pratt & Whitney Wasp engine of increased power. It was delivered in quantity during 1932.

Boeing began designing its Model 248 monoplane pursuit in 1931. It used a Pratt & Whitney Wasp power module similar to that employed by the F4B-4. Like its Navy counterpart, the P-26 had an open cockpit and utilized a ring cowl to reduce aerodynamic drag. There the similarity ended, however. Unlike the F4B-4, the P-26 was a low-wing monoplane incorporating fully faired landing gear and wheel assemblies. Landing flaps, just then coming into vogue, were incorporated to increase lift at low velocities and reduce landing speed. As a consequence, the P-26A enjoyed a nontrivial 24 percent increase in speed over the F4B-4. Landing speed for the Navy fighter was

Twenty-five P-12F pursuits were ordered during December 1931, the last of which was delivered in May 1932. The "F" model is readily distinguishable from earlier P-12s due to its extended and enlarged head rest. This Wright Field example is radio equipped as witnessed by the antenna masts and wires. Like a number of airplanes in this era, the P-12 marked an evolution or transition in design philosophy. The fuselage, tail, and control surfaces were of metal construction, indicative of future trends. Conversely, the biplane configuration was retained and the wings were fabric covered. Peter M. Bowers collection

A strong faction within the Air Corps became advocates of bombing aircraft, beginning in the early 1930s. Part of this enthusiasm derived from Martin's 1931 XB-907 two-engine bomber design, which incorporated much of the latest thinking in aerodynamics and construction. The prototype shown here still reflected traditional thinking, in that it had open cockpits. More important, however, was the monocoque all-metal construction and attention to streamline design. Peter M. Bowers collection

Until the Boeing P-26 entered service, Army pursuit squadrons were equipped with biplanes that were not significantly advanced over their World War I counterparts. The height of biplane pursuits was reached with the Curtiss P-6E, depicted here being readied for a night takeoff. The aircraft is painted in the markings of the 17th Pursuit Squadron, 1st Pursuit Group, from Selfridge Field. Walt Jefferies artwork

Table 5-4

Contemporary Army and Navy Fighter Aircraft

Model	Service	Type	High Speed Mph	Landing Speed Mph
YP-24	Army	Monoplane	214	73
P-26A	Army	Monoplane	234	83
YP-29A	Army	Monoplane	242	82
P-30	Army	Monoplane	239	77
XP-31	Army	Monoplane	184	81
F8C-4	Navy	Biplane	137	59
XFJ-2	Navy	Biplane	193	64
F9C-2	Navy	Biplane	177	65
F4B-1	Navy	Biplane	176	59
F4B-4	Navy	Biplane	188	61

Source: Ray Wagner, *American Combat Planes.*

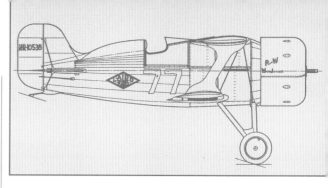

The Laird LC-DW-300 captured the 1930 Thompson Trophy. Although built specifically for racing, the design heritage of this airplane, immediately apparent, represents the traditional Matty Laird approach. It was the first and last biplane to win this premier race. In a real sense, the biplane racer went out on top when Speed Holman won the 1930 Thompson. It was without a doubt the end of an era. Monoplane configurations were becoming increasingly popular. Jack Abbott drawing, Garrett collection

just 73 percent of the Army pursuit, a factor of greater significance to Bureau of Aeronautics engineers considering its carrier application.

The rapidity of aeronautical design advancement during the early 1930s quickly reduced both the P-26 and F4B designs into obsolescence. Even so, there was no rush to rectify the situation. "Until Germany started rearming," as Brigadier General Benjamin S. Kelsey recalled, "there was cause for impatience but not alarm,"[5] The alarm sounded toward the end of the decade, as German insatiability for expansion became ever more obvious.

COMPARISONS

Any comparison of American fighters and contemporary racing planes is a precarious task, because of the differing design objectives for the two aircraft types. The racing machine is basically a single-point design. The only criterion is maximum speed for the duration of a given race or speed record trial. Virtually all other considerations are subordinated in the quest for speed. In contrast, the pursuit or fighter plane is an exercise in tradeoffs between maximum speed and other desirable or necessary qualities including: maneuverability, range or endurance, climb performance, armament requirements, landing speed, ease of maintenance, pilot visibility.

In spite of design requirement differences between the two types of craft, there is a natural tendency to compare racers and fighters specifically with

The Martin B-10 evolved from the prototype XB-907. The B-10B shown in this photograph reveals design improvements evolved over time. Crew positions were now fully enclosed. The landing gear retracted into the engine nacelles, although like the Douglas DC-3, a portion of the wheel was still exposed. Powered by Wright R-1820-33 engines, the B-10B was capable of 213 miles per hour at 10,000 feet, much better performance than standard Air Corps fighters of the time. Peter M. Bowers collection

respect to high speed. To the press and lay public, defeat of both the Army and Navy entries in Event 26 of the 1929 races by a commercially designed airplane was perhaps troubling if not altogether shocking. A closer examination of the race is warranted if only because it was an upset, and the basis for some criticism of the military. Objectivity requires consideration of the results in a broader context.

That the Travel Air *Mystery Ship* was somewhat faster *at sea level* than the Army XP-3A is not in question. Other performance characteristics, especially at altitude, cannot be compared due to a lack of available data. In terms of the race results, there was an average speed difference of 8 miles per hour. Davis' winning speed of 194.9 miles per hour was approximately four percent higher than Lieutenant

Certainly the B-10 bomber was an advancement compared to older Air Corps models, but the new state-of-the-art had plenty of room for improvement. This close-up reveals sheet metal fabrication techniques employed during the early 1930s. Note the corrugated structure used on top of the fuselage for stiffness. Adjacent metal skin sections are mated using lap joints rather than butt joints. Flush riveting was not yet available. Peter M. Bowers collection

Concurrent with the introduction of Martin B-10 bombers, pursuit pilots had to content themselves with World War I style biplanes. The Curtiss P-6E was perhaps the cleanest example of a biplane fighter. It was powered with a 700-horsepower Curtiss V-1570-23 engine, giving it a maximum speed of just over 190 miles per hour from sea level to 5,000 feet, measurably slower than Martin's new bomber. The engine coolant radiator was slung beneath the fuselage and nicely faired. The use of ethylene glycol allowed the radiator size to be reduced considerably, and Curtiss did a nice job of enclosing the appendage to minimize drag. Peter M. Bowers collection

Breene's second-place finish at 186.8 miles per hour, certainly not a tremendously large difference. Nor were these speeds particularly indicative of the maximum velocity of either machine. Most sources indicate that the *Mystery Ship* had a top sea level speed of 235 miles per hour. Assuming Davis flew the 50-mile triangular race course at essentially wide-open throttle, the 40 miles per hour difference between maximum straightaway speed and the average race speed was largely attributable to speed lost during 15 pylon turns of 120 degrees each. By the same rationale, the specially race-prepared XP-3A was probably capable of something in the vicinity of 225 miles per hour. (The unmodified XP-3A has a listed top speed of 171 miles per hour.) And finally, air racing is a three-dimensional arena, and as a consequence, variations in average speed between two airplanes is also dependent upon piloting technique. It is consequently difficult to more closely judge speed differences between the *Mystery Ship* and the XP-3A.

RACE PLANE TRENDS

Race planes continued to demonstrate higher maximum speeds than American service aircraft over the ensuing years. Beginning with Doug Davis' victory in the 1929 race, a new racing plane design captured the Thompson Trophy Race each year through 1933, as shown in Table 5-5. Davis' remarkable feat was followed by in succession by the Laird *Solution*, Gee Bee Z, Gee Bee R-1 and Wedell-Williams Model 44.

Charles Holman (Speed) flew the Laird LC-DW-300 *Solution* to victory in 1930. Holman's win

THOMPSON TROPHY WINNERS

YEAR	NO.	AIRCRAFT	MPH	ENGINE
1929	31	Travel Air Model R*	194.90	Wright J6-9
1930	4	Laird LC-DW-300	201.91	P&W Wasp Jr.
1931	77	Gee Bee Model Z	236.239	P&W Wasp Jr.
1932	11	Gee Bee Model R-1	252.686	P&W Wasp T3D1
1933	44	Wedell Williams	237.952	P&W Wasp T3D1
1934	57	Wedell Williams	248.129	P&W Hornet
1935	40	Howard DGA-6	220.194	P&W Wasp SE
1936	100	Caudron C-460	264.261	Renault Bengali
1937	301	Folkerts SK-3	259.910	Menasco C6S-4
1938	29	Laird-Turner LTR-14	283.419	P&W Twin Wasp S1B3G
1939	29	Laird-Turner LTR-14	282.536	P&W Twin Wasp S1B3G

* The Thompson Trophy was not created until 1930. The race in 1929 was listed as Event No. 26. However, it was sponsored by Thompson Products and is generally considered one of pre-World War II races under the Thompson name.

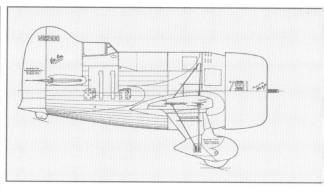

After the Gee Bee Model Z crashed on a record speed run outside of Detroit, the Granvilles regrouped and built two new racers, the R-1 and R-2. The R-1 was intended from the start for Thompson competition. Larger than the Z, the new Gee Bee R-1 proved to be a formidable competitor in the hands of Jimmy Doolittle. With very little time in the airplane, Doolittle captured the 1932 Thompson. Like the Z, however, there was little potential of converting the R-1 into a pursuit for the Army. Jack Abbott drawing, Garrett collection

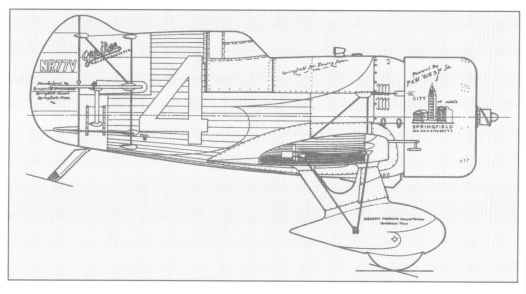

One year after Holman won the Thompson, a new and unique design appeared at the races. The yellow and black Gee Bee Model Z was the progenitor of a short series of racers produced by the Granville Brothers. It was squat, compact, and very close coupled. Its winning speed in the Thompson was 236 miles per hour and it was probably capable of something like 250 miles per hour. Although it was fast, it was hardly a design that could be translated into a pursuit plane for the Army. Jack Abbott drawing, Garrett collection

simultaneously marked an impressive triumph and the passing of a design standard. The compact Laird biplane racer was the last of its type to win this premier event.

Nineteen thirty-one witnessed the beginning of a new, albeit short-lived, era of the Gee Bee racers.

Designed and built by the Granville Brothers of Springfield, Massachusetts, the Gee Bee Model Z *City of Springfield* was a smash hit with racing fans. Lowell Bayles pushed the stubby close-coupled racer to a dazzling 236 miles per hour as he won the Thompson. When Bayles was killed later that year

during a record speed attempt in the same airplane near Detroit, Michigan, the Granvilles regrouped and designed yet another racer for the Thompson called the R-1. James H. Doolittle (Jimmy) flew a prudent and somewhat conservative pylon race in the rotund airplane, capturing the 1932 Thompson and posting yet another new record speed of 252 miles per hour. Doolittle's qualifying speed for the race was an impressive 296 miles per hour over the 3-kilometer straightaway Shell Speed Dash. (Note that the 44-mile per hour Gee Bee speed differential between the speed dash and pylon race closely parallels the corresponding 40-mile per hour difference between pylon and straightaway speed of the Travel Air *Mystery Ship*.)

Yet another fresh design appeared in the Thompson winner's circle during 1933. This was the Wedell-Williams Model 44. It was not a completely new design, but one extensively reworked and improved over a period of several years. By 1933, however, it was truly a sensation. A sister version of the Wedell was successful again in 1934. The next three years witnessed a decidedly different trend as the Howard DGA-6 high-wing cabin plane won in 1935,

The first of a new breed of Army Air Corps fighters was initially designated XP-900. It was designed and built in 1931 by Detroit Aircraft Corporation. Bob Woods, later Bell Aircraft chief engineer, designed the metal fuselage around a Curtiss Conqueror V-1570-23 engine of 600 horsepower. The wooden wing was basically a Lockheed Altair design with retractable landing gear. When the Air Corps purchased the first example, it was redesignated YP-24. Performance was impressive with a top speed of 214 miles per hour at sea level. Lockheed via Birch Matthews collection

Detroit Aircraft Corporation went bankrupt shortly after the YP-24 was delivered to the Air Corps, and an order for four more aircraft went by the boards. The design was next taken up by Consolidated Aircraft and produced as the turbosupercharged Y1P-25 with revisions that included all-metal construction. Production of the type was initiated in January 1935, first as the P-30 and later as the PB-1. The P-30A likewise became the PB-2A (pursuit biplane). Peter M. Bowers collection

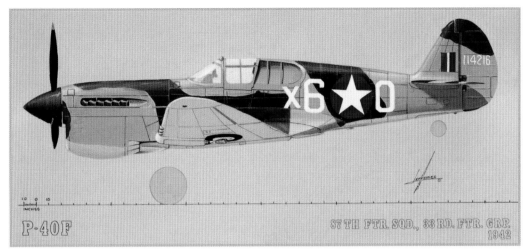

P-40F   87TH FTR. SQD., 33RD FTR. GRP.
                                                                                    1942

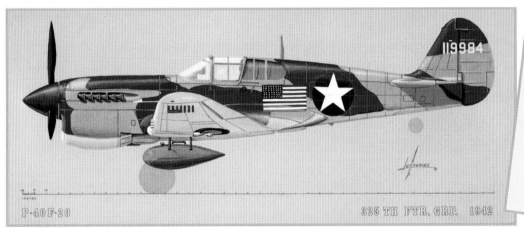

P-40F-20   325TH FTR. GRP. 1942

When the United States entered World War II, the Curtiss P-40 was the only Army fighter available in quantity. It was already on the verge of being obsolete, with performance marginally inferior to Japanese and German first-line fighters. A major deficiency was its Allison V-1710, which lacked high-altitude capability. Markings of these two profile drawings illustrate aircraft with the 87th Fighter Squadron, 33rd Fighter Group (top) and 325th Fighter Group (bottom) in 1942. Walt Jefferies artwork

while the diminutive Caudron C-460 and Folkerts SK-3 racers won in 1936 and 1937, respectively. The Howard was essentially a prototype for a commercial line of aircraft to be built by Benny Howard. Although a fast civil transport, it was a slow Thompson competitor, winning with an undistinguished speed of 220 miles per hour against a field crippled by mechanical problems. The Caudron and Folkerts machines were impressive in design and speed, but hardly comparable to, or potentially useful as, pursuit airplane designs.

The "big bore" class of pure racing planes like the Wedells and Gee Bees was absent until 1938,

when Roscoe Turner captured his second Thompson race, a feat he repeated the following year in the same airplane for this third trophy. His aircraft was the Barlow-designed, Laird-built LTR-14 powered by a big Wasp engine. Turner reverted to the tried and true method of utilizing copious amounts of horsepower to make his airplane faster than the competition.

PURSUIT PLANE TRENDS

A prototype of what would become the newest Army pursuit first flew six months earlier on March

20, 1932. This became the Boeing P-26A when it went into production.[6] Boeing's fighter had a top speed of about 215 miles per hour at sea level, some 80 miles per hour slower than Doolittle's qualifying time for the Thompson. The Pratt & Whitney R-1340-27 Wasp engine in the P-26A had a rated altitude of 6,000 feet. At this altitude, the all-metal Boeing could churn along at 234 miles per hour. Beyond this somewhat mundane observation, additional comparisons are meaningless. The general arrangement of the Gee Bee was hardly ideal for aerial combat. Other championship racers appeared

One potentially outstanding feature of the Consolidated PB-2A was its performance at altitude. A General Electric turbosupercharger (left side of the aircraft below the exhaust collector) gave the two-place fighter a theoretical service ceiling of 28,000 feet. Maximum speed at 25,000 feet was 275 miles per hour. Engine overheating problems apparently prohibited mapping the full altitude performance envelope. Peter M. Bowers collection

The U.S.S. Lexington (CV 3), shown here, and her sister ship the U.S.S. Saratoga (CV 2) were the next two carriers commissioned. This occurred five years after the Lexington entered the fleet. These two carriers had decks 866 feet long, 65 percent greater than the Langley. In spite of the increased deck area, space was at a premium. Approximately 65 airplanes appear on deck in this photograph. Peter M. Bowers collection

The first Navy carrier was the U.S.S. Langley (CV-1). It was commissioned on March 20, 1922. This vessel was not designed from the keel up as an aircraft carrier. Rather, it was to be a collier and therefore had to be converted into a carrier. Note the absence of any structure on the carrier deck for control and command operations. The 65-foot-wide deck was 523 feet in length. Peter M. Bowers collection

The first Thompson Trophy Race took place in 1930. The first winner was Charles W. Holman (Speed) in this Laird LC-DW-300 racer. Doug Davis' victory the previous year in Event 26 was for the Thompson Cup, precursor to the Thompson Trophy. A small, compact, and a reasonably well-streamlined biplane for its day, the Laird's Pratt & Whitney Wasp Jr. pulled Holman around the 1930 Thompson course at an average speed of just over 200 miles per hour. The biplane era was just about over, however. Subsequent Thompson winners were all monoplanes. John Garrett collection

In 1931 Lowell Bayles brought this exotic Granville brothers Gee Bee Model Z racer to Cleveland for the Thompson race. Small, lightweight, and powered by a Pratt & Whitney Wasp Jr., the Model Z proved very fast. This was demonstrated during the Shell Speed Dash. when Bayles urged the racer to a speed of 267 miles per hour. He subsequently captured the Thompson race at 236 miles per hour. John Garrett collection

For the 1932 race season, the Granvilles built two new Gee Bee racers, identified as Models R-1 and R-2 (pictured here). The R-1 was powered by a Pratt & Whitney Wasp and intended specifically for the Thompson. In contrast, the R-2 used the less-powerful Wasp Jr. and possessed greater fuel capacity, making it more competitive in the Bendix Trophy contest. The design philosophy was basically unchanged from the Model Z: lightweight airframes with powerful engines. James H. Doolittle won the Thompson flying the R-1. John Garrett collection

to be adaptable to the role, however. These were the Travel Air *Mystery Ship* and Wedell-Williams Model 44, which were not only fast, but of more conventional arrangement.

The early 1930s were crucial years with respect to pursuit aircraft development in context with America's coming involvement in World War II. Army and Navy single-seat fighter aircraft advancement languished for the most part, the result of low priority and even lower funding. Barely enough work was done to sustain a minimal degree of development without significant deployment of newer designs. By the middle of the decade, however, there was a noticeable turn around, albeit agonizingly slow at first. Nineteen thirty-five marked a rejuvenation of pursuit airplane fortunes as Bell, Seversky (later Republic) Lockheed and Curtiss laid down lines for newer generation pursuits. A glimmer of the future promised by the Detroit-Lockheed YP-24 at the turn of the decade now seemed attainable.

Had the process been any slower, the United States would have been even less prepared for war in 1941. One factor our enemies and perhaps even our citizens and political leadership underestimated, though, was the tremendous latent industrial capability this country possessed. This would turn the tide of World War II from early debacle to complete victory. Modern fighters began to roll off assembly lines from coast to coast. The eventual number was staggering: "There were over 100,000 of them, 100,000 U.S. fighter airplanes!"[7]

James Wedell evolved a truly fine race plane design over a period of years. In 1933 he achieved the pinnacle of success by winning the Thompson Trophy Race, after placing second in the previous two contests. The Wedell-Williams Model 44 was a more conventional airplane than the Gee Bee racers; however, the design details were executed to perfection. John Garrett collection

Roscoe Turner won the 1934 Thompson in the second of three Wedell-Williams Model 44 airframes. Turner constantly tinkered with his Wedell, and for the 1934 races installed a more powerful Pratt & Whitney Hornet engine. To keep the frontal area of the larger diameter Hornet to a minimum, the cowling incorporated "bulges" for the engine rocker arm housings. This airframe-engine combination produced a maximum sea level straightaway speed of 295 miles per hour. Emil Strasser photo via Gerry Liang collection

In 1935, Benny Howard's DGA-6, Mr. Mulligan, won both the Bendix and Thompson races. Designed as the forerunner of a commercial cabin plane series, Mr. Mulligan was hardly ideal for closed-course pylon racing. It succeeded in the Thompson race due to a lack of formidable competition. If American fighter aircraft entering World War II benefited from prewar racing designs, the advantages had to have been derived during the years 1930–1935, due to the military fighter procurement lead times involved. John Garrett collection

Performance Appraisal

Any comparison of military pursuits and contemporary race aircraft inevitably devolves to performance numbers, in particular maximum speed. A one-to-one comparison is hardly objective, however. To point out that the 1929 Thompson Trophy winning Travel Air *Mystery Ship* was capable of about 235 miles per hour at sea level while the fastest first-line pursuit biplane of the day could muster 200 miles per hour or less is not too meaningful for more than one reason. Racers are not encumbered with military equipment. Fighters, or pursuits as they were then called by the Air Corps, were designed with little anticipation of combat at sea level. Pure racing machines had but one basic requirement: maximum speed in a straight line or on a pylon race course. Pursuits were designed to multiple requirements. Although it seemed a potentially attractive possibility to a few pursuit plane advocates at one point in time, translating a race plane design into a military fighter necessitates equipping it for combat. Only then can performance estimates be made and compared with current or emerging pursuit aircraft.

Is it feasible to realistically *estimate* performance for a specific race plane hypothetically converted to military use? The answer is yes. To more suspicious temperaments it may appear a form of black art, a charlatan's tool to deceive the unwary. In reality, though, it is entirely feasible. Consider that in the world today, integrated computer-aided techniques permit a rather full appreciation of what a given design will do in the air before any metal is cut. Verification is partly if not fully confirmed using sophisticated software programs, wind tunnel experiments and flight simulators. Even before such advanced tools became available, designers were nonetheless able to predict airplane performance. That this could be done is attributable to the work of many scientists engaged in understanding and mathematically describing the aerodynamic phenomena and forces acting on an airplane in flight.

With Jimmy Doolittle in the cockpit, this Curtiss R3C-2 won the Schneider Trophy Race, held off the Baltimore shore in 1925. The compact little float plane was powered by a 500-horsepower V-1400 Curtiss engine. Its zero lift drag coefficient was only 0.0206. Had it been entered in Event 26 of the 1929 National Air Races, it could have easily beaten Doug Davis' winning Travel Air Mystery Ship! *Air Force photo via John Garrett collection*

HISTORICAL NOTE

The chronicle of aerodynamics began a very, very long time ago. Astounding as it may seem, the roots of aerodynamics took form before the birth of Christ. In his highly readable book entitled *A History of Aerodynamics*, John D. Anderson, Jr., traces the groundwork for this science to Aristotle and Archimedes a few hundred years B.C. Contributions by Leonardo da Vinci, Galileo Galilei, and Isaac Newton, to mention only a few, though highly recognizable names, added to a growing foundation of knowledge in this field.

George Cayley is recognized as a pioneer in modern aerodynamics. Born in Scarborough, England, in 1773, Cayley investigated and measured lift generated by a flat plate at various angles of attack. He also recognized that curved (cambered) surfaces produced more lift than flat plates at an equivalent angle of attack. The field of theoretical and experimental aerodynamics is studded with men like Cayley, each adding and refining our understanding of the field.

Jimmy Doolittle (left) poses along side the Curtiss R3C-2 racer with Lieutenant Cyrus Bettis, who won the 1925 Pulitzer Race in the landplane version of this airplane. Without floats, the racer was designated R3C-1. Note the generous fillet on the lower side of the upper wing. Similarly, Curtiss employed a small fillet at the juncture of the float struts and fuselage. Air Force photo via John Garrett collection

LIFT AND DRAG

Lift is the force generated by the flow of air about an airplane wing. Drag is the resistance encountered as the airframe moves through the air. At constant velocity, drag is offset by thrust delivered by the engine-propeller combination. Drag in subsonic flight consists of two components: parasite drag and induced drag. Parasite drag results from friction occurring between the airframe surface (wetted area) and the air through which it moves. Parasite drag

The 1929 Travel Air Mystery Ship was in part successful in capturing the major free-for-all race that year due to its relatively low-drag design. The zero lift drag coefficient for this racer was a respectable 0.03. Equally important, the Travel Air had a good power-to-weight ratio of 5.0, as well as a high aspect ratio wing. Air Force photo via John Garrett collection

also includes any local air flow separation from the airframe. Flow separation (also known as form drag) may occur at the intersection of the wing and fuselage, for example. Thus parasite drag is the sum of skin friction drag and form drag.

Induced drag results when lift is generated by the wing. Vortices form at the wing tips because there is a greater pressure on the lower wing surface. Conversely, air pressure on the upper wing surface is less. A vortex flow forms at the wing tip due to this pressure differential, as higher pressure air from the lower surface spills around the tip to the region of lower pressure. As lift increases, the strength of the vortex also increases. The vortices alter the pressure distribution over the wings such that a drag force is created. At the condition where lift is zero, the *induced* drag is also essentially zero because the vortices no longer exist. In summary, airframe drag is the sum of induced drag plus parasite drag. At the zero lift condition only parasite drag remains—skin friction and local flow separation.

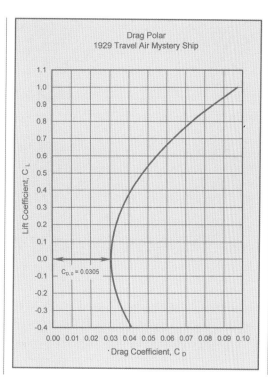

A plot of lift coefficient (C_L) as a function of drag coefficient (C_D) for the Travel Air Mystery Ship is shown in this illustration. The resulting plot is called a drag polar. When the lift coefficient is zero, the drag coefficient value is known as the "zero lift drag coefficient," and represents airframe parasite drag. It is a useful parameter when comparing the cleanliness of one design against another. As shown on the plot, the zero lift drag coefficient for the Mystery Ship was determined to be 0.0305, indicating it was a relatively clean design.

A zero lift drag coefficient, ($C_{D,0}$) may be determined for a particular airplane provided sufficient information is available.[1] One usefulness of this parameter is as a measure of the aerodynamic cleanness of a given design, because it relates only to surface skin friction and form drag. Thus one airplane configuration may be compared to another in this respect. Appendix C presents the methodology for calculating a zero lift drag coefficient. Suffice it to

The minimal frontal area of the 1922 Curtiss R-6 racer is shown to advantage in this view. It featured a Curtiss D-12 engine of some 375 horsepower, and single-piece streamlined struts between the wings. General Billy Mitchell flew the R-6 to a world speed record of 223 miles per hour during October 1922. Pilot Russell Maugham increased this record to 236 miles per hour during March 1923. Air Force via John Garrett collection

Never designed as a racing airplane, the Lockheed Orion nevertheless was a sturdy and very fast commercial airplane. A generous fillet was employed to minimize flow separation (form drag) at the point where the wing joined the fuselage contour. The Orion had a zero lift drag coefficient of 0.0210, a remarkably low number exceeded only by the Curtiss R3C-2. This particular airplane was in service with TWA when the photograph was taken. Birch Matthews collection

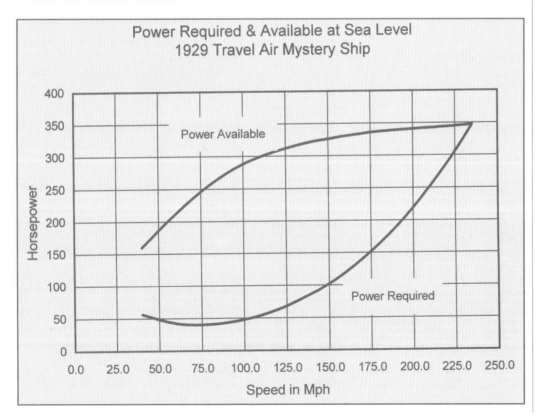

say this procedure requires determining the lift, drag, and induced drag (drag due to lift) coefficients. The drag coefficient is a function of the engine horsepower, ambient air conditions, forward velocity, and the wetted area of the airframe. Induced drag is related to the square of the lift coefficient, wing aspect ratio, and airplane efficiency factor, while the lift coefficient is calculated through knowing aircraft gross weight and speed, wing area, and ambient air conditions. Once these parameters are calculated, the drag coefficient at zero lift is readily ascertained by subtraction (see Appendix C). After the zero lift drag coefficient is determined, it is possible to calculate an array of drag coefficients corresponding to assumed lift coefficient values and then plot these data. An example of such a plot is shown in the accompanying Figure 6-1. This curve is called a "drag polar" and illustrates the variation in lift coefficient with changes in drag coefficient. This particular drag polar example was calculated for the Travel Air *Mystery Ship*, winner of the 1929 free-for-all race and forerunner of the Thompson Trophy. As shown in the curve, the $C_{D,0}$ value is slightly over 0.03.

As noted, the zero lift drag coefficient is a measure of aerodynamic cleanness. In his book, *Quest for Performance: The Evolution of Modern Aircraft*, Laurence Loftin determined this characteristic for 50 different aircraft.[2] Table 6-1 consists of data extracted from Loftin's work as well as zero lift drag coefficients independently calculated for several vintage racing aircraft. Note that the lowest coefficient value does not necessarily connote the highest speed, merely that form drag and skin friction are relatively low. Take for example a comparison between the 1923 Curtiss R2C-1 and the 1934 Wedell-Williams 44 racer listed in Table 6-1. The Wedell has a zero

These curves illustrate the engine power available and required over a range of Travel Air Mystery Ship speeds. The point at which the two curves cross indicates the maximum speed obtainable, about 235 miles per hour. Excess power is available at all points to the left of this crossover. This particular curve represents power available and required for sea level flight. New curve sets must be determined through calculation for each altitude of interest, usually in 5,000 feet increments.

Table 6-1

Characteristics of Selected Aircraft

Aircraft	Hp	Gross Wt(Lb)	Span (Ft)	Wing Area (Ft2)	Vmax Mph	CD, 0	Data Source
Curtiss R2C-1	500	2,071	22.0	140	267	0.0206	Loftin
Lockheed Orion 9D	550	5,400	47.8	262	226	0.0210	Loftin
Wedell-Williams 45	750	3,320	26.7	124	330	0.0211	Author
Wedell-Williams 44	550	2,677	26.2	108	305	0.0222	Author
Seversky P-35	850	5,599	35.0	220	282	0.0251	Loftin
Supermarine S-4	450	3,150	30.5	136	239	0.0274	Loftin
Northrop Alpha	420	4,856	43.8	312	177	0.0274	Loftin
Laird Turner LTR-14	950	4,923	25.0	95	330	0.0275	Author
Lockheed Vega 5C	450	4,033	41.0	275	190	0.0278	Loftin
Travel Air Mystery Ship	400	1,982	29.2	125	235	0.0305	Author
Wedell-Williams XP-34	750	3,320	26.7	124	330	0.0363	Author
Boeing P-26A	600	3,012	27.9	149	234	0.0448	Loftin

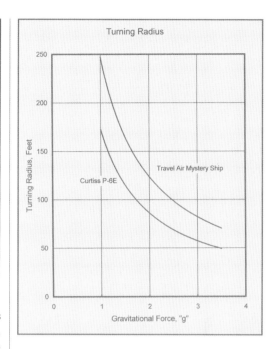

Even though biplanes were fading as a configuration of choice, the Army and Navy continued to use them for several years. The epitome of classic biplane pursuits was the Curtiss P-6E. As this set of curves illustrates, the biplane enjoyed one significant advantage over the monoplane: turning radius. Turning radii were calculated for both the P-6E and Travel Air Mystery Ship as a function of "g" load or force. Under all conditions, the elegant little biplane could turn inside the sleek Mystery Ship.

lift drag coefficient about 8 percent greater than the old Curtiss racer. Yet the Wedell had a top speed of 305 miles per hour versus the Curtiss speed of 267 miles per hour. The Wedell had 10 percent more horsepower, and this was a major factor.

The zero lift drag coefficient, in addition to assessing the aerodynamic cleanness, may also be utilized as a basis for calculating airplane performance. In this narrative, it was used to evaluate various performance parameters of several aircraft including the Travel Air *Mystery Ship*, the Wedell Williams racer and its hypothetical military derivatives, and the Boeing P-26A pursuit. The methodology is also outlined in Appendix C (for the Wedell-Williams racer), which provides a representative sample of the process; however, only results for the Travel Air *Mystery Ship* are presented and discussed here.

The 1929 *Mystery Ship* had a top speed of about 235 miles per hour at sea level. This is illustrated in the nearby graph showing curves of thrust horsepower required and available for a range of speeds. Thrust horsepower is brake horsepower, power delivered by the engine to the propeller shaft, multiplied by the propeller efficiency. (Propeller efficiency is always less than 100 percent.) The lower curve indicates the amount of power required at any given speed. Corresponding values of power available are shown by the upper curve. At 150 miles per hour, for example, the *Mystery Ship* needed a mere 102 (thrust) horsepower, although it had 326 horse-

power available at this speed. Power required as more speed is demanded begins to increase sharply. As a consequence, the lower curve rises toward the upper curve representing power available. Maximum aircraft speed occurs where the two curves intersect on the right. Beyond this intersection there is no more power available.

Power available and required varies with altitude, due to the changes in atmospheric pressure and density. The *Mystery Ship* engine, a nine-cylinder Wright Whirlwind, had minimal supercharging. As a consequence, thrust horsepower output declined with increasing altitude, as shown in Table 6-2. Speed increased slightly at 5,000 feet due to a reduction in skin friction drag at the lower air density, as the engine continues to deliver reasonable power. Although airframe drag continues to decrease with increasing altitude, a proportionately greater loss of horsepower occurs with increasing altitude. This becomes the larger and overriding factor.

The Travel Air *Mystery Ship* was faster than any U.S. Army or Navy fighter when it made its debut at the 1929 National Air Races. With a sea level speed of 235 miles per hour, it could show its tail feathers to the Curtiss P-6 biplane series of Army pursuits, first delivered in 1929. The P-6E model of this aircraft, the most numerous and best remembered of all the variants, had a top sea level speed of 193 miles per hour, considerably slower than the *Mystery Ship*. The P-6E did enjoy some advantages, however. It could turn inside

Table 6-2

1929 Travel Air *Mystery Ship* Estimated Performance

Altitude (Ft)	Thrust Hp Available	Maximum Speed, Mph
Sea Level	347	235
5,000	297	251
10,000	250	231
15,000	205	226

Jimmy Wedell's racers were almost always in contention during the early 1930s. The Model 44 shown here had a zero lift drag coefficient of 0.0222, right in the same class as the Curtiss R3C-2 and Lockheed Orion. This is the aircraft that won the 1933 Thompson Trophy Race. Doug Davis won the 1934 Bendix with this machine, but crashed fatally during the 1934 Thompson. Emil Strasser photo via Gerry Liang collection

the *Mystery Ship*, a decided benefit in combat. The difference in turning radii for these contemporary aircraft is shown graphically in the accompanying Figure 6-2. During a 2 g turn, for example, the *Mystery Ship* had a calculated turn radius of 124 feet while the P-6E had a corresponding radius of 86 feet. A second advantage of the P-6E was its lower stalling speed, and

therefore lower landing speed. Both values were less than the Travel Air machine. Stall speed of the racer was 61 miles per hour while the P-6E had a stall speed of 51 miles per hour. Landing speeds were usually defined as being 20 percent above the stall velocity, yielding speeds of 73 miles per hour and 61 miles per hour for the Travel Air and P-6E, respectively.

Regardless of any maneuvering advantages, the days of biplane fighters were numbered. Travel Air's beautiful monoplane racing aircraft presaged the future. The same was true in Europe, where Schneider Trophy winners were consistently monoplanes beginning with the 1926 Macchi M.39 racer, the first monoplane victor since the original contest in 1913.

The last Wedell-Williams racer was this Pratt & Whitney Wasp-powered Model 45, which appeared at the 1934 National Air Races. Although similar in layout to the Model 44, it featured two conspicuous improvements, full cantilever flying surfaces and retractable landing gear. Its zero lift drag coefficient calculated to 0.0211. Emil Strasser photo via Gerry Liang collection

In general, there is a paucity of performance data for racing planes. There are at least three reasons for this condition. Both private and corporate race plane designers were loath to divulge information fearing their competition might benefit. A second reason is that quite often no complete performance map was ever established due to a lack of time and money or need. And lastly, where more complete performance information was generated it has not survived the passage of time and thus forever lost to the historian.

Relatively meager amounts of race plane data may be augmented through performance estimation. This simultaneously offers the option of hypothetically converting a race plane design into pursuit plane of that era. This may be done in part by adding weight to cover various military requirements and components not found in pure racing machines. The amount of weight added was determined by reviewing a number of pursuit aircraft designs to determine what was standard at the time. The results

Monoplane configurations could clearly be made to go faster than biplanes.

The objective of this brief chapter is to demonstrate that aircraft performance may be calculated with some confidence, provided sufficient basic information is available for the airframe and engine. Data for a number of the more prominent American and European racing planes has been published in several books and popular magazines (see Bibliography). Much more information is available for contemporary military pursuit airplanes, making possible comparisons of the two types. The type of performance information which may be calculated in the absence of published data is shown in Table 6-3.

Table 6-3

Basic Aircraft Performance

Steady-State Performance	Accelerating Performance
Power required & available	Takeoff distance
Maximum speed versus altitude	Landing distance
Rate of climb	Turning rate and radius
Maximum altitude	
Range and endurance	

This Seversky P-35 was one of the first modern Army pursuit aircraft placed into service. This particular example belonged to the 1st Pursuit Group, 94th Pursuit Squadron, out of Selfridge Field. At the time this picture was taken on December 8, 1939, the airplane was at the Akron, Ohio, Municipal Airport. The P-35 had a zero lift drag coefficient of 0.0251. Emil Strasser photo via Gerry Liang collection

Table 6-4

Weight Additions for Military Pursuit Applications

Item	Wt. in lb.
Automatic mixture control (engine)	20.0
Radio shielding & spark plugs	10.2
Gun sight	8.0
Tail wheel	15.0
Added structure	200.0
Machine gun drive	1.1
Two .30-caliber machine guns	47.2
1,000 rounds, .30-caliber ammunition	60.0
Radio installation	60.0
Antenna and mast	20.0
Oxygen system	20.2
Furnishings	44.0
Total Weight Added	505.7

Equally interesting is the fact that winning speeds in succeeding Thompson contests increased rapidly. In other words, the Travel Air racer quickly became obsolete, as new and faster designs emerged. At first it was the Gee Bee designs of the Granville brothers. In 1933 Jimmy Wedell arrived on the scene with his exceptional Wedell-Williams Model 44 design and won the Thompson at 238 miles per hour. Roscoe Turner in another Wedell racer captured the premier race with a speed of 248 miles per hour a year later. The winning Thompson speed increased 28 percent in five years. Although the corpulent and close-coupled Gee Bees forever caught the public's fancy, it was the sleek Wedell designs that attracted Air Corps interest!

are presented in Table 6-4 and in general consist of armament, radio equipment and structural enhancement where necessary.

Again using the Travel Air *Mystery Ship* as the example, a gross weight was calculated by adding in the military items from Table 6-4. An upward adjustment was also made to the zero lift drag coefficient of four percent to allow for increased parasite drag in the military configuration. The racer wing loading was preserved by increasing wing area for the hypothetical pursuit. Maximum speed was then determined and compared with the pure Travel Air racer as well as the Curtiss P-6E then coming into service. The converted racer still has a speed superiority over the P-6E, but the disparity is lessened as one might logically expect. At sea level the Travel Air "pursuit" is capable of about 227 miles per hour. After climbing to 5,000 feet, where the air is less dense, its speed rises 238 miles per hour.

No serious consideration was given by Army or Navy bureaucracies to a pursuit derivative of the *Mystery Ship*. For one thing, bureaucracies move slowly in the absence of strong outside political pressure. Another consideration was money. Not long after the 1929 National Air Races ended, the stock market collapsed, marking the beginning of the Great Depression. Curtailed government military spending became the rule over the next several years. In spite of its dazzling performance, there was hardly room in Spartan military budgets for another pursuit development.

A contemporary of the P-35 was the Curtiss P-36. Like the P-35, this P-36C was all metal in construction and possessed a similar medium altitude performance. It was capable of 311 miles per hour at 10,000 feet, while the P-35 could manage only 282 miles per hour at the same altitude. This P-36 example was part of the Headquarters Squadron, 1st Pursuit Group. Emil Strasser photo via Gerry Liang collection

Had the Travel Air Mystery Ship *been adapted to a pursuit role, several modifications would have been necessary. About 500 pounds would have been added to meet structural and armament requirements. Drag would also increase in the military configuration due to gun ports, enlarged cockpit profile, larger wing area, and so forth. Top sea level speed would have decreased from 235 miles per hour to about 227 miles per hour as a consequence. John Garrett collection*

If the wing area is maintained equal to the racer in converting the Travel Air design to a military pursuit, high speed at sea level is still around 227 miles per hour, due to the increase in drag associated with the conversion. Due to the weight increase, however, wing loading and thus stall and landing speeds, increase significantly. This would probably have been unacceptable to the Air Corps in 1929. John Garrett collection

chapter 7

A Desire for Performance

Is it not strange that desire
should so many years
outlive performance?

William Shakespeare • *King Henry the Fourth*

At first glance, speed differentials between Air Corps pursuits and Thompson racers appears large. Comparing racing planes of the 1930s with contemporary pursuit aircraft is not straightforward, however. Because sheer speed is paramount in a pure racing plane, the designer sacrifices utility. This takes many forms. Race aircraft prior to World War II incorporated small wheels and tires to minimize drag. The utility of such landing gear in service applications would have posed obvious problems. Yet another streamlining technique involved a tightly designed cockpit windscreen or enclosure barely large enough for the pilot's head. This feature would have been a decided detriment to the fighter pilot whose life depends upon his ability to see the enemy.

Race plane fuel capacity was often limited to little more than what was needed for a given race. Long range and endurance were seldom a consideration for the designer of a pylon racer. More fuel meant added weight, a luxury the race pilot could ill afford. Added weight in any form required more lift from the wing, leading to greater wing surface area while simultaneously increasing drag. The ideal racer, from a weight and drag perspective, is one in which the airframe is reduced to the minimum necessary to contain the pilot and engine and a bit of fuel. It was a never-ending battle to maximize thrust horsepower and minimize the drag force.

If politics is the art of compromise, it surely is a handmaiden of pursuit aircraft designers as well. The fighting plane is constrained by many often-conflicting requirements. Consideration must be given to a multiplicity of factors such as range, endurance, armament, communications, landing speed, climb capability, maneuverability, and field maintenance, as well as speed. If these considerations were applied to a race plane design, performance would inevitably be degraded.

A military contemporary of the Wedell-Williams Model 44 was Boeing's P-26A pursuit. The Boeing fighter pictured here displays markings of the 1st Pursuit Group, based at Selfridge Field, Michigan. Although the blue and yellow paint scheme once employed by the Air Corps was colorful and attractive, it was abandoned in favor of camouflage before America entered World War II. Walt Jefferies artwork

To analyze this performance degradation aspect and simultaneously compare results with a contemporary military airplane, a series of calculations was made for both the 1934 Wedell-Williams Model 44 racer and Boeing P-26A pursuit of 1933. These two aircraft were chosen for several reasons. They were monoplanes and physically similar in size, as shown in Table 7-1. Both were powered by Pratt & Whitney Wasp engines of equal displacement. Each airplane utilized an externally braced low-wing design featuring fixed and fully streamlined landing gear.

Although the Wedell and Boeing aircraft were remarkably similar in general arrangement, there were some notable differences. The P-26A wore a Townend-style ring cowl, while the racer employed a full NACA-type cowling, a decided advantage. The racer also used a full-wing fillet while the pursuit airplane transition from wing to fuselage was surprisingly minimal. Pilot visibility from the P-26 cockpit was far superior to the racer. The military aviator sat higher and in an open cockpit in the Boeing. Visibility over the ring cowl was reasonably good. In contrast, the racer incorporated a low-profile windscreen and small enclosed cockpit canopy. Although beneficial from a drag standpoint, pilot vision was impaired. Another difference worth noting involved gross weight and wing loading. Although

the Boeing P-26A was 335 pounds heavier than the Wedell, its generous wing area produced a wing loading considerably less than the racer as shown in Table 7-1.

Aside from assessing physical characteristics, performance comparisons between the Wedell and the P-26A can also be estimated. To make the Wedell-Williams racer into a pursuit airplane in the 1933–1934 time frame, items such as armament and ammunition and radio equipment have to be added. A complete list of weight additions is shown in Table 7-2 which presents weight estimates for the racer and its militarized variants (about which, more later) and the P-26A pursuit.[1]

Of all the pre-World War II American racing planes, only the Wedell-Williams basic Model 44 and Model 45 were seriously considered by the Air Corps as potential pursuit airplanes. Three Model 44 designs were constructed, two for the Wedell-Williams racing team and one for Roscoe Turner. Turner's airplane is seen here shortly after arriving in California. Roscoe is shaking hands with his sponsor, E.B. Gilmore. John Garrett collection

Table 7-1

Design Characteristics
Wedell-Williams Racer and Boeing P-26A Pursuit

	Wedell-Williams 44	Boeing P-26A
Length, Ft	23.0	23.6
Empty Weight, Lb	1,702	2,271
Gross Weight, Lb	2,677	3,012
Wing Span, Ft	26.17	27.96
Wing Area, Ft2	107.81	149.50
Wing Loading, Lb/Ft2	24.83	20.15
Aspect Ratio	6.35	5.23
Airfoil	M-10 Modified	Boeing 109
Engine	P&W Wasp	P&W Wasp
Engine Model	T3D1	R-1340-27
Engine Horsepower	550	570
Propeller Gear Ratio	Direct Drive	Direct Drive

Sources: Wedell data was gleaned from several publications while Boeing data was taken from Ray Wagner's *American Combat Planes.*

Opposite, inset: The 1933 International Air Races were held in Chicago, coincident with the World's Fair Century of Progress exhibition. Cliff Henderson was called upon to direct the meet, and even his bag of tricks could not forestall financial disaster. Too many people flocked to the World's Fair and too few attended the races. Jimmy Wedell swept the big-bore events in his Model 44. John Garrett collection

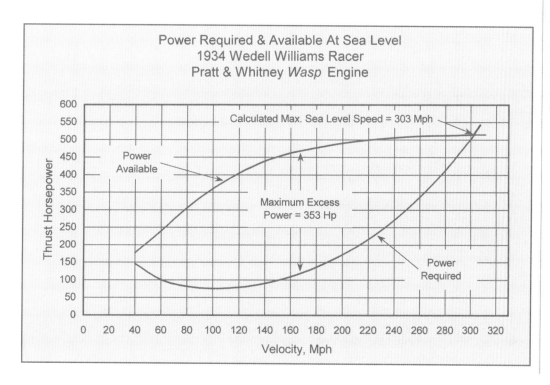

Two military conversions of the Wedell racer were considered. One preserved the racer wing area. In so doing, a higher wing loading was accepted. Wing loading is an important design parameter strongly influencing stall and landing speed. High wing loadings also produce higher top speeds, greater turning radii and lower turning rates. The converse is also true. Thus a second Wedell "pursuit" configuration was examined, in which the racer wing loading was preserved by proportionately increasing wing area. Wing chord was kept constant while span was lengthened.

Most of the weight additions in Table 7-2 are obvious, although one or two need comment for full understanding. In this regard, the line item titled "Additional Structure" represents a 200-pound allowance for: structurally modifying the airframe to accommodate two .30-caliber machine gun installations; providing ammunition storage containers and access; reworking the cockpit area for improved pilot vision; installing a tail wheel; and structurally reinforcing the airframe to meet military design load requirements. For the Wedell pursuit version in which the racer wing loading is preserved, 50 additional pounds is allocated to account for the added wing structure.

As the data in Table 7-2 show, equipping the Wedell Williams racer for military duty significantly increases gross weight. Holding the racer wing loading (24.8 pounds per square foot) by increasing wing area on the pursuit version results in a takeoff gross of 3,751 pounds, an increase of 1,074 pounds or 40 percent. Maintaining the racer wing area and allowing

Sea level power required and available points were calculated for the Wasp-powered 1934 version of the Wedell-Williams racer. When plotted, the data produce curves as shown in this illustration. The point at which power required and available curves cross on the right side of the chart is the maximum speed of the airplane. The calculated speed of 303 miles per hour agrees quite well with the measured speed of 305 miles per hour in the Shell Speed Dash. This chart also indicates the level flight speed at which maximum excess power (power available minus power required) is available. Maximum rate of climb for a given gross weight occurs when the excess power is at a maximum.

Table 7-2

Wedell-Williams Weight Estimates

Variation	Wedell Racer	Wedell Pursuit 1 Racer	Wedell Pursuit 2 Racer
	As Built	Wing Loading	Wing Area
Empty Weight	1,500	1,500	1,500
Less Wasp Jr. Engine	-596	-596	-596
Plus Wasp Engine	798	798	798
Automatic Mixture Control		20	20
Radio Shielding		10	10
Gun Sight		8	8
Tail Wheel		15	15
Additional Structure		200	200
Added Wing Surface		50	
Machine Gun Drive		1	1
Two .30-Caliber Guns		46	46
1,000 Rounds, .30-Caliber		60	60
Radio Installation		82	82
Radio Antenna and Mast		20	20
Oxygen		20	20
Furnishings		44	44
Adjusted Empty Weight, Lb	1,702	2,278	2,228
Fuel @ 115 Gallons	690		
Fuel @ 198 Gallons		1,188	1,188
Oil @ 14 Gallons	105	105	105
Pilot and Parachute	180	180	180
Useful Load, Lb	975	1,473	1473
Gross Weight, Lb	2,677	3,751	3,701
Wing Area, Ft^2	107.8	151.1	107.8
Wing Loading, Lf/Ft^2	24.8	24.8	34.3

Like the Travel Air Mystery Ship discussed in Chapter 6, two military conversions of the Wedell Model 44 racer (shown here) were analyzed. One maintained the racer wing area while the second increased wing area to retain the racer wing loading. Sea level speeds for the racer, Wedell pursuit with the racer wing loading, and Wedell pursuit with the racer wing area were 303, 266 and 302 miles per hour, respectively. John Garrett collection

the wing loading to rise produced a slightly lower gross of 3,701 pounds. Wing loading under this condition increased by 9.5 pounds per square foot, representing a hefty 38 percent increase. At 34.3 pounds per square foot with the racer wing area, a hypothetical Wedell Williams Model 44 pursuit conversion would have had a wing loading considerably above that of the Boeing P-26A at 20.2 pounds per square foot. In fact, such a high loading would almost certainly have been unacceptable to the Air Corps. Even the long wing version, in which the racer wing loading was preserved, yielded a 24.8-pound per square foot wing loading, about 19 percent higher than the Boeing airplane.

Converting a race plane design into a military pursuit is not just a matter of hanging two machine guns on the airframe. Tradeoffs are necessary to make the airplane suitable for complex and demanding combat missions. It is interesting to note that the reverse process is less tremulous and more easily done. Race aircraft in the Unlimited Class of today are fashioned from surplus fighter aircraft. Weight is removed, wing surface area reduced, and various other modifications made to reduce drag and increase engine power.

PERFORMANCE APPRAISAL

Total drag for a subsonic airplane is the sum of the parasite drag plus induced drag, the latter being drag associated with the creation of lift in the form of wing tip vortices. Parasite drag, in contrast, is composed of two forces. One is drag exerted on the airframe due to skin friction between the aircraft surfaces and the air through which it moves. The other parasite drag component derives from any flow separation from the surface of the airplane, such as flow about a wing airfoil. (It should be noted that flow separation can also occur on other parts of the airframe as well.) The flow separation phenomenon is known as form drag.

From a practical standpoint, some increase in parasite drag would be experienced if a Wedell-Williams racer is converted into a pursuit aircraft. This is due to necessary military requirements for a higher cockpit profile, for improved visibility; allowances for gun ports; access hatches, for servicing; radio antenna mast; and the like. The amount of this increase is debatable although quite possibly

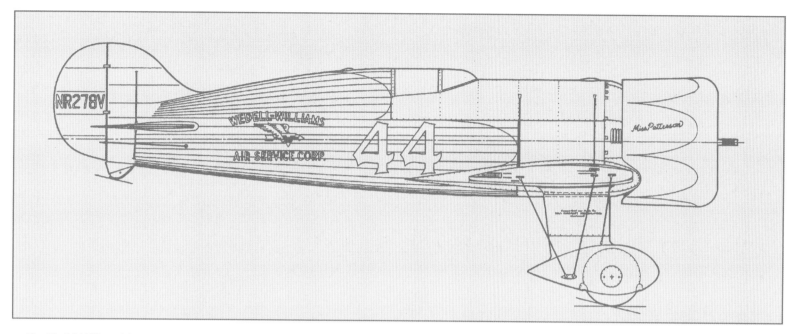

The Wedell-Williams Model 44 was the finest and most successful American racing airplane developed during the 1930s. In addition to Jimmy Wedell's Race Number 44, two additional airframes were built to the same design formula. Jimmy Wedell captured the 1933 Thompson Trophy in his racer. The 1934 Thompson race was won by Roscoe Turner, flying another Wedell-Williams. The airplanes were equally successful in the premier Bendix Trophy Race, with three victories in three consecutive years, 1932 through 1934.

Race 92 in this 1932 illustration was a sister ship to Jimmy Wedell's Model 44. Jimmy Haizlip is in the cockpit. Although the basic Model 44 racer and hypothetical military conversions of the Model 44 were indeed faster at all altitudes than the contemporary Boeing P-26A, limitations on Air Corps funding during the Depression era made it almost impossible for the Army to explore race plane derivatives. Emil Strasser photo via Gerry Liang collection

estimated with some confidence provided a design is available. Absent a specific design layout and a myriad of design decisions supporting the layout, another approach was selected. Zero lift drag coefficients (referenced in Chapter 6) were arbitrarily and consistently increased by five percent in all performance calculations for hypothetical military conversions of race planes.

Zero lift drag coefficients may be used to compare the relative aerodynamic cleanness of various airplanes. This is illustrated in Table 7-3. The magnitude of this coefficient for the Wedell racer calculates to 0.0222, indicating it was a relatively clean aerodynamic design, as one might intuitively conclude. Boeing's P-26A, on the other hand, had a zero lift drag coefficient of 0.0448, twice that of the Wedell racer.

Table 5-7 presents zero lift drag coefficients for a variety of representative single-engine civil and military aircraft from the two decades leading up to World War II. It can be seen that the Wedell racer compared very favorably with the sleek

Howell Miller, who previously worked with the Granville brothers, set his design talents to work in 1936 on a new racer for speed flyer Frank Hawks. The result was Time Flies, *sponsored by the Gruen Watch Company. For takeoff and landing, the pilot's seat and windscreen could be manually raised and lowered. For maximum speed, however, the windscreen was lowered until it was flush with the fuselage profile. This photo was taken in November 1937. Emil Strasser photo via Gerry Liang collection*

Pulitzer-winning Curtiss R2C-1 Navy racer of 1923, and the more modern Lockheed Orion of 1931 vintage. In reviewing Table 5-7, however, recall that this parameter is a measure of aerodynamic refinement rather than speed, which is highly dependent on the thrust horsepower available as well as drag under a given set of conditions.

The data contained in this table is revealing for another reason. It clearly shows that the newer P-35, XP-39 and P-40 aircraft were relatively clean designs. Although larger than the pure racing machine and equipped with all of the necessary military accouterments, these newer generation fighters compared fairly well with the Wedell, by having zero lift drag coefficients only 16 to 22 percent greater than the pure racing machine. They were markedly superior to the older P-6E and P-26A. Emphasis on aerodynamic cleanness was clearly a priority as these newer generation fighters were being designed and developed. The process of evolving a truly first rate fighter aircraft in this country was beginning to take hold.

Table 7-3

Aircraft Drag Comparison Using Zero Lift Drag Coefficient (Wetted Area Reference)

Aircraft	$C_{D,0}$
Curtiss R2C-1	0.0206
Lockheed Orion 9D	0.0210
Wedell-Williams 44	0.0222
Seversky P-35	0.0251
Curtiss P-40	0.0257
Bell XP-39	0.0272
Supermarine S-4	0.0274
Lockheed Vega 5C	0.0278
Curtiss Hawk P-6E	0.0371
Boeing P-26A	0.0448

Sources: Loftin, Laurence K., Jr., *Quest for Performance;* (Some data calculated using methodology presented in Appendix C of *Quest for Performance;* Lednicer, David A., *Aerodynamics of the Bell P-39 Airacobra and P-63 Kingcobra,* Society of Automotive Engineers Paper No. 00GATC-55, 2000.

Time Flies *was eventually converted by the Military Aircraft Corporation into a two-place fighter prototype, in hopes of attracting Army Air Corps interest. Notice the large cockpit canopy addition, compared to the flush racer windscreen of* Time Flies. *Because most race planes, if not all, have low-profile canopies, this is one of the changes absolutely necessary for any contemplated fighter conversion. The* Time Flies/MAC *cockpit comparison is starkly dramatic. Emil Strasser photo via Gerry Liang collection*

Although the military aircraft fighter version of Time Flies *gives the outward appearance of being a modern pursuit airplane, it was built more along the lines of an early 1930s vintage aircraft. It lacked all-metal construction, as was found on contemporary P-35 and P-36 pursuits, as well as the emerging P-38, P-39, and P-40 designs. This aircraft placed fourth in the 1938 Thompson. It is the only known example of an American race plane actually being converted to a fighter aircraft. Emil Strasser photo via Gerry Liang collection*

WEDELL CONVERSION

Estimates of performance were made for three versions of the Wedell-Williams airplane at each of four flight altitudes from sea level to 15,000 feet in 5,000 feet increments.[2] First was the as-built racing configuration powered with a 550-horsepower (possibly 600) Pratt & Whitney Wasp engine. Some may possibly argue that Jimmy Wedell was pulling more than 600 horsepower from his engine when he established the Shell speed record of 306 miles per hour. This may be a reasonable assumption, but if the basic design were to have been converted for military use, Pratt & Whitney or Army Air Corps

rated power outputs would have been adhered to for reasons of engine reliability and durability. Thus for pragmatic reasons and to be consistent, rated power levels have been used in all calculations. It should also be noted that published racing horsepower figures are frequently suspect, oft repeated and of questionable heritage.

The next configuration examined was a Wedell "pursuit" with a wing loading equivalent to the racer. Sufficient wing area was added to maintain a wing loading of 24.8 pounds per square foot. The area was added by increasing the span, which resulted in a higher aspect ratio as well. The third Wedell "pursuit"

retained the race wing plan form, resulting in a much higher wing loading of over 34 pounds per square foot.

Thrust horsepower required and available for various aircraft velocities were determined for each of the three Wedell versions. All calculations were made using standard atmospheric conditions from sea level to 15,000 feet. Horsepower data were plotted as a function of aircraft speed, an example of which is shown in Figure 7-1. The lower curve in this figure—for sea level conditions—indicates horsepower required to achieve a range of speeds, while the upper curve shows corresponding thrust

Seversky and Curtiss fought long and hard to win the 1935 Air Corps pursuit competition. Curtiss' entry was this company Model 75, precursor to the P-36. It was powered by a 900-horsepower Wright XR-1670-G5 engine, giving it a top speed of 281 miles per hour at 10,000 feet. Of all-metal construction and incorporating retractable landing gear, the Model 75 was representative of new technology applied to pursuit aircraft. Peter M. Bowers collection

Results of this analysis as presented in Table 7-4 show that the Wedell in any configuration possessed a superior speed compared to the P-26A at all altitudes. That advantage was less for the long-wing version of the Wedell pursuit as might be expected. Jimmy Wedell's design was faster because it was aerodynamically cleaner than the Boeing airplane. This was especially true with respect to engine cowling. Boeing used the ring or Townend cowl, while Wedell employed an NACA style cowl. This fact alone probably accounted for a 10-mile per hour advantage.

THE ARMY LOOKS AT RACE PLANES

A fleeting though direct, connection between American racing planes and pursuit-type aircraft occurred during the decade prior to World War II. It evolved at a time when Air Corps doctrine was predominantly bomber oriented. Pursuit development suffered accordingly, further aggravated by parsimonious Army budgets of the Depression era. "The disturbingly slow rate at which technological advance was being absorbed into American military aircraft," Brigadier General Benjamin S. Kelsey wrote, "became apparent

horsepower levels available.[3] Maximum speed occurs at the point where the two curves cross one another. In this instance, maximum sea level speed for the Wedell racer is calculated to be 303 miles per hour, a velocity very close to that obtained with the airplane during the Shell Speed Dash competition of 1934. Note that aircraft velocity in all configurations increases at 5,000 feet over that obtained at sea level. There are two reasons for this. The Wasp engine was rated at 550 horsepower from sea level up to 5,000 feet. Power was accordingly not diminished due to a reduction in the local ambient air density, because the engine supercharger was capable of delivering sea level manifold pressure up to that altitude. Lower air density at this altitude reduces drag, however. A combination of the these two factors produces a speed somewhat in excess of what the racer could achieve at sea level. Wasp output at altitudes above 5,000 feet diminishes at a rate approximately equal to a ratio of the air density at the altitude of interest to that found at sea level.

The Curtiss Hawk Model 75 is shown here in its final form. This company-owned prototype carried civil registration X17Y. Although Curtiss lost out to Seversky in the 1935 pursuit competition, the basic Model 75 was a worthwhile company investment. From this design evolved extensive export orders, as well as the P-36 and P-40 production contracts. Peter M. Bowers collection

Table 7-4

Calculated Performance
Wedell-Williams Configurations & Boeing P-26A

Configuration Altitude	Model 44 Racer Maximum Speed	Wedell Pursuit Racer Wing Loading Maximum Speed	Wedell Pursuit Racer Wing Area Maximum Speed	Boeing P-26A Pursuit Maximum Speed
Sea Level	303 Mph	266 Mph	302 Mph	215
5,000 Feet	317 Mph	278 Mph	315 Mph	226
7,500 Feet				231
10,000 Feet	298 Mph	259 Mph	292 Mph	209
15,000 Feet	294 Mph	216 Mph	279 Mph	203

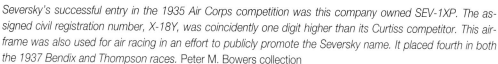

Seversky's successful entry in the 1935 Air Corps competition was this company owned SEV-1XP. The assigned civil registration number, X-18Y, was coincidentally one digit higher than its Curtiss competitor. This airframe was also used for air racing in an effort to publicly promote the Seversky name. It placed fourth in both the 1937 Bendix and Thompson races. Peter M. Bowers collection

The production P-35 airframe illustrated in this 1938 photograph was quite similar to the prototype SEV-1XP. Shown here in the markings of Headquarters Squadron of the 1st Pursuit Group, it was powered by a Pratt & Whitney R-1830-9 engine, delivering 850 horsepower. The SEV-1XP used a Wright R-1820-G5 engine of the same power output. Emil Strasser photo via Gerry Liang collection

only by comparing them with newer civilian transports and recent racing planes."[4]

In November 1933, the Air Corps Materiel Division evinced early if passing interest in the Wedell Model 44 racer design (which carried Race Number 44 as well) as the basis for a pursuit aircraft. In response to an inquiry, Harry P. Williams, president of the Wedell-Williams Air Service Corporation, provided the Air Corps with data and specifications for the racer. Because the corporation had no aeronautical engineering capability per se, Williams turned to Howard Walter Barlow of the University of Minnesota for assistance. It was Barlow "who engineered this job for us originally for a 'Wasp Jr.' developing 530 horsepower . . ." Williams explained.[5] In all probability, Barlow ran an engine mount stress analysis as well as a weight and balance check to insure the integrity of the modified airplane when the heavier and more powerful Wasp engine was installed. Certainly he determined the load factors presented in the Williams correspondence to the Air Corps. Data provided to Wright Field are shown in Table 7-5.

Table 7-5

Wedell-Williams Model 44 Racer Data Forwarded to Wright Field		
Wing Span	25 ft 8 in	
Wing Chord	60 in	
Wing Area	103 ft²	
Aspect Ratio	6.38	Actually 6.40, see note 1
Overall Length	22 ft 3 in	
Flat Plate Equivalent Drag	2.02 ft²	Less wings
Flat Plate Equivalent Drag	2.56 ft²	Including wing profile
Empty Weight	2,000 lb	
Gross Weight	3,500 lb	
Wing Loading	34 lb/ft²	
Power Loading	4.7 lb/hp	
Engine	P&W Wasp Special	"Similar to (P&W) Model E-1"
Horsepower	745 @ 2,200 rpm	
Supercharger Gear Ratio	12:1	
Compression Ratio	6:1	
Propeller	Ham. Std.	
Type	Controllable Pitch	
No. of Blades	Two	
Propeller Diameter	8 ft	
Limit Load Factor	5.43	(Pursuit requirement = 8.5)
Factor of Safety	1.5	
Design Load Factor	8.15	

Source: Williams correspondence to Wright Field dated December 19, 1933.

Note: Aspect ratio (wing span² â wing area) calculates to (25.67)² / 103 = 6.40, not the listed value of 6.38.

Another source indicates that Jimmy Wedell installed a Wasp Model T3D1 in his racer.[7] Curiously, a Pratt & Whitney engine index lists only Wasp T1D1 and T2D1 models, both sea level engines developing 525 and 420 horsepower, respectively. Regardless of the precise engine model identification, the most surprising statistic presented by Williams is the stated Wasp output of 745 horsepower at 2,200 rpm. This number was not a typographical error on Williams' part, for it was used in calculating the power loading figure (Table 7-5). The 745 horsepower amounts to a whopping 35 percent increase over the nominal 550 horsepower produced by numerous Wasp engine models during the mid-1930s![8] Calculations show that this power output required a manifold pressure of about 44 inches of mercury, rather improbable and far in excess of the rated value of 32 inches. The only other

Jackie Cochran acquired a civil version of the Seversky P-35 which was designated AP-7. She used it for air racing as well as personal transportation. In 1938 Jackie won the Bendix Trophy Race with an average speed of just under 250 miles per hour. Her closest competitor was wealthy sportsman pilot Frank Fuller, in another Seversky racer. Emil Strasser photo via Gerry Liang collection

THE ENGINE ENIGMA

There are two interesting aspects to the data in Table 7-5. First is the vague identification of the Wasp engine. Williams described it as being "similar to the Model E-1" Wasp, but using a supercharger gear ratio of 12:1. There were two Pratt & Whitney "E" models. These were the SE and S1E Wasps, equipped with supercharger gear ratios of 12:1 and 10:1, respectively. The SE was a production engine widely employed in various Boeing P-12 models and certain Lockheed aircraft. It was rated at 500 horsepower from sea level to 11,000 feet. This engine, with a 14:1 supercharger gear ratio, was used to good advantage by Ben Howard in his 1935 Bendix Trophy-winning DGA-6, *Mr. Mulligan.* The Wasp S1E, in contrast, was a one-off variant with 12:1 supercharger gearing (rated to 9,000 feet) built for Roscoe Turner's Wedell-Williams racer.[6]

Frank Fuller's Seversky SEV-S2 racer was quite similar to Jackie Cochran's airplane. This is the 1938 version, photographed at the Cleveland Municipal Airport after he placed second in the Bendix that year. The civil versions of the P-35 were probably a bit lighter than their military counterparts. Most if not all used Pratt & Whitney Twin Wasp engines. Emil Strasser photo via Gerry Liang collection

feasible answer to this small mystery is that Williams may have been referring to the new Twin Wasp Jr. engine which ultimately developed 750 horsepower.

A WEDELL WEAKNESS

The second matter of interest in the data given to Wright Field involves the load and safety factors as listed in Table 7-5. Key to the Air Corps evaluation of the Wedell design and what subsequently transpired is an understanding of the "limit load factor." This is the "maximum load factor which the airplane is expected to be subjected in any type of maneuver."[9] For pursuit aircraft, which must be highly maneuverable at all speeds, the limit load factor is relatively high. A characteristic limit load factor for pursuit aircraft is 8.5. Where maneuvering is a secondary consideration (bombers, for instance) limit load factors can be reduced. At high limit load

factors, the airframe structure is, of necessity, designed proportionally stronger to meet the requirement. This almost always results in a heavier airframe in context with consistent materials of construction and fabrication techniques.

The "factor of safety" indicated by Williams in his correspondence to Wright Field (and listed in Table 7-5) is also crucial to understanding how Wright Field assessed the Wedell racer. As the term implies, this requirement is intended to account for uncertainties that inevitably exist in structural analyses.[10] Williams identifies a factor of safety equal to 1.5 which is quite standard even today. The factor of safety is applied by multiplication, in which the limit load factor is multiplied by the factor of safety to give the design load. In the case of the Wedell racer, Williams did not provide the limit load value; however, he did note the design load factor and factor of

safety, thus enabling a determination of the limit load, which calculates to be 5.43. With a 1.5 factor of safety, the design load factor is 8.15 (5.43 x 1.5). Comparable numbers for pursuits of that era are a limit load factor of 8.5, a factor of safety of 1.5 with a resulting design ultimate load value of 12.5 (8.5 x 1.5). With a design load factor, the Wedell racer was at a substantial disadvantage in any evaluation.

THE CRITIQUE

Wright Field politely rejected the concept of converting the Wedell racer into a pursuit airplane. The heart of their finding involved the design load shortcoming just discussed. In a letter to Harry Williams in early 1934, Captain A. J. Lyons, acting chief of the Engineering Section, wrote to the company explaining the situation. He noted that their airplane "would require a complete redesign to bring

Fuller won the Bendix in 1937 and again in 1939. His second victory was achieved at an average speed of 282 miles per hour. Jackie Cochran was entered in the 1939 Bendix, but did not start. This is the 1939 version of the airplane. Fuller was the scion of a family that owned the Fuller Paint Company. He was a great aviation enthusiast and loved the long-distance races. William F. Yeager photo via Gerry Liang collection

[it] up to the requirements for pursuit airplanes." This was the crux of the problem. "By the time this had been done a great deal of time and money would have been spent," Lyons continued, "and your airplane would undoubtedly suffer a great impairment in performance by the increased strength, vision, and equipment, and the decrease in landing speed which would be required to make this a service airplane."[11]

The Wedell-Williams saga continued, however. About the time Captain Lyons replied to Harry Williams, another then-obscure Air Corps captain entered the arena. His name was Claire Lee Chennault, who would go on to lead the famous Flying Tigers and subsequently the 14th Air Force during World War II. A dedicated and thoughtful fighter pilot, Chennault's ancestry traced back five generations to Etienne de Chaneau who arrived in the United States from France via England in 1701. When he poked his nose under the Wright Field

tent, Chennault was an instructor at the Air Corps Tactical School at Maxwell Field, Alabama. He was a fervent advocate of pursuit aircraft, a conviction not shared by many of his Air Corps peers and superiors, who were bomber devotees.

Chennault's enthusiasm for the Wedell racer centered on its blinding speed, which was well documented. Jimmy Wedell captured the official landplane speed record of just under 305 miles per hour flying Race Number 44 during timed trials at Cleveland on September 4, 1933.[12] As the first pilot to break the 300-mile per hour barrier in a landplane, Wedell's feat was justly acclaimed. While the previous Wright Field assessment of a Wedell racer involved characteristics of Race Number 44, Chennault's interest was caught by the latest racer, commonly referred to as the Model 45.

Chennault visited Patterson, Louisiana, for a first-hand look at the new racer. In appraising the

airplane, Chennault wrote to the Chief of the Air Corps, saying he "was impressed both by its extraordinary speed and by the fact that it appears to be readily adaptable as an interceptor type, pursuit airplane."[13] The Model 45 was a further refinement of Wedell's previous designs, but with markedly modern innovations including, as Chennault pointed out, "an internally braced, low wing with retractable landing gear."[14] He was convinced that the general arrangement would easily facilitate installing two synchronized machine guns arranged to fire between engine cylinders. He also believed that bomb racks could be mounted on the lower surface of the fuselage making the aircraft equally useful in a ground attack role.

From the perspective of aircraft performance, Chennault was informed by Wedell that the plane would "cruise at approximately 300 miles an hour at a throttle setting of about 1,800 rpm . . . and

The Navy finally abandoned any new biplane carrier fighter design when it ordered development in 1936 of the Brewster XF2A-1 (pictured here) and the Grumman XF4F-2. Like their Army counterparts, the new monoplane Navy fighters were fully cowled and basically of all-metal construction. They incorporated retractable landing gear and featured completely enclosed cockpits. U.S. Navy via Peter M. Bowers collection

will climb to 10,000 feet in three minutes."[15] This level of performance must have been music to Chennault's ears. He closed his letter to the Chief of the Air Corps with a positive recommendation that the airplane be examined and considered for use as an interceptor.

Jimmy Wedell had to estimate Model 45 performance for Claire Chennault's benefit because the full extent of what the airplane could do was yet to be determined. Wedell began evaluating the Model 45 using a Wasp Jr. engine, which left the airplane underpowered. With an R-1340 Wasp under the hood, performance improved, although it never matched the older Model 44 fixed-gear racer. It remains unclear why the apparently cleaner Model 45, with its cantilever wing and retractable landing gear, was unable to match, let alone exceed, the top speed of the older fixed-gear Model 44.

Wedell demonstrated the Model 45 at New Orleans during February 1934. Over a 100-kilometer course, he averaged 266 miles per hour with the larger (Wasp) engine. The intended powerplant for this machine was a Pratt & Whitney Twin Wasp Jr., but this was not yet available to Wedell. Originally developed for the Navy in an effort to generate more power while maintaining minimum frontal area, the two-row Twin Wasp Jr. had a displacement of 1,535 cubic inches and was initially rated at 650 horsepower. Subsequent models were increased to 750 horsepower output. One example, the S2A5-G, produced 825 horsepower and was used by Earl Ortman in the Marcoux-Bromberg racer of 1937.

Unfortunately, Jimmy Wedell was killed in an airplane accident on June 24, 1934. Harry Williams and Jimmy's brother Walter carried on the racing program, though one suspects with a heavy heart. In any event, the Model 45 was never mated to a Twin Wasp Jr. engine. It was instead campaigned during the 1934 racing season with both the Wasp Jr. and larger Wasp engines.[16]

Were the Model 45 performance figures (a 300 miles per hour cruise speed and sea level to 10,000 feet time-to-climb of 3 minutes) that Wedell quoted to Chennault realistic? Without test data there is no way of positively knowing. Performance estimates suggest that Wedell was at least in the ballpark. Sea level high speed was calculated to be 322 miles per hour with the twin-row engine. Time-to-climb to 10,000 feet with the Model 44 racer was calculated to be 3.3 minutes using the Williams data (Table 7-5) given to the Air Corps. With a more powerful engine and only a modest gross weight increase the Model 45 should have been able to reach altitude in approximately 3 minutes.

ROUND TWO

Air Corps interest in a new pursuit airplane resurfaced early in 1935. Invitations to bid in a design competition were sent out to numerous designers and aircraft manufacturers. Although the exact number of bids solicited is unknown, 16 proposals were received! This large number of responses testifies to the economic and political environment of the time. The economic depression was still severe within the aviation community and airplane orders were few and far between. Equally significant, if not more so, Air Corps procurement policies were under close Congressional scrutiny. Competition was the byword.

When the bids were opened on May 16, 1935, an evaluation that continued for five months commenced. Finally on October 1, the secretary of war announced an award. Wedell-Williams Air Service Corporation was declared the winner. Contract W535 AC-8392, including Air Corps specification X-603A, was for the design (only) of what would be designated the XP-34.[17]

The required minimum performance for the XP-34 was 286 miles per hour at 10,000 feet using a Pratt & Whitney R-1535 Twin Wasp Jr.. In the meantime, however, a second pursuit competition later that same year resulted in submission of two sample aircraft at Wright Field for evaluation: a Curtiss Model 75 powered by an experimental 900-horsepower Wright XR-1670-5; and the Seversky

Grumman's chubby Wildcat fighter was a mainstay in the Pacific theater during the early part of World War II. Shown here is the F4F-4 model, with a 1,200-horsepower supercharged R-1830-36 engine up front. An advantage of the wing intersection placement at midfuselage is that it requires essentially no wing fillet. Peter M. Bowers collection

SEV-1 using a Wright R-1820-G-5 of 850 horsepower. The Model 75 was the prototype for what became the Curtiss P-36. Similarly, Seversky's SEV-1 was the forerunner of the P-35. A curious circumstance arose when the sample aircraft appeared at Wright Field. Both incorporated more powerful engines than planned for the XP-34 design. Not surprisingly, Seversky's SEV-1 achieved the design speed objective (268 miles per hour) of the XP-34, while the Curtiss Model 75 exceeded the requirement with a high speed of 281 miles per hour.

THE CATCH 22

Proceeding with an XP-34 design possessing inferior performance was nothing if not ludicrous as a consequence of the Curtiss and Seversky flight test results. Common sense dictated a new direction or abandonment of the project altogether. When the Air Corps attempted to change the Wedell contract to incorporate a new engine, the Judge Advocate General objected: "An award could not legally be made for such a modified design," he decided, "without obvious detriment to the other competitors."[18] In reality, Wedell-Williams was under a severe disadvantage. Without a more powerful engine upon which to base its design, the small Patterson, Louisiana, organization could not possibly generate a product competitive with the faster Curtiss design. It was truly a "Catch 22."

Political conditions at that time posed a problem for the Air Corps in context with the Wedell design. The original XP-34 contract resulted from competitive bidding. A simple change order to incorporate a more powerful engine, however, would be a noncompetitive process negotiated between the government and the contractor. The absence of competition in this instance caught the attention of the Judge Advocate General, even though recompeting the project would have been costly in time and money, and made no technical sense for something as straightforward as an engine change.

As foolish and trivial as this issue may seem today, it was a serious matter in 1935. The political environment was heavily shaded by the "merchants of death" mentality surrounding Congressional investigation of the munitions industry, its alleged profiteering and illegal foreign military sales. Out of this came an insistence on competitive procurement to avoid "favoritism alleged to color the use of negotiated experimental contracts." It should be pointed out that negotiated contracts—through which the Air Corps selected a single contractor, as opposed to soliciting competitive bids from several firms—were legal under provisions of existing procurement regulations.[19]

The dilemma was complex in detail because procurement policies were inadequate for every situation that might arise. The Air Corps wanted

The Air Corps expressed interest in the Wedell-Williams Model 44 racer. In response to a Wright Field inquiry, Harry Williams forwarded a set of data on the Pratt & Whitney Wasp-powered version. The Wasp power module is installed on the racer in this photograph, recognizable by the rocker arm bumps on the engine cowl. Emil Strasser photo via Gerry Liang collection

and needed advanced combat aircraft of superior performance. Political and bureaucratic interests demanded low cost through extensive competition. The two objectives were often remarkably incompatible when it came to new experimental designs. A particularly egregious example of how this policy could go awry occurred when a decision was made to procure lower-cost Douglas B-18 two-engine bombers instead of the more expensive yet demonstrably better performing Boeing B-17 four-engine bombers.

The initial Wedell-Williams XP-34 procurement was competitive. When it quickly became obvious the product would be obsolete before the design task was even finished, the Air Corps chose to issue a new contract on a negotiated basis (sole source) incorporating the more powerful 850-horsepower Pratt & Whitney R-1830 Twin Wasp. "To proceed with a contract for constructing an experimental aircraft according to the winning [original] design was obviously futile."[20] The thought of not doing this raised the ire of the Judge Advocate

Further Air Corps interest in Wedell-Williams designs centered on the Model 45. The R-1340 Wasp power module was interchangeable with the Model 44. The Wedell XP-34 design contract was based on the Model 45, with suitable modifications to make it acceptable for military operations. Unfortunately, the XP-34 went no further than a design study. Its performance was inferior to the Curtiss P-36 prototype already in existence. Emil Strasser photo via Gerry Liang collection

With the war already raging in Europe, race pilot Harry Crosby turned his attentions to a lightweight interceptor for the Air Corps. The design was influenced by his CR-4 race plane. Unlike the all-metal CR-4, however, Crosby's CIP-5 proposal was based upon wood, a nonstrategic material. The CIP-5 was to be powered by an air-cooled Ranger V-770. The Air Corps was not interested. Birch Matthews collection

General, however. In the end, a new contract (W535 AC-8815) was issued. No hardware was involved. Wedell-Williams was obligated only to deliver a design, albeit with a more powerful engine.

The XP-34 story ended with delivery of the design to Wright Field in fulfillment of the second contract. In final form its general layout closely resembled the Model 45 in both appearance and construction. Based on later renditions of the general arrangement (the design layout apparently no longer exists) the aft fuselage was fabric covered. One distinguishing feature was a vast improvement in pilot vision from the cockpit. It was an enlarged both in

profile and width compared to the standard arrangement on Wedell's racers.

Why did the XP-34 recede into the dustbin of history? There were probably several contributing factors, one of which was the estimated high speed for the design. To calculate this number, some assumptions had to be made in the absence of data. For instance it was assumed that the wing area approximated the Model 45 racer (124 square feet), and the gross weight is thought to have been somewhere around 4,250 pounds. If these numbers are representative, the XP-34 would have a sea level maximum speed in the neighborhood of

280–285 miles per hour. Thus the XP-34 would not have been any faster than the Curtiss Model 75. Both the Curtiss and Seversky designs were of all-metal construction, whereas the Wedell was not. More importantly, the Curtiss and Seversky models already existed in sample form and both companies had manufacturing and engineering capabilities that Wedell-Williams Air Service did not. It was hardly a contest.

There were other government flirtations involving pursuit derivations of race aircraft designs. Noted designer Keith Rider submitted a version of his Rider R-3 (nee Marcoux Bromberg) racer in the

Table 7-6

Proposed 1935 Rider R-5 Pursuit

Characteristic	Air Corps Requirements		Rider R-5
	Desired	Minimum	Performance
Gross Weight, Lb			4,050
Equivalent Flat Plate Parasite Drag, Ft^2			5.3
Propeller Efficiency, %			80
Span Efficiency Factor, e			0.8
High Speed @ 10,000 Ft, Mph	325	260	276
Cruise Speed @ 10,000 Ft, Mph	285	225	243
Landing Speed, Mph			68
Endurance @ Cruise Speed, Mph	3.0	3.0	3.0
Takeoff Over 50 Ft Obstacle, Ft	500	1,500	1,420
Landing Over 50 Ft Obstacle, Ft	500	1,500	1,170
Service Ceiling, Ft	30,000	25,000	29,500
Time to Climb to 10,000 Ft, Min	3.0	5.0	3.6

Source: Specification sheet for the R-5 pursuit dated April 30, 1935.

XP-34 competition. Rider's offering, like the initial Wedell design, was to be powered by a Pratt & Whitney Twin Wasp Jr. Table 7-6 provides a glimpse not only of the Rider design characteristics, but what the Air Corps wanted in the way of performance. Note in particular that a high speed of 325 miles per hour at 10,000 feet was desired, and the minimum acceptable speed at that altitude was 260 miles per hour.

Keith Rider's bid to the Air Corps lost to the Wedell proposal. It would appear that on paper, at least, the Wedell design was a shade faster. Ironically, the Rider R-3 upon which the proposal was based was eventually converted to accept a Twin Wasp Jr. engine, a goal that forever eluded the Wedell-Williams group.

A LIGHTWEIGHT INTERCEPTOR

Race pilot Harry Crosby submitted a lightweight interceptor design concept to Wright Field during 1940. The genesis for this proposal was Crosby's elegant little Menasco-powered, all-metal CR-4 racer that first appeared at the National Air Races in 1938. Crosby originally intended to use an air-cooled, 12-cylinder V-770 Ranger engine in the CR-4. The airframe was designed and stressed accordingly. Unfortunately he was never able to acquire the Ranger, and instead settled for a Menasco C6S-4.

Crosby's experience with the CR-4 racer were less than ideal. He was forced out of the 1938 Thompson race, and placed a relatively slow fourth in the 1939 race with an average speed of 244.52 miles per hour. Within another year or two, Crosby may well have ironed out the numerous problems typically encountered with any new design. It was not to be, however, because Germany invaded Poland in September 1939. Europe was quickly enveloped in war. Air racing in the United States ground to a halt as the country's attention gravitated, albeit reluctantly, to rearming the military.

Harry Crosby turned to the task of evolving a military derivative of his racer. His possible entre to military sales appeared to reside within a category of Air Corps planes known as interceptors. The term interceptor appears to have first entered the Air Corps lexicon somewhere around late 1933. This was at a time when pursuit aircraft development money was at a low ebb. If a mission developed requiring a new aircraft type, however, this deplorable situation might change. Implicit in the "interceptor" nomenclature, at least in the beginning, was a reduction in design load factors over that of pursuit aircraft. The objective was a fast, lightweight airplane capable of a superior rate of climb. It was in this context that Claire Chennault considered the Wedell-Williams racer potentially suitable for the interceptor role. The interceptor concept was finally put to the test when the Bell Aircraft Corporation won a contract to build the XFM-1 Airacuda.[21]

Crosby designated his preliminary design the CIP-5.[22] Unlike the massive 18,492-pound gross weight Bell XFM-1, powered by two Allison V-1710-13 engines, the CIP-5 could be described as diminutive and delicate by comparison. It had a gross weight of only 2,700 pounds. Power was to be supplied by a single Ranger Model SGV-770C-1 engine with a sea level rating of 450 horsepower (520 horsepower for takeoff). Perhaps the most startling aspect of the Crosby design was that it would be constructed out of wood. This was a complete departure from his innovative all-metal racing planes, the CR-2 and CR-4. The lightweight airframe and *Ranger* engine combination produced a calculated maximum speed of 368 miles per hour. Armament consisted of two synchronized .30-caliber machine guns.

Unfortunately, Crosby's timing was wrong. War in the air over Europe rapidly demonstrated a need for more and heavier fire power. In addition, maximum speed of the CIP-5 was essentially unremarkable. Using wood as the primary material of construction was not particularly intriguing in 1940. The United States was not yet in the war, and a perceived shortage of aluminum had yet to materialize. And like the Wedell effort, there was no experienced manufacturing organization behind Harry Crosby. As a consequence, the Crosby interceptor died aborning.

Chapter 8

R-2-C-I NAVY CURTISS RACER.
LANDING GEAR MOTOR INSTALLATI
9-6-23.
T-253

Piston Power: Liquid-cooled Engines

I once facetiously remarked that the four-stroke engine has one stroke for producing power and three for wearing the engine out!

Sir Stanley Hooker • *Not Much of an Engineer*

The piston engine in its various forms was the source of power for both civil and military airplanes from the inception of powered flight through World War II. It was and still is the primary engine in the sport of air racing. As with any broad statement, of course, there are exceptions. Turbine-powered fighter aircraft were used during the late 1940s, when military participation in both cross-country and pylon racing returned to the National Air Races after a 17-year absence. Jets briefly reappeared in 1973 as part of the Mojave race program, this time in the hands of civilian pilots. The mainstay of all air racing classes to this day remains the piston engine, however.

Invention of the four-stroke internal combustion engine is generally attributed to the German experimenter Nicolaus August Otto, who built his first engine in 1876. In truth, the four-stroke concept originated with a Frenchman, Alphonse Beau de Rochas during 1862.[1] He accordingly applied for patent protection, and had it been granted, we would most likely refer to the four-stroke engine concept as the "de Rochas" cycle. Unfortunately for de Rochas, he neglected to pay taxes associated with the patent process. As a consequence, the French bureaucracy invalidated his patent as a penalty.[2] The honor of inventing the four-stroke engine thus passed some 14 years later to Germany and Nicolaus Otto, perhaps to the sorrow of many Frenchmen.

To this day the operating cycle describing a four-stroke piston engine is known as the Otto cycle. The four strokes consist of intake, compression, ignition or power and exhaust. During the intake stroke, a mixture of vaporized fuel and air is drawn into the engine cylinder. At the bottom of the stroke, the piston reverses direction and compresses the mixture. The power stroke occurs when the compressed mixture is ignited, and the expanding high-pressure gas drives the piston downward again. Once again the piston reverses course and drives the burned mixture out of the cylinder through the exhaust valve

The 1923 Curtiss R2C-1 Navy racer utilized a Curtiss D-12A engine. Like the Packard 1A-2025, the D-12A produced 500 horsepower, but it was lighter weight. The R2C-1 with its D-12A engine proved to be a winning combination. Al Williams flew this sleek racer to victory in the 1923 Pulitzer at a speed of 244 miles per hour. Navy via Peter M. Bowers collection

EARLY AIRCRAFT ENGINES

The Wright Brothers' 12-horsepower water-cooled engine in their *Flyer* was the product of thoughtful design and development testing. Though it lacked refinements now taken for granted, and was prone to lose power as it heated, the 1903 engine nonetheless proved adequate. This in itself is remarkable. A number of contemporary aviation pioneers, including Otto Lilienthal, Percy S. Pilcher, Samuel P. Langley and Alberto Santos Dumont, attempted to fashion lightweight airplane engines. Only the Wrights succeeded.

One factor contributing to the success of the Wright Brothers engine was an acceptable engine weight to horsepower ratio. Existing stationary and automotive engines were simply too heavy to be used in a flying machine. Charles E. Taylor, who helped build the 1903 engine for the Wrights, recalled that: "We tried to get a motor built there [at the Oldsmobile company] but they couldn't make one near the low weight we wanted."[3] Faced with this situation, the Wrights exercised their customary methodical approach to a problem and began engine design experiments. As a weight

A liquid-cooled engine was the first to power a controlled manned flight. The coolant was water. The Wright brothers, not finding a suitably lightweight automobile engine to use, designed and built this four-cylinder gasoline engine. Gasoline was gravity fed in a stream, which impinged on a portion of the heated water jacket where it was vaporized. John Garrett collection

The first Wright engine produced 12 horsepower at 1,090 rpm. As the engine heated, this dropped to something like 7 horsepower. It had a bore and stroke of 4 inches, yielding a displacement of 201.1 cubic inches. The most prominent feature of this engine was its light weight. Including the water coolant, it weighed just over 200 pounds, much lighter than any contemporary automobile engine of comparable size. John Garrett collection

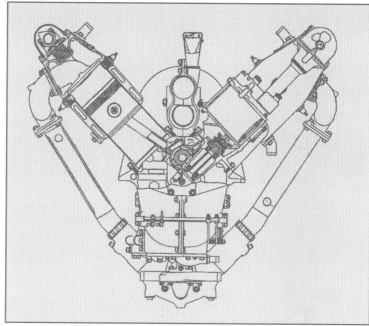

The Hispano-Suiza was the design inspiration of Swiss automotive engineer Marc Birkigt. Originally a V-8 configuration producing 150 horsepower in 1915, the Hispano-Suiza's cylinders were arranged with a 90-degree included angle between banks, giving frontal area more width and less depth. Compare this with the nearby front view of the 60-degree included angle configuration of a Curtiss V-1570 engine.

One month before the 1933 International Air Races, another race program was inaugurated in Chicago. Known as the American Air Races, it was promoted by the Chicago Tribune newspaper and a group of civic leaders. Held on the same dates as the 1933 National Air Races in Los Angeles, the American Air Race program was not sanctioned by the National Aeronautics Association, which caused many problems. John Garrett collection

saving measure, they used an aluminum alloy to cast a one-piece crankcase and water jacket. In its final configuration the Wright engine (dry) weight-to-power ratio was around 15 pounds per horsepower. To their everlasting credit, the brothers approached the problem of fashioning an engine in the same meticulous way they designed and built the *Flyer*.

By 1906, through further development the Wright engine weight-to-power ratio was essentially cut in half (8 to 1). Two years later the Wrights achieved a ratio of 4.6 to 1 as their engine development continued. The decline in weight-to-power was a trend that would continue unremittingly through World War II, when this figure of merit would become slightly less than 1.0.

QUEST FOR HORSEPOWER

Early engines were normally aspirated, that is manifold pressure was contingent upon atmospheric pressure plus any ram air pressure (very minor at low aircraft speeds of the times), and minus pressure losses through the carburetor and induction system. Before the advent and common use of piston engine supercharging, power increases were achieved in basically two ways. One was to increase the swept volume (displacement) of the engine. This could be done by increasing the cylinder bore diameter, lengthening the piston stroke, and adding more cylinders. There were practical limits to this approach involving engine size (frontal area in particular), engine weight, and the strength requirements of the moving parts.

A tendency toward greater swept volumes is illustrated by the Glenn Curtiss line of engines. The 50-horsepower engine designed by Curtiss for the

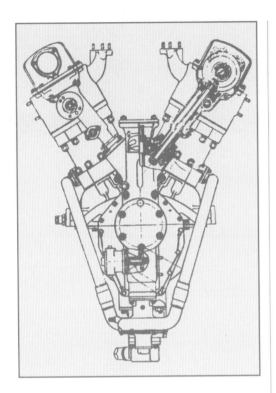

The GV-1570-F Conqueror 600-horsepower engine shown in this illustration had a 60-degree included angle between cylinder banks. This feature allowed airframe designers to minimize frontal area and thus drag. One of the better known pursuit airplanes powered by this engine was the Curtiss P-6E.

1908 Silver Dart utilized a bore and stroke of 3.75x4 inches in each of its eight cylinders. Its displacement was 353.4 cubic inches. Both bore and stroke dimensions increased over time as more power was required. The Curtiss OX series of 1912–1914 incorporated a 4-inch bore and 5-inch stroke, resulting in a 502.7-cubic-inch displacement. These engines developed from 75 to 100 horsepower, virtually all of which resulted from a 42 percent increase in swept volume relative to the Silver Dart engine (these engines all ran at about the same crankshaft speed). This trend continued with the later Curtiss D-12 and Conqueror engines of the 1920s and 1930s. The D-12 had a 4.5-inch bore and 6-inch stroke plus four more cylinders (it was a V-12) yielding 1,145.1

cubic inches. The Curtiss Conqueror design pushed these numbers still higher, with a bore of 5.125 inches and a nominal stroke of 6.250 inches. This yielded a displacement of 1,547.2 cubic inches; however, the working displacement was actually more because 6 of the 12 cylinders employed articulated connecting rods, producing a stroke of 6.426 inches. The effective displacement was thus 1,569 cubic inches. By this innovative piece of machine design, Curtiss added about 22 cubic inches of volume at essentially no increase in engine physical dimensions and very little increase in engine weight.

The other way to develop greater horsepower in a normally aspirated engine is to increase crankshaft speeds. Early engines were limited to about 1,100 to 1,400 revolutions per minute (rpm). Later engines such as the D-12 were routinely running as high as 2,300 rpm and the Conqueror was rated at 2,400 to 2,450 rpm. Higher crankshaft speeds were the result of improved metallurgy, strengthened components, and larger and better bearings. Racing engines were often run at higher crankshaft speeds

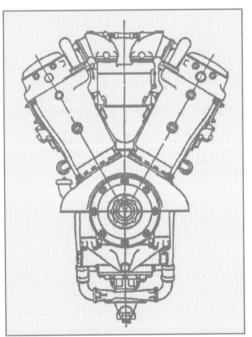

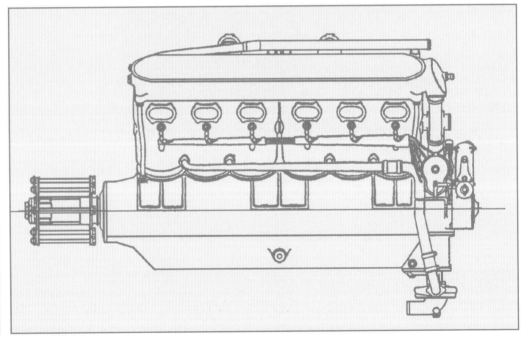

Most people associate air-cooled radial engines with the Wright name; however, during the early 1920s, the company also built a number of water-cooled V-12 engines. Depicted here is a direct drive Wright T-3 model, capable of delivering 800 horsepower at 2,000 rpm. This was the end of the Wright liquid-cooled engine series. The company went on to develop a solid line of air-cooled engines popularized initially by the J-6, used by Lindbergh when he crossed the Atlantic.

power output; rather, it improved thermodynamic efficiency yielding better fuel economy. Higher compression ratios were facilitated by improvements in fuel quality with additives suppressing fuel detonation tendencies.

A final factor worth mentioning with respect to improved aircraft/engine performance is the evolution of the propeller. No matter how much brake horsepower is delivered to the propeller shaft, it must be converted into thrust. Early propellers were fixed pitch and constructed of wood. In an attempt to obtain greater thrust, designers resorted to increased propeller diameters. Larger propellers process air more efficiently with each revolution. Higher crankshaft revolutions coupled with larger diameters propellers also lead to tip speeds approaching or exceeding sonic velocity. Under this condition a sharp rise in propeller drag occurs, defeating the objective of higher aircraft speed. The answer to this dilemma was reduction gearing, allowing the propeller to turn at a slower speed than the engine. The solution to sonic tip speeds was obvious, but implementing it proved troublesome. It

Grover Loening designed and built two R-4 racing planes for the Army to enter in the 1922 Pulitzer Trophy Race. They were powered by Packard Model 1A-2025 water-cooled engines. This engine delivered a maximum of 500 horsepower. Notice the large flat-face radiator core just behind the wooden propeller. Such designs were a significant source of drag. John Garrett collection

in an attempt to obtain a competitive advantage around the pylons.

Two other aspects of engine progress are worthy of mention. One was a tendency to increase engine compression ratio. As one might expect, early engines typically employed relatively low compression ratios of less than 5:1 due to the quality limitations of available fuel. When the Conqueror went into production, it had a compression ratio of 5.8:1, and some high-compression models were rated at 7.25:1. The latter ratio was an extreme. When superchargers were perfected and came into common use, compression ratios stabilized at around 6:1. Increased compression ratio contributed little increased

Another view of the Loening racer and Packard 1A-2025 engine. The R-4s were plagued with wing flutter problems. Fabric covering on the wings was removed and replaced by wood veneer to stiffen the structure. This photo is believed to have been taken during that rework. In an effort to save weight, Loening used the two wing spars as engine mounts, transmitting vibration directly to the wing and contributing substantially to the flutter problem. John Garrett collection

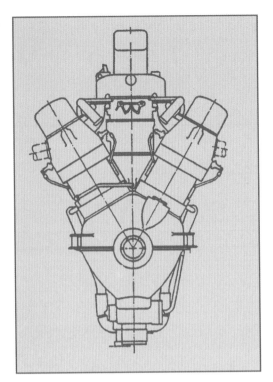

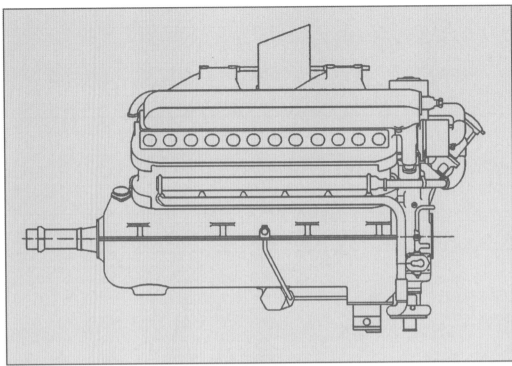

The last of the Curtiss production liquid-cooled engine series was the Conqueror. In its original form, it had a 1,569-cubic-inch displacement, producing 600 horsepower. Later development increased output to as high as 700 horsepower. As a civilian racing engine, it was plagued by a number of problems.

became a matter of perfecting the type, design and material of the gearing to achieve acceptable reliability and durability. Toward the mid-1930s, these solutions were pretty much in hand.

ENGINE DEVELOPMENTS

In spite of drastic demobilization following World War I, the Army and Navy air services maintained a healthy interest in aircraft engine development for a variety of aircraft types and missions. (This interest was largely frustrated by miserly budgets and an abundance of war surplus engines.) In 1921, the National Advisory Committee for Aeronautics summarized military needs into three development categories: engines of mutual interest to both the Army and Navy; engines specifically desired by the Army; and, engines specifically needed for the Navy.[4] At that point in time the services shared a mutual interest in both air-cooled and water-cooled piston engines ranging from 50 to as high as 1,000 horsepower, although the latter was only

A kingpost was mounted on the fuselage centerline. Large struts extended from the post to the wing panels to further stiffen the wing structure. Engine cooling problems also troubled the R-4 design, and the planes were raced without cowlings to alleviate this problem. Numerous test flights confirmed that the R-4 had fundamental design flaws. Although they raced in the 1922 Pulitzer, finishing eighth and 9nineth, one machine was immediately grounded and the other broken up three years later. John Garrett collection

then in a design phase. Engines existing or planned in excess of about 250 horsepower were water-cooled. The breadth of interest on the part of the air services was amazing, including not only gasoline-powered engines, but diesel, steam, and turbine engines as well! History would show that diesel and steam power-plants were better left to trucks and trains; however, the recognition of turbine engines for potential use in aircraft was truly prescient.

The number of companies marketing aircraft engines in the United States exceeded 60 in 1929.[5] A total of 110 models were represented, and by this time fully 83 percent of available models were air-cooled, a dramatic turn around from the beginning of the decade, when many, if not most, were water-cooled. The mix of engine brands included indigenous designs and some foreign types merely assembled and sold in this country. Engine power output ranged from the minuscule Moorehouse Model M-42, producing all of 12 horsepower, to the gigantic one-off Allison experimental air-cooled X-4520, developing 1,200 horsepower.[6] Competition between air-cooled and liquid-cooled engines continued through World War II; however, commercial applications were dominated by air-cooled designs.

Table 8-1

American Racing Aircraft Using Water-Cooled Engines 1920–1939

Manufacturer	Model	Race No.	Year	Engine	Hp
Orenco	D	45	1920	Hispano-Suiza	300
Verville-Packard	VCP-R	63	1920	Packard 1A-2025	600
Thomas Morse	MB-3	4	1920	Wright Hispano H-2	325
Vought	V.E.7	22	1920	Wright E-3	180
Loening	M-81-S	46	1920	Wright-Martin H	325
Curtiss Aeroplane Co.	Curtiss CR-1	4	1921	Curtiss CD-12	400
Curtiss-Cox	Texas Wildcat		1921	Curtiss C-12	340
Curtiss-Cox	Cactus Kitten	3	1921	Curtiss C-12	340
Thomas Morse	MB-7	1 & 7	1921	Wright Hispano H-2	340
Thomas Morse	MB-6	2	1921	Wright Hispano H-2	325
Curtiss Aeroplane Co.	Curtiss R-6	69	1922	Curtiss D-12	375
Curtiss Aeroplane Co.	Curtiss CR-2	8	1922	Curtiss D-12	375
Curtiss Aeroplane Co.	Curtiss CR-2	40	1922	Curtiss D-12	470
Loening	R-4	45 & 46	1922	Packard 1A-2025	500
Thomas Morse	R-5	47 & 48	1922	Packard 1A-2025	500
Verville-Packard	R-1	42	1922	Packard 1A-2025	500
Aerial Engineering Corp.	Bee Line BR-1	6 & 18	1922	Wright H-3	325
Verville-Sperry	R-3	70	1922	Wright H-3	340
Verville-Sperry	R-3	49 & 50	1922	Wright H-3	340
Wright	NW-1	9	1922	Wright T-2	525
Curtiss Aeroplane Co.	Curtiss R2C-1	9 & 10	1923	Curtiss D-12	500
Verville-Sperry	R-3	70	1923	Curtiss D-12	375
Wright	F2W-1	7 & 8	1923	Wright T-3	600
Curtiss Aeroplane Co.	Curtiss PW-8A	71	1924	Curtiss D-12	460
Verville-Sperry	R-3	70	1924	Curtiss D-12A	500
Curtiss Aeroplane Co.	Curtiss R3C-1	40 & 43	1925	Curtiss D-12	500
Curtiss Aeroplane Co.	Curtiss PW-8B	50	1925	Curtiss D-12	440
Curtiss Aeroplane Co.	Curtiss P-1		1925	Curtiss D-12	470
Curtiss	F6C-3	27	1929	Curtiss D-12	435
Curtiss	XF6C-6	27	1930	Curtiss D-12	700
Walter Carr	Carr Special	36	1932	Curtiss OX5	
Jamieson			1933	Curtiss D-12	435
Northrop	Gamma 2G		1934	Curtiss SGV-1570-F4	705
Reggie Robins Racer			1934	Wright-Hispano	320
Delgado Trade School	Delgado Maid	6	1935	Curtiss D-12	435
Wittman	Bonzo	4	1935	Curtiss D-12	475
Delgado Trade School	Delgado Maid	6	1936	Curtiss Conqueror	700
Hosler	Fury		1938	Curtiss D-12	450
Pearson-Williams PW-1	Mr. Smoothie	11	1938	Curtiss Conqueror	825

Source: Don Berliner, *The Complete Worldwide Directory of Racing Airplanes*, Vol. 1, Aviation Publishing, Inc., Destin, Florida, 1997.

Table 8-2

U.S. Army Pursuits Using Water-Cooled Engines
1920 – 1929

Manufacturer	Model	Year	Engine	Hp
Verville	VCP-1	1921	Wright Hispano H	300
Curtiss Aeroplane Co.	PN-1	1920	Liberty 6	220
Engineering Division	PW-1	1921	Packard 1A-1237	350
Engineering Division	PW-1A	1921	Packard 1A-1237	350
Loening	PW-2	1921	Wright H	320
Loening	PW-2A	1922	Packard 1A-1237	320
Loening	PW-2B	1922	Packard 1A-1237	350
Orenco	PW-3	1922	Wright H	320
Gallaudett	PW-4	1922	Packard 1A-1237	350
Fokker	V-40	1922	Wright H	334
Fokker	PW-5	1922	Wright H-2	300
Fokker	PW-6	1922	Wright H-2	315
Fokker	PW-7	1924	Curtiss D-12	440
Curtiss	PW-8	1923	Curtiss D-12	440
Boeing	PW-9	1924	Curtiss D-12	440
Curtiss	P-1	1925	Curtiss V-1150-1	435
Curtiss	P-2	1925	Curtiss V-1400	505
Boeing	XP-4	1926	Packard 1A-1500	510
Curtiss	P-5	1927	Curtiss V-1150-3	435
Curtiss	P-6	1928	Curtiss V-1570-17	600
Boeing	XP-7	1928	Curtiss V-1570-1	600
Boeing	XP-8	1927	Packard 2A-1530	600
Boeing	XP-9	1928	Curtiss V-1570-15	600
Curtiss	XP-10	1928	Curtiss V-1570-15	600

Source: Ray Wagner, *American Combat Planes*, 3rd Edition, Doubleday & Co.

LIQUID-COOLED ENGINES

Large water-cooled engines were popular in the United States through the 1920s. This was generally true with respect to both military pursuit and racing aircraft. Prominent American racing aircraft and Army pursuit planes using water-cooled engines during this period are shown in Table 8-1 and 8-2, respectively.

By way of clarification, it should be noted the liquid cooling medium used into the 1930s was water because of its excellent heat capacity. There was a very pragmatic reason water-cooled engines were employed in the early years of aviation. It proved considerably easier to achieve uniform cylinder cooling by this mechanism, especially in larger engines. There were penalties associated with water cooling,

though, because it added weight, complexity and drag (due to the radiator). Nonetheless, several outstanding water-cooled engines were developed during World War I and for several years thereafter. (Later engineering development at Wright Field led to the use of pure ethylene glycol and subsequently glycol-water mixtures.)

HISPANO-SUIZA ENGINES

A leading European engine of this type was the Hispano-Suiza, the design product of a young and quite talented Swiss automotive engineer named Marc Birkigt. The Model A Hispano-Suiza aircraft engine (140 horsepower) was prototyped in late 1914 and placed in production during 1915. Its compact V-8 production version produced 150 horsepower at 1,450 rpm with a (dry) weight-to-power ratio of

about 3.1. Continued development over the next year increased horsepower to 215 by running the engine at steadily higher revolutions. Hispano also increased the swept volume (displacement) and number of cylinders from 8 to 12, resulting in power outputs up to 300 horsepower. Approximately 50,000 Hispano-Suiza engines of all models were produced during World War I. Among the many manufacturing licenses granted was one to the Wright-Martin company in the United States.[7] The Hispano-Suiza, known colloquially as the "Hisso," had come to America.

Birkigt's contribution to water-cooled technology centered on forming the basic engine structure from a single-block aluminum alloy casting. Forged steel barrels were then threaded full length into the aluminum. Each steel barrel was open at the bottom (crankcase) end and closed at the top to form the combustion chamber. A lightweight crankcase was bolted to the aluminum engine block, completing the overall assembly. The *Hisso* proved relatively dependable, light weight and compact, and it possessed a small frontal area. A primary disadvantage, however, was a less than efficient waste heat transfer from the hot gasses in the combustion chamber to the cooling water. This derived from the closed-end steel cylinder

The ill-fated Curtiss R3C-3 was perhaps the finest example of the company's biplane racing machines. Every effort appears to have been made to tightly cowl the engine and streamline the remainder of the airframe. Intended for the 1926 Schneider contest, the airplane was destroyed in an accident before the race on November 12, 1926.
John Garrett collection

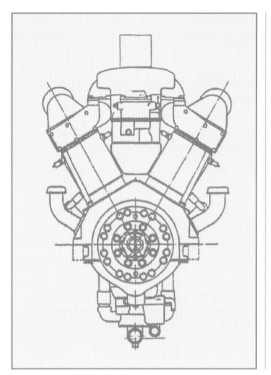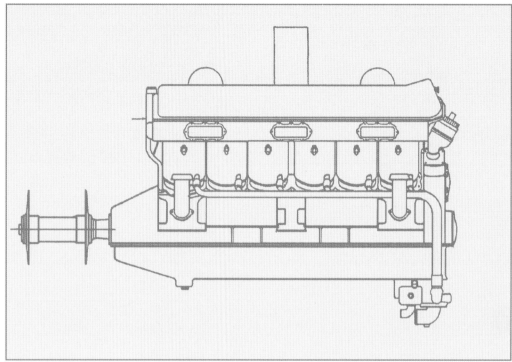

Packard was the third major producer of liquid-cooled engines in the United States during the 1920s. The other two, of course, were Wright and Curtiss. Shown in this illustration is the Packard Model 2A-2500, an engine rated at 800 horsepower, turning 2,000 revolutions. Packard and Wright got out of the liquid-cooled engine business as Curtiss eventually cornered the military market.

design. Waste heat had to be conducted through a somewhat torturous path including the closed-end steel barrel, across the threaded joint, through the aluminum and finally into the cooling water.[8] It was not the best resolution, but one that sufficed.

Some understanding of the design problem inherent in dealing with waste heat of combustion in piston engines can be appreciated from the temperatures involved. Peak flame temperature resulting from combustion of the fuel-air mixture is about 3,500 degrees Fahrenheit. This occurs during the engine power stroke. More meaningful from the designer's perspective, however, is the mean gas temperature in the cylinder head region because, there are four strokes and only one involves ignition and combustion of the fuel-air mixture. The mean temperature in the cylinder head is somewhere around 1,200 degrees Fahrenheit. (The mean temperature in the barrel of the cylinder is perhaps 600 degrees Fahrenheit.) Thus, the critical design area from a

temperature perspective is the cylinder head. Heat must be transferred rapidly enough from this region to prohibit the material of construction from reaching its yield point–the temperature at which the metal begins to deform.

Birkigt's innovative approach was counter to standard engine design practice up to that time. Typically a strong rigid crankcase was fabricated onto which individual steel cylinders were fastened. Water jackets were then assembled around each cylinder for cooling. The entire approach tended to be quite heavy, yielding a high weight-to-power ratio. To Birkigt's credit, one-piece cast engine blocks became the accepted norm.

CURTISS ENGINES

Curtiss became the dominant manufacturer of large water-cooled aircraft engines up to the middle of the 1930s. Its history in this field traces to 1908 and the pioneering days of aviation (Appendix D).

The most prolific and perhaps successful of these early engines was the OX series culminating in the water-cooled 8-cylinder, 90 horsepower OX-5 in 1917. In 1917, however, Curtiss rolled out its first V-12 engine, identified as model V-4. With a 1,649-cubic-inch displacement, equivalent to a World War II Merlin, this engine developed 250 horsepower at a crankshaft speed of 1,400 rpm. The supercharged Merlin, in contrast, put out 1,500 horsepower at 3,000 rpm with the same swept volume.

When Wright Aeronautical (formerly Wright-Martin) secured a manufacturing license to produce Hispano-Suiza engines, Curtiss Aeroplane & Motor Company accurately foresaw stiff competition. Fortuitously, Charles B. Kirkham was chief motor engineer in the Curtiss organization and an established engine designer in his own right. At management direction, Kirkham set about designing an engine that would outperform the Hisso. His objective was a 12-cylinder vee-type engine capable of 300

horsepower at 2,250 rpm—the Hisso had only 8-cylinders. Kirkham appreciated the benefits derived from a lightweight aluminum casting, and utilized this design approach in what became the Curtiss Model AB, although with significant improvements over the Birkigt's Hispano-Suiza.

Recall that with Birkigt's *Hisso* design, waste heat from the combustion process had to traverse a steel liner plus a wall of aluminum before reaching the cooling water. Not unnaturally, this became known as "dry sleeve" construction. Kirkham's approach, however, directly exposed most of the steel sleeve to the cooling water and thus the "wet-sleeve" concept was born. He accomplished this by shrink fitting the closed-end steel sleeves into an aluminum cylinder head. The primary aluminum casting providing the outer wall and the steel sleeve the inner wall of the cooling passages. A packing ring completed the water passage seal at the lower end of each cylinder sleeve. Kirkham's innovation was a masterful piece of design engineering, and one that would be widely imitated in the future.

Several Curtiss water-cooled engines materialized during and after World War I, two of which

This close-up photograph depicts the Curtiss R3C-3 engine installation. In a departure from most Curtiss racers, this aircraft was adapted to a Packard Model 2A-1500 water-cooled engine. What power output this particular racing engine achieved is not precisely known. Various models of the 2A-1500 produced between 760 and 880 horsepower. Note the metalwork covering the left engine bank and the three exhaust port fairings. John Garrett collection

Wright and Packard dropped out of the large liquid-cooled engine market for more than one reason. Curtiss dominated the military market when it won Army contracts for its D-12 engine and the later Conqueror engine. One reason was that Curtiss typically built lighter weight engines, as this chart illustrates. The pounds of engine weight per horsepower generated for the various Wright and Packard engines showed identical linear trend lines. Both were substantially higher than Curtiss products.

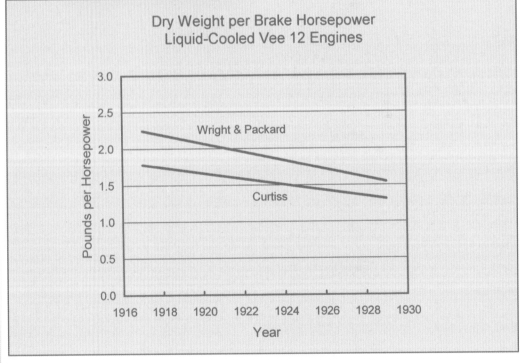

The Curtiss R-6 was designed and built in 1922 for the Pulitzer Race. Using a wooden A-frame and chain hoist, Curtiss workers wedge a Curtiss D-12 into one of two airframes. Russell Maughan and the R-6 won the 1922 Pulitzer at over 200 miles per hour. The D-12 provided Maughan with at least 375 horsepower. John Garrett collection

CIVILIAN D-12 RACING APPLICATIONS

The Curtiss D-12 was used to great advantage by Steve Wittman during the 1930s. Wittman began his racing career in 1926. He designed and built his first pure racing airplane in 1931, appropriately named *Chief Oshkosh* after the Wisconsin city where he lived and worked. The *Chief* was variously powered by (in chronological order) a 90-horsepower Cirrus; a 115-horsepower Cirrus Hermes; and a Menasco C4S Pirate normally rated at 150 horsepower, although with racing upgrades it could develop 220–230 horsepower.[9]

Wittman's next racing design venture was begun in 1934, this time with Curtiss' splendid D-12 liquid-cooled engine. This effort resulted in the *Bonzo* (named for a cartoon character), a typically compact utilitarian design in the best Wittman tradition. The heritage of this particular D-12 is nebulous. It was, according to author Hugo Byttebier, a second-hand engine "purchased from an aircraft engine dealer in the East . . . without logbook or previous history."[10] Wittman carefully rebuilt his newly acquired D-12 and proceeded to convert the cooling medium from water to ethylene glycol.

The conversion project was no mean task though potentially rewarding. Ethylene glycol (sold commercially under the trade name "Prestone") offered a much higher sea level boiling point, 387 degrees Fahrenheit versus 212 degrees Fahrenheit for water, allowing engine operation at higher coolant temperatures.[11] Army Air Corps work at Wright Field during the late 1920s and early 1930s established a maximum coolant temperature of 300 degrees Fahrenheit for ethylene glycol.[12] Engine coolant temperature using water was typically restricted to 160 to 180 degrees Fahrenheit, resulting in a 120-degree operating advantage with ethylene glycol. Wittman ran his coolant temperature as high as 325 degrees making the differential even greater at 145 degrees Fahrenheit.[13] The result was a reduction in radiator size because the glycol coolant at that temperature had a greater heat capacity.

In its original 1934 configuration, Wittman placed a blunt-faced rectangular radiator in front of the engine with the propeller shaft extending through a cutout in the core. Although a larger radiator would have been needed had water been used in

were prominent. Perhaps the best-known model was the D-12 series with ratings from 435 to 552 horsepower. This engine enjoyed fairly wide use in Army pursuits including the elegant Curtiss P-6 series (see Table 8-2). Navy air service applications were essentially nonexistent; their preference for air-cooled engines prevailed throughout the 1930s and World War II.

CURTISS RACING ENGINES

Curtiss racing engine laurels reached a pinnacle in the early and middle 1920s and for a while, the D-12 engine was king of the pylons. When coupled with sleek Curtiss biplane racers the combination was unbeatable. These machines captured the Pulitzer three years running, beginning in 1921. Curtiss racers fitted with floats were equally successful in the 1923 and 1925 international Schneider races. The 1924 Schneider race was canceled when

David Rittenhouse's R2C-2 was the only racer able to run the course. In an ultimate show of sportsmanship, the Americans declined to accept the trophy because of a lack of competition. Ironically, the Schneider Trophy would have been retired to the United States in 1925 because Jimmy Doolittle once again swept to victory flying the R3C-2 that year. Unlike previous D-12-powered Curtiss racers, Doolittle's airplane was equipped with a Curtiss V-1400 engine developing well over 600 horsepower. Table 8-3 identifies Curtiss racers and engines of this era.

Nothing could match the speed of the Curtiss racers during this period, and several closed-course speed records were established in the process. Beyond the middle of the decade, however, the government lost interest in air racing and the Schneider Trophy was eventually retired in 1931 by the British and their magnificent Supermarine racers.

place of ethylene glycol, the entire installation was still not particularly clean from an aerodynamic perspective. A year later this high drag installation had been partially remedied. A smaller radiator was partly enclosed in a smooth shroud which was then faired into the engine cowl. Cooling proved inadequate, however, as Wittman experienced engine heating problems in the 1935 Thompson race. He nonetheless finished second at a respectable 218.94 miles per hour.

Whether or not Wittman overcame heating problems of the previous year will never be known. On his way to Los Angeles for the 1936 National Air Races, the engine backfired on the runway at the Cheyenne, Wyoming airport. A small fuel leak caught fire and *Bonzo* was badly damaged before the fire was extinguished.

A 1937 facelift resulted in an entirely different look for the nose of the racer. The radiator was now completely shrouded. Cooling air passed through a large port in the propeller spinner and then through the radiator core. Heated air leaving the radiator flowed out of the engine cowling through a series of louvers. A ducted radiator fan was used to distribute incoming air across the radiator face. No apparent cooling system alterations were made for 1938. Wittman placed third in the Thompson that year with 259.2 miles per hour, though coolant leaks handicapped his racing efforts. He did no better the following year, coming in fifth at 241.36 miles per

Great Britain won the 1931 Schneider Trophy Race with a combination of brute horsepower and a very clean Supermarine S6.B airframe designed by Reginald J. Mitchell. This photograph shows the Rolls-Royce "R" racing engine being fitted to one of the S6.B airframes at the Supermarine factory. This engine/airframe combination was potent. After winning the Schneider, the airplane was used to set a world speed record of 407 miles per hour. It was the first time the 400-mile per hour barrier had been exceeded. John Garrett collection

The gigantic Fiat AS.6 consisted of two AS.5 engines joined end to end. Designed by Tranquillo Zerbi, the AS.6 had 24 cylinders and reportedly developed 3,100 horsepower at 3,200 rpm. These were prodigious numbers in 1933–1934. The AS.6 was installed in the Macchi-Castoldi MC.72; it set a world speed record of 440.681 miles per hour in 1934.

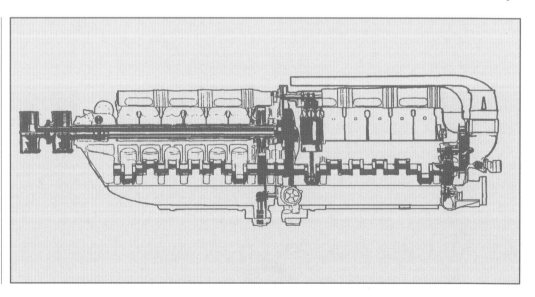

The extremely long slender fuselage of this Macchi-Castoldi M.C.72 seaplane racer housed two Fiat A.S.6 engines coupled in tandem. The two engines drove counterrotating propellers, a unique innovation a the time. Unfortunately for the Italians, the racer was not ready in time for the 1931 Schneider Race. Had it been able to race, the Supermarine S6.B would have had some stiff competition. John Garrett collection

hour. Nonuniform cooling resulted in burned valves in the front cylinders; however, this was attributed to mixture ratio distribution problems.

Bonzo never reached its potential high speed of well over 300 miles per hour. Many of the problems were associated with engine cooling, a perennial malady that still plagues racing aircraft. Wittman's efforts were innovative and commendable. He was, however, working with an engine never designed for high temperature cooling. When the D-12 (and Conqueror) used water cooling with a maximum liquid operating temperature

of 160 to 180 degrees, reliable performance was achieved. Three hundred-degree coolant temperatures produced differential thermal expansion between the cast aluminum banks and steel cylinder sleeves that could create a coolant leakage path. Ethylene glycol systems were also prone to leak, in part because its viscosity diminished rapidly at elevated temperatures; in contrast, water viscosity changes slowly with increasing temperature.

The capability of higher coolant temperature operation meant that a smaller radiator (heat exchanger) could be used, yielding a corresponding

decrease in aerodynamic drag and airframe weight. Radiator (oil and coolant) drag considerations were nontrivial, as illustrated by NACA testing at the request of the Army Air Corps. The test vehicle was a Conqueror-powered Curtiss YO-31A installed in the Langley full-scale wind tunnel. Test results revealed that oil and coolant radiators comprised 11.8 percent of total airplane drag at 120 miles per hour. Of this total amount, 8.3 percent was represented by the coolant radiator, the remainder attributable to the oil cooler.[14]

CONQUEROR RACING APPLICATIONS

The next significant water-cooled engine produced by Curtiss was the V-1570 Conqueror. With 37 percent more swept volume than the D-12, the Conqueror began life with a rating of 600 horsepower. Within five years, the basic design was producing as much as 750 horsepower (see Appendix D). It was produced in direct drive version; with propeller reduction gearing; with and without supercharging; and in upright and inverted versions. The Conqueror was used primarily in Curtiss pursuit aircraft, most notably the P-6 series, as well as a number of experimental and limited-production machines. Curtiss installed this engine in a variety of attack and observation planes as well.

Unlike the Curtiss D-12, racing applications of the Conqueror engine were very limited and singularly unsuccessful. The first use of a Conqueror for racing was by the well-known woman pilot, Jacqueline Cochran. When the 1934 London-to-Melbourne MacRobertson Race was announced, Jackie ordered a Northrop Gamma with a late model 705-horsepower Curtiss SVG-1570F-4 Conqueror. The "SVG" prefix identified the engine as supercharged (an experimental General Electric device), a vee-shaped cylinder arrangement, and propeller reduction gearing.

Normally powered by air-cooled radials, the water-cooled engine markedly changed the appearance of the Gamma. This was in part due to a need to transition from a round fuselage cross-section to the oval shape of the Conqueror engine cowling, coupled with a chin radiator beneath the cowling. With the water-cooled engine installation, the Gamma overall length was slightly greater from tail cone to propeller spinner than its radial engine-powered counterpart.

The supercharger in Jackie's airplane proved troublesome. A planned tune-up flight in the 1934 Bendix Race had to be abandoned.[15] There was no hope of using it in the MacRobertson. The airplane was subsequently reequipped with a Pratt & Whitney Twin Wasp Jr. for the 1935 Bendix. Unfortunately, Jackie was unable to finish this race due to weather. Shortly afterward, she leased the Gamma to Howard Hughes, who ultimately established a transcontinental speed record with the airplane.

Curtiss Racing Engines

Aircraft	Engine	Hp	Rpm
CR-1	Curtiss D-12, Hi CR	460	2,300
CR-2	Curtiss D-12	410	2,250
CR-3	Curtiss D-12 Hi CR	460	2,300
R2C-1	Curtiss D-12A, Hi CR	500	2,300
R2C-2	Curtiss D-12A	502	2,300
R3C-1	Curtiss V-1400	600	2,350
R3C-2	Curtiss V-1400	600	2,350
R3C-4	Curtiss V-1550	705	2,600
XP-6	Curtiss V-1550, Hi CR	730	2,600
XO-13	Curtiss V-1550, Hi CR	730	2,600
XO-13A	Curtiss V-1550, Hi CR	720	2,560
XP-6A	Curtiss V-1550, Hi CR	730	2,600
Wittman Bonzo	Curtiss D-12, Hi CR	485-500*	2,550–2,600

*Estimated. See Hugo T. Byttebier, *The Curtiss D-12 Aero Engine*, Smithsonian Institution Press, 1972, p. 83.
Source: Curtiss Aeroplane & Motor Co., Aircraft Characteristics Sheets

Table 8-3

The Delgado Trade School of New Orleans entered into some interesting student projects students during the 1930s. Two of these activities consisted of designing and constructing race planes for the prewar National Air Races. The smaller of their two racers was the Delgado *Flash*, powered by a four-cylinder 125-horsepower Menasco C-4 engine. The second and larger racer was the Delgado *Maid*. In 1935 the *Maid* flew with a Curtiss D-12 at Cleveland. It never did compete in a race. Engine cooling problems and excessive heat entering the cockpit from the engine compartment made flying untenable for pilot Clarence McArthur, and the *Maid* was ignominiously trucked back to New Orleans.

A decision was made to replace the D-12 with the more powerful Curtiss Conqueror (reportedly capable of about 700 horsepower). As with the previous engine installation, cooling continued to be a problem, although McArthur pronounced the airplane ready for the 1936 races. A last-minute change in pilots before departing for Cleveland resulted in the untimely demise of the Delgado *Maid*. Art Davis, who had never flown the airplane, stepped into the cockpit for what would prove to be his first and last flight in the racer. His takeoff was satisfactory, after which he made a high-speed run over the airport. Smoke began pouring from the engine cowling during the high-speed pass. Apparently believing the airplane was on fire, Davis took to his parachute and the *Maid* plummeted to earth.

Like the Delgado *Maid*, the third Conqueror-powered racer would never compete in any event. This was the 1938 Pearson-Williams PW-1 *Mr. Smoothie*, designed around the big Curtiss engine by Rodney Nimmo, and built by Bud Pearson and Lee Williams.[16] Both Pearson and Williams harbored dreams of using one of the new Allison V-1710 engines for their racer, "but because of military secrecy and red tape, it was impossible to secure one."[17] This is partly true. The Allison was a classified Army program. Equally important, however, was the fact that the engine really was not in production. Only seven V-1710 Allison engines were delivered in 1937. Just 12 more were shipped during the entire year of 1938. All were desperately needed by the Army Air Corps for aircraft development programs. Mass production was still a year or two away.

The Pearson-Williams racer was a well-streamlined aircraft featuring retractable landing gear, a tightly cowled engine and radiator installation. The latter was patterned after Steve Wittman's D-12-powered racer, *Bonzo*. Cooling air entered through a truncated conical propeller spinner, swirled (for good distribution) using propeller-rotated fan blades, passed through the radiator, and then exhausted via

Table 8-4

WRIGHT & PACKARD WATER-COOLED V-12 ENGINES*

MODEL	YEAR	DISP IN3	RATED HP	RPM	WEIGHT LB	LB/ HP	REMARKS
Wright-Hispano E	1916	718	180				V-8
Wright E-2 Tempest	1921	718	220	2,000	485	2.20	
Wright E-3 Tempest		718	200	1,800	476	2.38	
Wright E-4 Tempest		718	200	1,800	480	2.40	
Wright E-4A Tempest		718	240	2,100	480	2.00	
Wright-Martin H		1,127	325	1,800	632	1.94	
Wright H-2	1921	1,127	358	2,000	620	1.73	
Wright H-3	1921	1,127	340	1,800	610	1.79	
Wright T-2 Tornado		1,947	600	1,900	1,110	1.85	
Wright T-3 Tornado		1,947	800	2,000	1,166	1.46	
Packard 1A-1116	1919	1,116	353				Direct Drive
Packard 1A-1237	1920	1,237	398				Direct Drive
Packard 2A-1500		1,498	600	2,500	760	1.27	Direct Drive
Packard 2A-1500		1,498	600	2,500	880	1.47	Geared
Packard 2A-1500		1,498	600	2,500	780	1.30	Inverted
Packard 2A-1500	1928	1,498	600	2,500	915	1.53	Geared
Packard 3A-1500	1928	1,498	600	2,500	800	1.33	Direct, Inverted
Packard 2A-2500		2,490	800	2,000	1,150	1.44	Direct Drive
Packard 2A-2500		2,490	800	2,000	1,370	1.71	Geared
Packard 3A-2500	1928	2,490	800	2,000	1,220	1.53	Direct Drive
Packard 3A-2500	1928	2,490	800	2,000	1,435	1.79	Geared

* Unless otherwise noted.

ports on the side of the engine cowling. As with so many race plane projects, time ran out before the inevitable problems could be resolved. The racer did not qualify for the 1938 races and was subsequently returned to California, never to compete again.

OTHER WATER-COOLED ENGINES

Long before Wright Aeronautical developed its benchmark J-5 air-cooled radial engine, used by Charles Lindbergh for his famous solo flight across the Atlantic, the company (first as Wright-Martin) was engaged in developing large water-cooled engines. The basic technology was derived from the Hispano-Suiza built under license. Wright soon incorporated its own embellishments and the Wright Model E Tempest series began, the most powerful of which was the E-4A at 240 horsepower. All of the E series engines were V-8 in configuration. A larger engine (1,127-cubic-inch displacement) known as the Model H series, also

a V-8, followed the 718-cubic-inch Tempest design (see Table 8-4). The Model H developed 340 horsepower in its final (H-3) configuration, 42 percent more than the highest rated Tempest. Following the formation of Wright Aeronautical, the company designed yet another and still larger V-12 engine called the Tornado. Production versions of this engine, the Model T-2 and T-3, produced 600 and 800 horsepower, respectively. The T-3 was basically the end of the Wright water-cooled line, however. Curtiss engines had been selected by the Army Air Service and the market was insufficient to support three companies (the third being Packard) producing water-cooled engines.

The Packard Motor Car Company first engaged in aviation manufacturing activities during World War I. Its first production aircraft engine was the famous 225-horsepower Liberty V-12. Two 60-degree V-8 engines of modest power followed. Packard quickly standardized on the V-12 arrangement when

it introduced the Model 1A-1116 in 1919 (Table 8-3). With a bore of 4.750 inches and stroke of 5.250 inches (giving a 1,116.4-cubic-inch displacement), the direct drive 1A-1116 delivered from 313 to 350 horsepower over the course of development. Subsequent 1A-1237 and 2A-1237 models stretched the 1A-1116 bore of 4.750 to 5.000 inches, but avoided boosting crankshaft revolutions above 1,800 rpm. Horsepower was limited to only 300.

Various versions of the next engine series developed between 500 and 600 horsepower. These were identified as the 1A-1500, 2A-1500 and 3A-1500 models. The engine displacement, as the model numbers imply, was just under 1,500 cubic inches (1,497.6, to be exact). A boost in displacement was achieved by increasing both the engine bore and stroke, 5.375 inches and 5.500 inches, respectively. The 1500 series design was augmented by the 2500 model variants. Once again, Packard increased both engine bore and stroke. With a 6.375 inch bore and 6.500 inch stroke, displacement grew to 2,489.7 cubic inches. The big Packard 2500 series engines were capable of 800 horsepower at 2,200 rpm. Like the Wright and Curtiss liquid-cooled engines, Packards were available in both direct drive or with propeller reduction gearing. Some experimental work was devoted in 1927–1928 to supercharging (Model 4A-2500), resulting in a power output of 950 horsepower.

The final liquid-cooled engine built by Packard was the 1927 Model 1A-2775. This was essentially a marriage of two 1A-1500 engines (same bore and stroke) using a common crankshaft, and arranged into an "X" configuration. Two development engines were built, one being equipped with a supercharger. Packard rated this 2,722.9-cubic-inch monster at 2,750 horsepower. Built for the Navy, one was installed in the Kirkham-Williams floatplane entered in the 1927 Schneider Trophy Race. Development problems with the aircraft

Table 8-5

Race Aircraft Powered by Packard & Wright Liquid-Cooled Engines

Year	Event	Aircraft	Engine	Remarks
1920	Pulitzer	Loening M-81-S	Wright-Martin H	Forced out, coolant leak
1920	Pulitzer	Thomas Morse MB-3	Wright Hispano H-2	2nd place
1920	Pulitzer	Vought V.E.7	Wright E-3	5th place
1920	Pulitzer	Verville-Packard VCP-R	Packard 1A-2025	1st place
1921	Pulitzer	Thomas Morse R-5	Packard 1A-2025	11th place
1922	Pulitzer	Bee Line BR-2	Wright H-3	Did not start
1922	Pulitzer	Bee Line BR-1	Wright H-3	Forced out, oil leak
1922	Pulitzer	Loening R-4	Packard 1A-2025	8th place
1922	Pulitzer	Loening R-4	Packard 1A-2025	9th place
1922	Pulitzer	Thomas Morse R-5	Packard 1A-2025	10th place
1922	Pulitzer	Verville Sperry R-3	Wright Hispano H-3	5th place
1922	Pulitzer	Verville Sperry R-3	Wright Hispano H-3	Forced out, mechanical problem
1922	Pulitzer	Verville Sperry R-3	Wright Hispano H-3	7th place
1922	Pulitzer	Verville-Packard R-1	Packard 1A-2025	6th place
1922	Pulitzer	Wright NW-1	Wright T-2	Forced out, oil leak
1923	Pulitzer	Wright F2W-1	Wright T-3	4th place
1923	Pulitzer	Wright F2W-1	Wright T-3	3rd place
1923	Schneider	Naval Aircraft Factory TR-3A	Wright E-4	Did not start
1923	Schneider	Wright NW-2	Wright T-2	Crashed before race
1926	Schneider	Curtiss R3C-3	Packard 2A-1500	Crashed before race
1927	Schneider	Kirkham-Williams	Packard X-2775	Withdrawn before race
1929	Schneider	Williams-Mercury	Packard X-2775	Withdrawn before race

eventually forced Charles Kirkham and Al Williams to withdraw from the event.

PACKARD & WRIGHT RACING ENGINES

The Pulitzer and Schneider races of the early 1920s were for the most part dominated by aircraft powered by Curtiss engines. In addition to the ill-fated Kirkham-Williams racer mentioned above, there were a number of racers equipped with Wright and Packard engines. Grover Loening designed his Loening M-81-S racer around a Wright-Martin H engine, for instance. A coolant line broke during the 1920 Pulitzer Racer, causing the engine to seize. Nineteen twenty-two saw the Booth Bee Line (BR-1 and BR-2) racers compete in the Pulitzer using a 325-horsepower Wright H-3 engines. The BR-1 was forced out of the race due to mechanical problems while the BR-2 was withdrawn. Quite a few other racer powered by Wright engines competed during these early years, with results ranging from mediocre to dismal (see Table 8-5).

With one exception, Packard enjoyed no more success in air racing than the Wright company. Race pilot Corley Moseley flew a Packard-powered biplane racer designed by Alfred Verville and built by the Army Engineering Division to first place during the 1920 Pulitzer. Another Verville-designed machine placed 6th in the 1922 Pulitzer. In reality, only a handful of racers ever used Packard engines. One of them was a Curtiss R3C3-3 racer, which received a Packard 2A-1500 engine for the 1926 Schneider. Unfortunately, it was destroyed in an accident on November 12, 1926.

Both Packard and Wright drifted out of the liquid-cooled engine business. Packard departed in 1928 after a squabble with the Army over design and manufacturing policies.[18] The Army withdrew all development support from the company and Packard saw little or no profitability in continuing. Wright merged with Curtiss in 1929. Emphasis soon turned to air-cooled engines, although Curtiss continued work on the Conqueror engine line for a few years.

The Packard and Wright liquid-cooled product lines were essentially not competitive with that of Curtiss. Although there may be some question of engine reliability with respect to Packard and Wright, they both suffered a quantifiable disadvantage. Their engines were on average quite a bit heavier than the Curtiss line. An examination of 21 Curtiss engine variants as well as 19 each for Wright and Packard between the years of 1917 and 1927 revealed the following. Curtiss engines averaged 1.53 pounds per horsepower while Wright and Packard averaged 1.87 and 1.77 pounds per horsepower, respectively.

Power output for various models were generally comparable between the three companies at any given time. However, Curtiss led the way in producing lightweight engines, and this may have been one strong reason it essentially cornered the liquid-cooled engine business with the military. A comparison of engine weight per horsepower trends over time for all three companies is shown in Figure 8-1. Trend lines for both Wright and Packard were virtually identical. Curtiss clearly had

the advantage. The fact that Curtiss engines were quite successful in competition undoubtedly added to their luster, especially in the eyes of the Army.

Whatever luster existed toward the end of the 1920s was soon dulled as the market for this type of engine declined. The Navy made a conscientious decision about this time to use only air-cooled engines in future aircraft. Commercial aircraft designs had also swung heavily to air-cooled engines. The only remaining market was the Army and even this customer had limited resources once the Depression took hold at the dawn of the next decade.

The situation was different in Europe. Government sponsorship during the 1930s allowed companies like Rolls-Royce, Hispano Suiza, Fiat and Daimler-Benz to develop liquid-cooled engines to a high state. Even though Army Air Corps budgets were inadequate to promote development of the type through the manufacturers, it did exhibited interest in and devote funds toward internal studies of such things as cylinder design and glycol cooling.

It was then believed (circa 1930) that air-cooled engines were for all practical purposes limited to something like 600 horsepower. Higher output would simply result in larger diameter engines, making them impractical for pursuit aircraft. This perception was mistaken, of course, for it failed to foresee the practicality of multiple-row radial engines, the evolution of supercharging, great improvements in fuel quality, and dependable propeller reduction gearing. In that context the liquid-cooled engine was still looked upon favorably. It was considered the only route to achieving 1,000 horsepower or more, while at the same time keeping frontal area within reasonable limits. It was in this environment and time frame that the Allison V-1710 was born, an engine that would become a mainstay in the war to come.

This unusual overhead view of the two Fiat A.S.6 engines in the M.C.72 explains the extra long airframe needed for this racer. The engine combination reportedly delivered a massive 2,800 brake horsepower to the propellers. In 1934, Francesco Agello, in the M.C.72, raised the world speed record to over 440 miles per hour, a piston engine seaplane record that remains unbroken to this day.
John Garrett collection

chapter 9

128

Piston Power: Air-cooled Engines

There is no country in the world where machinery is as lovely as in America. I always wished to believe that the line of strength and the line of beauty are one.

Oscar Wilde (1854–1900) • *Irish poet, novelist, critic*

Well-functioning machines more often than not exhibit an aesthetically pleasing form. Had Irish poet and novelist Oscar Wilde lived to see the great air-cooled engines of Pratt & Whitney and Wright Aeronautical, it surely would have reconfirmed his impression "that the line of strength and the line of beauty are one." For the mighty radial engines from these two manufacturers were at once strong and functionally elegant. They were produced by the tens of thousands during World War II and represented the truest form of American precision mass production. This was not always the case, however. Liquid-cooled powerplants dominated the large aircraft engine scene for a long time during the early years; persistent cooling limitations and large frontal areas arrested air-cooled engine applications, particularly for very high-speed aircraft.

ROTARY ENGINES

Air cooling engine cylinders proved a difficult challenge for designers as horsepower requirements increased. The first practical solution was the rotary engine, wherein cylinders, crankcase, and propeller rotated about a stationary crankshaft. The approach was conceived in 1907 by Laurent Seguin of France; the first working five-cylinder, 34-horsepower model took form the next year.[1,2] Its first usage was for auto racing. It was not long before this unique engine design was used to power flying machines. By virtue of the fact that the engine rotated as it ran, there was always a strong flow of cooling air passing through the cylinder fins.

Other rotary engines appeared during this period, but the acclaimed French Gnôme engine was certainly one of the most popular. These engines were manufactured by the Société des Moteurs Gnôme run by the Seguin family, and went rapidly into quantity production (see Table 9-1). Over 3,600 of the type were produced in a six-year run leading up to World War I. Various configurations were built having from 5 to 14 cylinders in single and two-row arrangements.

In an attempt to derive more power from a radial engine, yet minimize frontal area, Pratt & Whitney built the Twin Wasp Jr. engine. This two-row radial developed up to 750 horsepower from 1,530 cubic inches. It was used in several Navy aircraft. Pictured here is a Great Lakes BG-1 R-1535-82 installation. Earl Ortman used a special R-1535 in his Marcoux-Bromberg with some success. Birch Matthews collection

Table 9-1

Gnôme Rotary Engine Production

Year	Quantity
1908	3
1909	35
1910	400
1911	800
1912	1,000
1913	1,400

Source: Gunston, *The Development of Piston Aero Engines*, p. 111.

French pilot Jules Vèdrines came into racing prominence in 1912. In January of that year, Vèdrines commenced what would become a frenetic assault on the world speed record. By September he had broken it no less than seven times. His aircraft was a beautifully streamlined Deperdussin powered by a Gnôme rotary engine. With this combination he steadily advanced the record from 90.199 miles per hour to over 108 miles per hour by September. In so doing, he became the first man to fly at a speed in excess of 100 miles per hour. To add to his laurels, Vedrines also won the 1912 Gordon Bennett Trophy competition. Rotary engines of several manufacturers in Great Britain, France and Germany would go on to play a major role in World War I.

As popular as rotary engines were for several years, there were detractions and limitations with the type. For one thing, the amount of mass rotating about the crankshaft was considerable, thus limiting engine speeds to something like 1,300 to 1,400 rpm.[3] This placed a decided limit on the amount of horsepower that could ever be generated by this type of engine. Designers partially circumvented this limitation by increasing the number of cylinders from five to seven and then adding a second row of cylinders, increasing the rotating mass even more, however.

Rotary engines were not particularly fuel efficient either. A rich fuel mixture was introduced into the crankcase to minimize the possibility of unwanted combustion or explosion (a decidedly unhealthy risk), before the mixture was introduced to the combustion chamber through a poppet valve in the piston dome. The rotary also consumed lubricat-

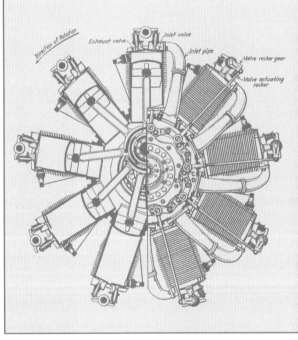

Liquid-cooled engines dominated the aviation scene for several years, until the advent of the rotary engine concept. One of the first truly successful air-cooled engines was the Wright Aeronautical Model J-5 shown here. It featured sodium-cooled exhaust valves, a technology breakthrough in valve cooling. An improved J-6 model set the standard in air-cooled engines for several years. John Garrett collection

ing oil in large quantities. Because the lubricant had to be miscible with gasoline, castor oil was employed, much of which exited through the single exhaust valve in each cylinder. The result was a swirling laxative mist enveloping everything and everyone in its wake. One way to protect the pilot from this unwanted medicinal ingestion was to place the engine in back of the cockpit in a pusher configuration. For tractor engine arrangements, cowls were quickly added to trap the castor oil and let gravity remove it through an opening in the bottom of the cowl. So while the rotary was an acceptable interim solution to cooling radial engines, its inherent limitations induced continued development.

WRIGHT AERONAUTICAL ENGINES

The Wright name and Wright engines date, of course, to the first successful powered flight in 1903.

In 1909 the brothers incorporated their Dayton, Ohio, operations and continued building "aeroplanes" and "motors." Wilbur Wright died of typhoid fever in 1912 and within two years, Orville was entertaining overtures to sell the company. Finally in September 1915, he accepted an offer for the patents and the business. It was sold to a group of prominent eastern investors. Orville was tired of being a businessman:

"I sold in order to devote my time to research work. The cares of modern business little encourage the tastes of one who feels that his work is not done. I have wanted to study, to think, to take up the work again in that little shop and study over on West Third Street. The world wouldn't let me."[4]

The financial syndicate now running the Wright Company also acquired Glenn L. Martin's

Rotary engines were an attempt to gain more uniform cylinder head cooling during the early years of aviation. Shown here is the Le Rhone 110 engine. The crankshaft was stationary and affixed to the airframe, while the cylinders rotated about the shaft. The mass of this much-rotating machinery restricted rpm to about 2,000, thereby placing an upper practical limit on the amount of horsepower that could be developed. Dan Whitney collection

Wright Aeronautical dominated the large air-cooled engine field until the formation of Pratt & Whitney in July 1925. With a core of key people from Wright, the new company designed and built the 1,344-cubic-inch displacement Wasp engine. It was a winner from the start and became the powerplant of choice for the Navy and many commercial applications. Production continued on various models through World War II. Birch Matthews collection

California enterprise during 1916. The Wright-Martin Corporation was thus born, though is was destined for a relatively short life. It was, however, the genesis of a product line of aircraft engines that would eventually make the successor company, Wright Aeronautical Corporation, both profitable and famous. Wright-Martin chief engineer Henry Crane started the ball rolling when he successfully negotiated a license to build the water-cooled Hispano-Suiza during a 1915 European trip. This proved to be an entre into the large engine field that heretofore did not exist for the company.

Following World War I, the Wright-Martin Corporation was dissolved. The surviving organization was renamed Wright Aeronautical in 1919, with operations concentrated on the East Coast. The new company retained the manufacturing rights to the Hispano-Suiza, but soon veered (some might say backed) into the air-cooled engine marketplace through acquisition of the Lawrance Aero-Engine Company. It was almost a shotgun marriage for Wright, happily engaged in growing its liquid-cooled engine line with little thought of building air-cooled models.

Charles L. Lawrance was admired as an "engine man." His background was in the design of automobile engines and racing engines for race cars. Lawrance turned his talents to designing and developing aircraft engines during World War I. His first successful design was a modest two-cylinder air-cooled engine of 28 horsepower, designated the Model A. This was followed by the 40-horsepower Model N, which subsequently evolved into a three-cylinder radial motor (Model L) for the Navy producing 65 horsepower. Duly impressed, the Navy asked Lawrance for an even larger engine, this time with nine radial air-cooled cylinders and capable of 150 horsepower. This became the Model R-1; only four were ever built, and these exclusively for development purposes. What followed,

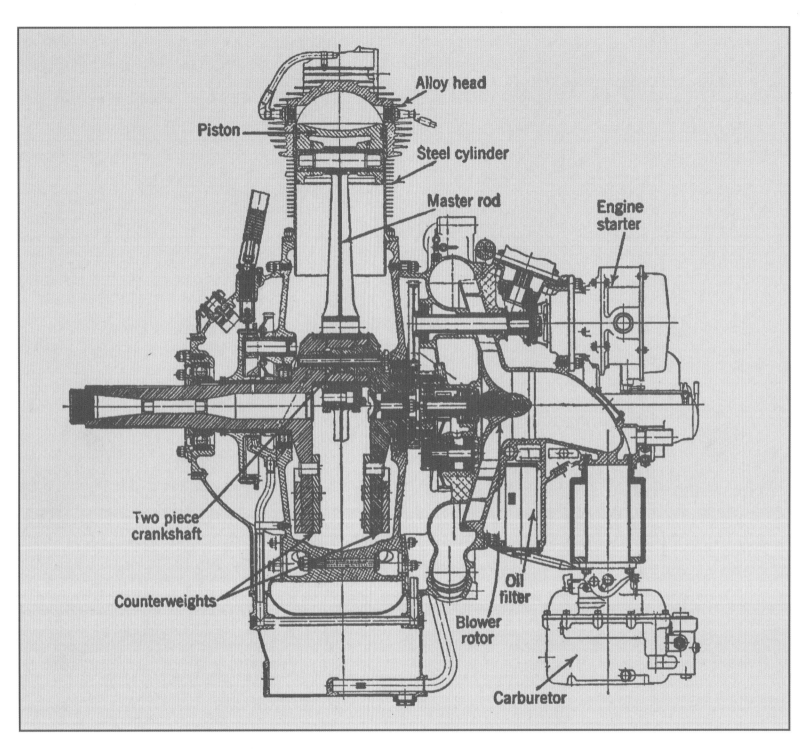

Piston

Alloy head

Steel cylinder

Master rod

Engine starter

Two piece crankshaft

Counterweights

Oil filter

Blower rotor

Carburetor

The first engine built by Pratt & Whitney was the Wasp, a progenitor of a long line of famous piston engines. The original Wasp developed 400 horsepower from 1,344 cubic inches of displacement. With improved fuels and metallurgy, succeeding Wasp models reached an output of 600 horsepower. These engines are still in use today and may be seen in the T-6/SNJ race class at the Reno Air Races every year. Dan Whitney collection

Table 9-2

Model	Year	Hp	Cu In	Remarks
R-1	1920	350	1,454	Designed for U.S. Army
R-2	1923		1,454	Improved air-cooled cylinder design
J-1		200	787	Designed by Charles Lawrance
J-2		250	787	Only 2 built
J-3			787	Structurally strengthened version of J-2
J-4		215	787	Improved cylinder tie-down, engine named Whirlwind
J-4B			787	Improved fuel economy
J-5			787	Redesigned cylinders, sodium-cooled valves
J-6		300	787	Increased cylinder bore

Early Wright Air-Cooled Engines

however, was Lawrance's Model J-1 engine, progenitor of what would become the Wright Aeronautical J-5 engine, a benchmark in aircraft engine design.

The J-1 was designed to produce 200 horsepower at 2,000 revolutions. Failing its first 50-hour endurance test, the new engine finally passed this requirement in January 1922. The Navy looked forward to its first really powerful air-cooled engine. What Lawrance Aero-Engines lacked, though, was adequate financial and manufacturing resources to produce the engine in quantity while at the same time improving its reliability and developing it further. A merger was needed to accomplish this objective, and the Navy finally convinced Wright Aeronautical to buy Lawrance's small company in the spring of 1923. As reluctant as Wright was at first, it ultimately proved to be a happy and profitable union.

Wright air-cooled radial engines were infrequently used in air racing during the 1930s. The company demonstrated scant interest in promoting its engines through the sport, relying instead upon more conventional means such as advertising in trade and popular aviation magazines. As a consequence, not many race planes of the 1930s era flew a Wright decal on their engine cowls. Closed-course pylon racing witnessed a few entries with Wright engines, however. Doug Davis was the most successful contestant using a Wright radial engine. He won the 1929 National Air Race's "Free-for-all Speed Contest," Event No. 26. His splendid racer, the Travel Air Model R *Mystery Ship*, was powered by a Wright J6-9 Whirlwind. A handful of other racers were powered by Whirlwinds, but none again reached the winner's circle in the prestigious Thompson Trophy Race. Indeed, after the 1931 Thompson, only one Wright engine powered a racer in this event. Lee Miles ran the 1935 Thompson pylons in a lumbering Seversky SEV-3 amphibian, completing the 15 laps with an average speed of just under 194 miles per hour. A Wright R-1820 provided the power for Miles' ersatz racer.

PRATT & WHITNEY ENGINES

The genesis of Pratt & Whitney Aircraft began when Wright Aeronautical president Frederick Brant Rentschler resigned from the corporation, effective September 1, 1924. He had become increasingly at odds with Wright Board Chairman Richard F. Hoyt on matters of policy.

"There had been several matters of dispute, but the essential one was the bland indifference Rentschler felt that the board [of directors] held for any true appreciation of the highly technical engineering problems that formed the basis of an aircraft engineering company. None of the directors owned any substantial personal stock interest in the company, and none of them appeared to understand Rentschler's philosophy that to reach, hold and surpass the field, money had to be plowed back into experimental and development engineering."[5]

The investment bankers who made up the Wright board of directors were much more concerned with maximizing shareholder return. This attitude persisted even after Wright Aeronautical became the Curtiss-Wright Corporation. (Wright merged with Curtiss Airplane and Motor Company on August 9, 1929.) Once management had a successful product line, it tended to undernourish future design and development activities. Once the dominant airframe and engine manufacturer in the country, Curtiss-Wright eventually drifted out of the aviation business and into relative obscurity during the mid-1960s.[6]

Within months of leaving Wright, the 37-year old Rentschler was actively seeking financial backing and facilities to launch a new aircraft engine company. His efforts were rewarded when an old family friend, James K. Cullen, president of Niles-Bement-Pond Company, agreed to help Rentschler's startup effort. Fortuitously, Cullen also knew of unused plant capacity in one of the Niles-Bement-Pond subsidiaries, the semiautonomous Pratt & Whitney Company, manufacturers of machine tools. Armed with finances, plant and a new air-cooled radial engine design laid down while Rentschler was putting the deal together, Pratt & Whitney Aircraft Company was incorporated on July 23, 1925.

Key officials in the new company all came from Wright Aeronautical. Rentschler became president.

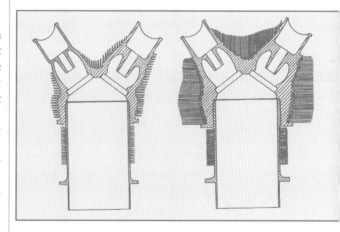

Obtaining more power from radial air-cooled engines was in part a matter of removing additional waste heat from the cylinder walls. Improved fabrication techniques resulted in a significant increase in fin surface area. More surface area exposed to the slipstream aided heat removal. This is shown in the cylinder sketches of this figure. On the left is an old-style cylinder, while on the right is the improved cylinder, with vastly increased fin area.

One key to successfully cooling radial engine cylinders was the incorporation of cooling fins on both the cylinder barrel and cylinder head. Heat transferred from the cylinder into the fins by conduction, and cooling air passing between the cylinder fins removed the heat by convection. It was therefore important to maximize the cooling fin surface area. This photo provides a good example of the number and arrangement of the cooling fins. Birch Matthews collection

George J. Mead was appointed vice president, and Andrew Van Dean Willgoos (Andy) assumed the position of chief engineer. It was a talented trio. They not only successfully founded the new enterprise, but assured its viability well into the future.

The first product of the new company was a nine-cylinder, direct drive air-cooled radial engine of 1,344 cubic inches. Through clever design, the new engine was light in weight and more powerful at 400 horsepower than its 325-horsepower Wright competitor, then under development. Rentschler and his team had, figuratively speaking, given birth to a winner. It was run for the first time on December 28, 1925. Type testing was completed early in 1926, and the engine was flight tested in May of that year. The magnitude of what Rentschler and company had accomplished is partly confirmed by the fact that Wright Aeronautical abandoned plans to put its 325-horsepower engine into production. The new Pratt & Whitney engine, named the Wasp, was simply far superior—it developed 75 more horsepower yet weighed no more than its Wright counterpart. The Wasp became a military and commercial success. It was continually developed over the years into a variety of models. It also served as a starting point for new engine designs.

Pratt & Whitney *did not* build racing engines. It would, of course, sell an engine to any domestic customer including owners of racing planes. There was also a policy of providing race teams with leased engines. Company technical support representatives were also present at the races and quite willing to aid anyone using a Pratt & Whitney engine.

In some instances the company "customized" an engine setup for a particular race pilot or owner. It should be emphasized that the term customized meant using standard proven parts, but building a unique engine configuration. This often resulted in changing the supercharger drive gear ratio or perhaps altering the compression ratio. The Twin Wasp Jr. Model S2A5-G engine in Earl Ortman's 1937 Marcoux-Bromberg racer is an example. Originally built for the Army as an R-1535-11(company Model S1A5-G), this particular engine suffered a major failure on the test stand while lubrication improvements were being evaluated.[7] A replacement engine was manufactured for the Army, and the failed unit rebuilt for Ortman. The major change involved increasing the supercharger gear ratio from 8.7:1 to 11:1. A new model number was assigned to Ortman's engine thus documenting the modification. It became the S2A5-G and was the only Twin Wasp Jr. so configured. The Pratt & Whitney model ratings for the S1AG-5 and the S2AG-5 make an interesting comparison. The Army engine was rated at 750 horsepower turning 2,500 revolutions at sea level. With a new supercharger setup in Ortman's engine, the factory rating was increased from 750 to 825 horsepower at 2,580 rpm for takeoff, the result of higher manifold pressure and a modest increase in engine speed.

MENASCO ENGINES

One entrepreneur who did on occasion apply his talents to racing engine development was Albert Menasco. Born shortly before the turn of the century, Al Menasco was a gifted and mechanically inclined youngster. A high school dropout in an era when this was hardly unusual, Menasco learned to fly in 1915 under the tutelage of pioneer aviator Art Smith, out of Fort Wayne, Indiana. Menasco was destined to make his name not as a pilot, but as a builder of inverted in-line, air-cooled aircraft engines. Urged on by Jack Northrop, his first creation was the Model A4 Pirate, a 326-cubic-inch displacement, inverted four-cylinder engine delivering 90 horsepower. This was followed by the 145-horsepower, six-cylinder A6 model. The A series engines were produced in very limited numbers, but were followed in rapid succession by the more familiar B and C series. Like the A series engines, the B and C

MODEL	YEAR	HP	CU IN	REMARKS
Wasp	1925	400	1,344	
Hornet A	1926	525	1,683	
Hornet B	1930	575	1,908	
Twin Hornet	1935	1,400	2,180	Not put into production
Wasp Jr.	1930	300	985	
Twin Wasp	1932	750	1,830	
Twin Wasp Jr.	1932	750	1,535	
Double Wasp	1936	2,000	2,800	

Early Pratt & Whitney Engines

Table 9-3

Douglas DC-3 transports used a variety of engines. Many were built with Wright R-1820 models developing 1,000 to 1,200 horsepower. This particular photo, however, represents a Pratt & Whitney R-1830 Twin Wasp engine installation. The size of the engine is readily seen here by comparing it to the man standing by the landing gear. The scoop at the bottom of the cowling contains the oil cooler. United Technologies via the Peter M. Bowers collection

models were built in both four- and six-cylinder versions. Unlike the A models, the B and C series were available in either normally aspirated or supercharged configurations. The B and C series engines achieved lasting fame in the sport of air racing during the 1930s.

The pinnacle for Menasco racing engines occurred in 1937, when Rudy Kling drove his Menasco-powered Folkerts SK-3 *Jupiter* to victory in both the Greve and Thompson Trophy Races. The beginning of Menasco's participation in air racing, however, was less than auspicious. A small A4 Pirate was the engine of choice for Keith Rider's very first racing plane design, which made an appearance at the 1930 National Air Races. The diminutive 875-pound airplane lost an aileron during its first race and crashed. Fortunately the pilot, John A. Macready—who with Oakley G. Kelly, gained fame during the nonstop Fokker T-2 cross-country flight of 1923—miraculously survived the accident. The same cannot be said for the first Rider racer.

The history of Al Menasco and his company (in its various incarnations) has been well documented. The journal *Skyways* presented a particularly well-written synopsis authored by Larry M. Rinek.[8] The original Menasco Motors in Los Angeles was a 1926 partnership between Al Menasco and fellow Californian, Karl Weber of Weber Showcase & Fixture Company. Weber's interest in the partnership was eventually bought in 1928 by a wealthy Santa Monica, California, businessman, Harry J. Tucker. Tucker gained celebrity when he and Art Goebel flew a fast Lockheed Vega 5C called *Yankee Doodle* in various races and cross-country flights. Tucker was killed in this same airplane in 1929.

Without financial support from either Karl Weber or Harry Tucker, Al Menasco eventually had to look elsewhere. He turned to financing in the equity markets in 1929 through the brokerage firm of Moffet & White. The partnership was (or was intended to be) converted into a corporation. [9, 10] Unfortunately, Moffet & White failed not long after the beginning of the Great Depression.

Menasco struggled on as the Depression deepened. William E. Boeing stepped forward and provided some interim financial assistance. With support and encouragement from Bill Boeing, Jack Northrop and Claude Ryan, Al Menasco's company limped along on what at times was little more than a shoestring existence.

During this early 1930s period, Menasco became more involved with air racing. Historian and author John Underwood, who interviewed Al Menasco on several occasions, states that air racing "kept the business going, really. Later, it got to be too much of a nuisance, with the racing crowd constantly expecting support in one form or another."[11]

Although air racing certainly offered exciting publicity opportunities, it was anything but profitable. By early 1934, Menasco's business needed yet another cash infusion. This time, Al Menasco worked through the brokerage house of G. Brashears & Company located at 510 Spring Street, in the heart of the Los Angeles financial district. Concurrent with this stock offering, his business was once again renamed (on June 11, 1934) and became the Menasco Manufacturing Company, Inc. At this point, the company was closely held by seven people, including Al Menasco's brother Milton; future Bendix Trophy Race victor and wealthy sportsman pilot Frank Fuller, Jr.; and the head of the Douglas Aircraft Company, Donald W. Douglas. The financial health of Menasco remained tenuous. Of the engine purchase contracts Menasco held, only the one with Ryan Aeronautical Company ever resulted in any significant production. By 1936, the company was pushing a new stock offering as yet more money was needed.

In 1935, Al Menasco was introduced to an idea that quickly appealed to his acknowledged mechanical aptitudes. Lockheed Aircraft Corporation was then exploring the potential of a new design to complement its existing Model 10 Electra series. Lockheed President Robert E. Gross knew that to survive and grow, his company had to enlarge its product line. Competing head-to-head with Boeing and Douglas in the large commercial transport field was financially unrealistic. Instead, Gross pushed his small engineering group in a different direction. He wanted a smaller twin-engine transport capable of carrying six to eight passengers (the Electra seated 10) together with a pilot and copilot. He envisioned a sizable market for aircraft which could economically serve smaller towns and rural communities. Gross called his idea the "baby Electra" (it would later be commonly referred to as the Electra Jr.), and it was to be designed "possibly around two seven-cylinder, 325-horsepower Wrights, or even two Menascos."[12]

The two major domestic large engine manufacturers, Pratt & Whitney and Wright Aeronautical, had engines in the desired horsepower range. What each of their engines lacked was adequate supercharging for Lockheed's needs at altitude. Nor were they willing to commit scarce financial resources to bring existing models to the performance level desired. Both companies were pursuing development of higher horsepower engines. Unfortunately for

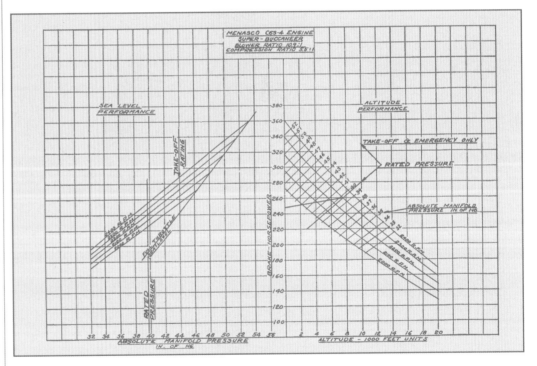

The Menasco C6S-4 was one of the most popular air-cooled engines used in Thompson and Greve Trophy race competitions. Sea level horsepower output was 360, although some contestants managed to increase this level to a certain degree by running the engine above its rated 2,400 rpm. The left-hand side of this power curve depicts sea level brake horsepower as a function of manifold pressure and rpm. Power output up to 20,000 feet may be read from the right-hand side of the chart.

This side view of a DC-3A engine cowling illustrates the adjustable cowl flaps. These were opened to allow greater airflow through the cowled engine at low speeds and during run-up on the ground. Also shown in this photograph is the downdraft carburetor scoop, just aft of the cowl flaps on the top of the nacelle. The projection on the bottom of the nacelle is the oil cooler scoop. United Technologies via Peter M. Bowers collection

Lockheed, manufacturers of smaller engines had nothing to offer either.

It was a vexing problem. What appeared a likely solution occurred to Hall Hibbard during late 1934 or perhaps early 1935. Hibbard, Lockheed chief engineer, conceived of uniting two engines to a single propeller drive train.[13] The key to this approach was devising a freewheeling clutch mechanism enabling either or both engines to drive a single propeller shaft, thus achieving two-engine reliability.[14] Such an engine arrangement mounted in the nose of an airplane insured that propeller thrust would always be along the airframe longitudinal centerline axis. No yaw condition would occur should

one of the engines fail. It was also believed that a more favorable drag condition would result by completely eliminating one engine nacelle.

Hibbard and Gross sought out Menasco Manufacturing to explore this unique engine configuration. Why did Lockheed turn to Al Menasco? Most likely it was a simple process of elimination. Menasco was already working on an air-cooled engine in the 250-horsepower class. If the power output could be pushed higher it might well do the job. Furthermore, Menasco's engines traditionally presented a very small frontal area, a decided aerodynamic advantage. Also attractive was the fact that Menasco was located in close proximity to Lockheed.

What Gross found was an organization possessing attractive technical capabilities and conservatively designed products. Without doubt he also recognized that they were not strong financially—not too many companies were during the Depression. Gross may also have looked at Menasco as a future acquisition should the contemplated engine configuration prove successful.

Two other factors played a role in the events that were to unfold. Regardless of other conservative business traits, Bob Gross was not adverse to taking business risks. He demonstrated this on several occasions, and this in part explains why Menasco's weak financial underpinnings were a secondary consideration. Second and perhaps more important, the idea of uniting two engines to a single propeller shaft took on a charismatic life of its own in Gross' mind. He and some of his close associates were fascinated with the concept. It was an addiction that persisted for almost five years, despite problems and disappointments along the way.

Lockheed issued a contract to Menasco Manufacturing on June 6, 1935, for the "experimentation and development of a free wheeling device to be used in conjunction with twin Menasco engines geared to the drive shaft for a single propeller." Oddly enough, proof-of-principle work proceeded not with Menasco engines, but with two air-cooled, four-cylinder 90-horsepower Wright Gipsy engines. The Gipsy design was of British origin, originally license-built in this country by the Wright Aeronautical Corporation. Manufacturing rights were later obtained by American Cirrus. When American Cirrus went under in 1930, Al Menasco bought a number of residual engines and spare parts. It was from this stash of hardware that the first experiments were made.[15] Nevertheless, the end objective was always centered on using Menasco C6S-4 powerplants then under development. This was the origin of the Menasco Unitwin engine and the relationship between the two companies that was to have a profound impact on Al Menasco's personal future.

Menasco jumped at the opportunity of devising a mechanism coupling two engines to a single propeller shaft. Shortly after experimental activities began, Lockheed's Cyril Chappellet and Hall Hibbard visited the Menasco plant. Afterward, Chappellet cheerfully reported to Gross that Menasco "is getting along well with his design work for the clutch and free wheeling device and is going to let me know . . . just how soon they will have the test rig set up and ready to go. Al is becoming more and more interested in the possibilities of this device and has been pleasantly surprised so far, that the problem has presented so few difficulties." Chappellet, Lockheed corporate secretary, went on to say, "We discussed with Al the possibility of changing our program somewhat and revising the Electra for an eight-place job with two 350s in the wing. He stated that he could have two 350-horsepower geared engines ready for us to use for flight tests within four months, and that by the end of six months he was sure he would have an entirely satisfactory engine in production for commercial usage." [16] Menasco's enthusiastic response proved totally unrealistic. The C6S-4 did not receive government certification for another *three years.*

Buoyed by Menasco's optimism, Lockheed issued a purchase order on July 1, 1935, for two Menasco engines (to be derivatives of the C6S-4) for the Unitwin project. There were two fateful provisions in the purchase agreement. First, the engines were to develop 350 horsepower. Second, although the basic power package was then essentially a sea level engine, it was expected that further development would enable sea level performance to be extended up to 5,000 feet.[17] (As a historical footnote, the Lockheed contract identified the engine as a "G-350" model, presumably meaning a geared engine of 350 horsepower.) The requirements set forth in the purchase agreement were challenging to say the least. The specified engine characteristics, undoubtedly furnished by Al Menasco, were listed as follows:

Altitude performance was vitally important to Lockheed. As a consequence, a specific caveat was imposed in the purchase order: "Every effort must be made to supercharge to 5,000 feet as single engine

Table 9-4		
Maximum Hp		350
Maximum Rpm		3,500
Maximum Propeller Rpm		2,000
Rated Altitude, Ft.		2,000
Fuel Octane		80
Engine Dry Wt., Lb.		Less than 675

ceiling with the sea level engines [2,000 feet as indicated in the above specification] will be very poor." [18] The stated design characteristics together with the caveat are critical to what eventually transpired, for they reveal a naiveté on the part of both Lockheed and Menasco with respect to what realistically might be achieved. Lockheed needed an ATC-rated engine capable of economic operation. Yet it was starting with a powerplant package still in early development, coupled with very imposing requirements.

For his part, Al Menasco failed to appreciate the dimensions of the task. He was overly confident in his ability to couple two engines to a single drive; supercharge the altitude rating of the engine to 5,000 feet; and, simultaneously increase the C6S-4 nominal power output from 250 to 350 horsepower.[19] To paraphrase author Cornelius Ryan, it was simply a bridge too far for Menasco to cross.

Up to this point, all of Menasco's engines, excluding specific racing configurations, developed considerably less power than the Unitwin objective. For this application, however, Al intended to achieve the horsepower rating by running the engine at a very high speed, namely 3,500 rpm, and by increasing manifold pressure, partially through greater supercharging. Admittedly some of his racing engines operated in regimes approximating these parameters, though often at the expense of reliability—a condition frequently confirmed in air racing events.

In spite of this, the early results from Menasco's proof-of-principle experiments convinced all concerned that the approach was sound. But these early results focused only on demonstrating a freewheeling clutch and drive mechanism with the two Gipsy engines. Indeed, a patent was eventually granted to Al Menasco for a "multiple motor drive" and a second one to both Al and Lockheed's Hall Hibbard for a "multiple motor drive for airplane propellers."

The company promoted the small transport concept with a number of air line executives and potential private customers during the fall of 1935. Two designs were presented. One utilized the two-in-the-nose Menasco Unitwin (the Lockheed Model 11) while the other was a conventional design derivative of the Model 10 Electra offered with 300-plus horsepower Menasco C6S-4 engines or various Wright and Pratt & Whitney powerplants. Bob

Gross wryly summarized the essence of this marketing foray in a letter to his brother, Courtlandt Gross: "The reactions were quite interesting but they all simmered down to one unalterable law, namely, that if the Menasco Company had only $50,000 in the bank, they didn't want the engine under any circumstances, whether it was located in the nose, in the wings or out back of the tail wheel." [20]

It was now totally apparent to Lockheed that Menasco Manufacturing Company was a liability in the view of many in the aviation community. The concern was not one of technical competence; rather, the company was perceived to be a financial risk. Should it go under, anyone using Menasco-powered airplanes would have immediate problems.

Bob Gross was worried and becoming disenchanted with Menasco. "The company's position," he told his brother, "is no more encouraging than it was. They are plugging along on their 250-horsepower engine, which they hope to have putting out from 300 to 350 horsepower some time next year. This, of course, is not sufficient to warrant our counting on them, because our present two-in-the-nose airplane now indicates it will have to have 300 to 350 horsepower" to be practical.[21] Gross assumed a watch-and-wait attitude for a little longer, but ultimately admitted to himself that it would be "a physical impossibility for Menasco to give us dependable enough power" to proceed with building the Model 11.[22]

As Unitwin engine development dragged on, Lockheed prudently turned to a second and totally conventional transport design. This was the Lockheed Model 12. Toward the end of November 1935, Lockheed firmly committed to the Model 12 allowing engineering design work on the Unitwin-powered Model 11 to proceed at a greatly reduced pace, ultimately no further than wind tunnel testing.

Interestingly, both designs were submitted for consideration in a Bureau of Air Commerce competition. Lockheed hedged its proposal by bidding the Model 11 Unitwin design at a much higher price than the Model 12. Should the Model 11 be selected, Lockheed reasoned, it would have to invest heavily in Menasco if it was ever going to get an engine with suitable performance. In the end, the Model 12 (the Electra Jr.) was the winner, although Air Commerce Bureau chief Gore Vidal's proposal

A few prewar racing aircraft used Pratt & Whitney Twin Wasp engines. One notable racer was Roscoe Turner's *LTR-14* Meteor. This photo of the engine installation shows the tubular steel engine mount and exhaust collector ring details. The LTR-14 replica is under construction in Bill Turner's hangar in Southern California.
John Garrett photograph

evaluators were, like Bob Gross, enamored with the Menasco-powered Model 11. Ironically, the heavily touted competition was somewhat disappointing for Lockheed. Initially, the department informed the company that it lacked sufficient funds to buy even one airplane, let alone to offset any development expense. In mid-June 1936, however, Lockheed did sell one Model 12 to the Commerce Department.[23]

Despite inevitable problems and delays, the Unitwin concept somehow remained alluring within Lockheed. Unfortunately, Al Menasco's company was perpetually drenched in red ink. Progress on the engine development slowed. This, in turn, adversely effected future Lockheed plans. For example, Lockheed was then working hard to sell Transcontinental & Western Air, Inc. (TWA), its new small feeder transport design (Model 12 version) by offering a number of powerplant options, including Menasco C6S-4 engines. Lockheed referred to this configuration as the Model 12M (Menasco-powered). TWA president Jack Frye expressed interest in the 12M and requested firm data. It was an embarrassing moment for Gross. The expected data from Menasco was not forthcoming and Gross was forced to tell Frye that "due to a delay in receiving adequate power curves from Menasco," he was regrettably unable to furnish the information.[24]

The Menasco situation failed to improve with time. Acknowledging this, Bob Gross and Cyril Chappellet began taking a financial stake in Menasco during the late spring of 1936.[25] These were personal investments. Lockheed Aircraft Corporation did not buy any Menasco stock. At first, this was looked upon as a way to assist Al Menasco and keep the project going. It would later become the basis for exerting a drastic management change.

In August 1937, Gross and several associates formed the AiRover Company for the express purpose of completing an aircraft design utilizing the Unitwin engine. By this time it was apparent to all concerned that the basic C6S-4 power package was never going to reliably produce the 350 horsepower originally specified. Even 300 horsepower was beyond reach. As a consequence, the Lockheed Model 11 design, which was intended to accommodate six-passengers plus a pilot and copilot at a gross weight of 7,500 pounds, was scaled down by AiRover to accommodate the available Unitwin power (two engines each delivering 160 horsepower). The result was a 6,000-pound gross weight airplane carrying only five passengers and one pilot. This amounted

Not all air-cooled engines were radial arrangements. Ranger and Menasco Motors both built a series of in-line air-cooled engines. Shown here is an unusual assembly of two Menasco C6S-4 engines powering a common propeller shaft. Known as the Unitwin engine, it was built for Lockheed. Menasco engines successfully powered a large number of racing planes during the 1930s. Birch Matthews collection

to a 20 percent reduction in gross weight compared to the intended Model 11.

Model 11 performance estimates in 1935 were based upon a Menasco Unitwin delivering a total of only 580 horsepower up to 5,000 feet. At the time Lockheed developed Model 11 performance predictions, it believed this was an attainable power rating in comparison with what it first asked Menasco to provide—700 horsepower. Interestingly, high speed for the Model 11 and AiRover designs was approximately the same (around 200 miles per hour). Range for the AiRover airplane, however, was less than the Lockheed Model 11 because of a diminished fuel capacity.

The AiRover Unitwin was subsequently designated the Vega Model 2 (still later the Model 22) when the small AiRover organization evolved into the Vega Airplane Company, a wholly owned subsidiary of Lockheed Aircraft Corporation.

Menasco suffered progressively increasing losses in 1936 and 1937. The situation became critical in 1938 with a fiscal year-end net loss of $97,000 (Menasco's fiscal year ended in June).[26] Gross was stunned at the magnitude of red ink. "The Menasco Company practically blew up in our faces," Gross said, "and it became important to Lockheed that

something be done to insure a dependable supply of reliable engines."[27]

Gross had to take action. "The Menasco Company," he later wrote, "has been the subject of a good deal of work and worry on my part . . . [and] I got into the picture by virtue of the fact that our experimental development subsidiary [AiRover, later Vega] is committed to a design which in turn is solely predicated on the Menasco motor. When we laid out the plane, we knew that the Menasco Company was hardly a seasoned or tested organization, but we did have reason to believe that the company would keep going and would gradually perfect an acceptable power unit. As we got into the airplane design, it became apparent that the engine company needed more help than we supposed."[28]

Although Unitwin development was nearing completion, getting the engine into production was now in jeopardy. Under development for several years, certification of the C6S-4 had only just occurred during March 1938. Gross saw his investment in grave peril. As Menasco's desperate situation became clearly evident during late May, Gross moved to retrieve the situation. He hastily contacted several potential investors in San Francisco,

including Randolph C. Walker (one of the original 1932 Lockheed investors).

Gross induced Walker and the others to invest $75,000 in Menasco. In return, he agreed "to be responsible to them for the expenditure of this money by joining the Board of Directors of the Menasco Company."[29] Menasco management had no option but to accept the rescue plan put forth by Gross. It was either this or go under. Two of the three Menasco directors, William K. Scott and W. R. Atwood, abruptly resigned on June 1, 1938. They were replaced by Bob Gross and Cyril Chappellet. Al Menasco continued as the third director, but his influence was now greatly diminished.

Having gained control, Gross immediately turned his attention to the company presidency. Menasco had to be replaced. As far as Gross was concerned, it was inconceivable that Menasco could lead the company away from financial ruin. Gross chose Gardner W. Carr as president. Carr had risen through the production ranks at Boeing Airplane Company to vice president and plant manager. From Boeing, Carr moved to The Glenn L. Martin Company as vice president and general manager. His stay with Martin was less than a year when Gross approached him to head Menasco Manufacturing.

It was not Bob Gross' intention to drive Al Menasco out of the company. He respected other attributes of the company founder and offered him the position of "vice president in charge of sales." There is every reason to believe Menasco initially accepted his new role.[30] Within a month or two, though, he apparently had second thoughts and suddenly retired by the end of that summer.[31] Menasco's retirement was accepted and he followed Scott and Atwood out the door. The formal reason given for Menasco's departure was his personal health. Possibly. Undisputedly, the well-being of Menasco Manufacturing was in serious jeopardy!

Why did Al Menasco leave his company? Quite conceivably he couldn't accept the reorganization imposed by Gross including his own demotion. The basic problem, however, was a conflict with Gardner Carr.[32] One senses that Menasco's departure left him with an indelible scar. In later years he *never* publicly referred to Bob Gross or Gardner Carr when reminiscing about his personal experiences and the history of Menasco Manufacturing.

The novel Unitwin-powered Vega Model 2 was a technical success and marketing failure. None were ever sold. In less than two years, the project was swept aside by the terrible winds of war, as Lockheed and Vega turned to aircraft production for the Army Air Corps and the Royal Air Force.

Why did the Unitwin engine ultimately become no more than an engineering curiosity and the final straw that forced Al Menasco from the company that bore his name? After all, the concept was eventually proven. It first flew experimentally in a modified Lockheed Model 8G Altair during December 1937. By April of the following year, the Unitwin successfully took the Vega Model 2 aloft, where it accumulated 85 hours of flight time. Although the airplane met its design objectives, it was not a triumph. It was now too small for the market first envisioned in 1935. The commercial airline business had passed it by.

The problem resided primarily with the basic engine selection. The Unitwin engine design approach was fundamentally flawed from the very beginning *in context* with Lockheed's 1935 plans for a 7,500-pound passenger transport. Both Lockheed and Menasco failed to appreciate that obtaining a reliable 350 horsepower from 544 cubic inches was (then) an unrealistic goal. Unquestionably, Al Menasco knew his C series engines were capable of generating this much power, based upon his air racing experiences, but that was hardly transferable to commercial aviation ratings. It is only necessary to look at contemporary air-cooled engine characteristics to understand the current state-of-the-art.

One method of comparing engines is to look at the power produced by each cubic inch of displacement. Consider that the Wright Whirlwind, publicly renowned for its sterling reliability and excellent economy (Lindbergh used it for his epic 1927 flight across the Atlantic), produced just over one-third horsepower per cubic inch of displacement. In contrast, the Unitwin C6S-4 power packages were expected to generate nearly twice that much power (Table 9-5). Admittedly there was a trend in the air-cooled engine industry toward greater power per cubic inch, but nothing close to the magnitude then envisioned for the C6S-4. Even the most advanced liquid-cooled engines of that general era (the Allison V-1710 and Rolls-Royce Merlin) were incapable of generating that much power from a cubic inch.[33]

Also consider that most air-cooled engines of that generation operated at a maximum of 2,000 to 2,400 rpm. Menasco was counting on a whopping 3,500 rpm to reach maximum power. Higher revolutions result in more waste heat, increased wear, and increased stress on critical engine parts. These weren't attractive features to commercial airline managers, who continually focused on economy and reliability.

The only realistic solution for Lockheed and Menasco in 1935, would have been to design and develop an entirely new engine of greater displacement. Considering the perpetual money problems at Menasco and the limited resources available to Lockheed for such a project, this avenue was as impractical as reliably getting 350 horsepower out of the C6S-4. In this instance, one can only conclude that Al Menasco's reach most definitely exceeded his grasp.

Nineteen thirty-eight found Menasco Manufacturing facing a number of problems, including the aborted M-50 engine. The Unitwin was only the proverbial straw that broke the Menasco camel. Ironically, had it not been for the Unitwin and Bob Gross' vested interest in the project, the Menasco company might well have then entered bankruptcy. Only Gross came forth with a rescue plan.

Perhaps more fascinating to racing historians is the question of Menasco's involvement with air racing. Was this a positive or negative factor to company fortunes? Did his race projects contribute to the financial woes and near downfall of Menasco

Manufacturing? As a general response, one may say that it was a contributing factor—insofar as these activities diverted funds and management focus away from Menasco's core business. Conversely, racing engine work helped keep the company going during the darkest Depression years.

One deduction that can be made from the Unitwin project is that Menasco's achievements with racing engines clouded his judgment into believing that he could meet the Lockheed requirement of 350 horsepower from the basic C6S-4 power package.

Even Robert Gross' last-minute resuscitation of Menasco Manufacturing in 1938 failed to stem the company decline. Gross, still involved in company management oversight, continued to fret about Menasco's future. In mid-1939, Gardner Carr departed as president—he joined Lockheed Aircraft—and was replaced by A. E. Shelton. Gross realized Menasco's future in the engine business was bleak. Another product line was needed. Coincident with the war production build-up at Lockheed, Gross turned to Menasco for landing gear subassemblies. It was an excellent match with their manufacturing capabilities. In a very real sense, Gross saved the company from extinction. Menasco Manufacturing ultimately built some 58,000 aircraft landing gears by the end of World War II.[34] Like the Unitwin engine, this product line had an air racing heritage too. Al Menasco had earlier built retractable landing gears for Keith Rider's racing planes.

Horsepower Developed Per Cubic Inch
Various Contemporary Engines

Mfgr.	Model	Hp	Hp/In³	Rpm	Year
Wright	Whirlwind	285	0.377	2,000	1927
P&W	Wasp	525	0.391	2,200	1934
P&W	Wasp Jr.	400	0.406	2,200	1934
P&W	Twin Wasp	750	0.410	2,400	1934
P&W	Twin Wasp Jr.	700	0.456	2,400	1934
Menasco	C6S-4[A]	260	0.478	2,300	1938
Allison	V-1710-C6	1,000	0.585	2,600	1937
Rolls	Merlin E	955	0.579	2,600	1935
Menasco	G-350[B]	350	0.643	3,500	1935

Notes: A. Based on ATC rating
B. Anticipated in 1935 purchase agreement.

Table 9-5

chapter 10

Necessities

He that loves a rosy cheek,
Or a coral lip admires,
Or, from starlike eyes doth seek
Fuel to maintain his fires;
As old time makes these decay,
So his flames must waste away.

Thomas Carew • *Disdain Returned*

In evaluating the progress and interrelationship of racing planes and military fighters, ancillary necessities such as fuel for the engines and waste heat management as a result of combustion, are sometimes overlooked.[1] Yet the evolution of both played vital, even pivotal, roles in facilitating rapid advances in high-speed flight in the two decades leading up to World War II. Without high quality aviation fuels, powerful liquid-cooled and air-cooled engines could not have been developed. At the same time adequate cooling technology had to evolve in parallel. This is the other side of the coin because high-speed, high-power engines using detonation-resistant fuels generate copious amounts of heat very rapidly.

STAYING COOL

Piston engine waste heat management must be considered, whether the engine is liquid-cooled or air-cooled. Early aircraft engines were typically water-cooled (water and much later, ethylene glycol-water mixtures) because well-designed passages in the cooling jacket successfully removed waste heat rather uniformly from the cylinder walls and heads. This alleviated the problem of local hot spots that could lead to detonation and rapid engine failure.

Large quantities of thermal energy (heat) are released as fuel chemical energy is transformed into mechanical energy by the piston engine. All of the heat generated through the combustion of gasoline does not need to be dealt with by supporting cooling systems, as shown in Table 10-1. Something like one-fourth of the combustion heat release is consumed in generating engine power. Another 40 to 45 percent is released to the atmosphere in the form of hot exhaust gasses. A small fraction (5 to 10 percent) is absorbed by the lubricating oil while another 15 to 20 percent soaks into the engine cylinder walls and cylinder heads. Both oil and cylinder heating loads must be removed by active cooling.

Pioneer aviators relied almost exclusively on water-cooled engines to power their early airplane designs. Shown here is a 1912 two-place Curtiss airplane with a V-8 pusher engine. Waste heat from the jacketed water-cooled cylinders was circulated through the large vertically mounted automobile style radiator. Drag was obviously not a paramount issue. John Garrett collection

Heat of Combustion Distribution Air-Cooled Engines	
Useful Power	25– 30 Percent
Exhaust Gases	40– 45 Percent
Lubricating Oil	5–10 Percent
Ambient Air	15– 20 Percent

Table 10-1

Source: Pratt & Whitney Report No. PWA 01.100

During 1920, the Army elected to participate in air racing. One of the designs built by the Army Engineering Division was this Verville-Packard VCP-R powered by a Packard 1A-2025 engine. Compared to the 1912 Curtiss illustrated in the previous photo, the VCP-R was a dramatic technology advance accomplished in an elapsed period of just eight years. One design detail remained essentially unchanged. A large cooling radiator was suspended between the landing gear struts. John Garrett collection

Regardless of the type of engine cooling, the amount of heat generated by combustion is a bit staggering at first glance. Before the advent of detonation-resistant 100-octane gasoline, high-performance racing engines often used a 50–50 mixture of gasoline and benzene with a thermal energy content of around 17,900 British thermal units (Btu) per pound. (A Btu is the amount of heat necessary to raise the temperature of one pound of water by 1 degree Fahrenheit.) This is precisely the fuel mixture used in 1922 in the Navy CR-2 racer powered by a Curtiss CD-12 racing engine. At wide-open throttle, the engine reportedly developed 460 horsepower with a corresponding total heat release of about 68,000 Btu per minute, approximately 17 percent of which was imparted to the cooling water.[2] To achieve a 10-degree Fahrenheit water temperature drop through the radiator before it was pumped back to the engine cooling passages required a water flow rate of 2.4 gallons per minute.[3]

EARLY RADIATORS

Water-cooled aircraft engines employed cooling radiators essentially patterned after automobile designs, often of the honeycomb type. Heat dissipation capability ranged from about 30 to 60 Btu per horsepower per minute.[4] Fin and tube radiators required something like 6 to 8 square inches for each Btu to be dissipated per minute. The location of the radiator installation varied, although many were placed ahead of the engine, producing the familiar blunt-nose appearance as seen, for instance, with the SPAD 13, S.E.-5A and Curtiss JN-4 Jenny. In other instances, fully exposed radiators were suspended between biplane wings or side-mounted on the fuselage. Little imagination is needed to intu-itively understand that early radiators created a lot of aerodynamic drag. As aircraft speeds increased the problem became magnified.

LAMBLIN RADIATORS

One man took note of the aircraft radiator drag issue and realized there had to be a better way. He was A. Lamblin and his firm was located at 36, Boulevard Bourdon, Neuilly-sur-Seine, France. Early in 1918, Lamblin decided to streamline the radiator package, simultaneously making it a more efficient heat transfer device. In this he succeeded. Author Thomas Foxworth relates that "tests in the Eiffel laboratory indicated the Lamblin radiator had twice the radiating [sic] effectiveness of standard honeycomb radiators with the same capacity."[5] (The intent of Foxworth's recounting was to emphasize that the Lamblin device was more efficient; however, the terminology used is somewhat misleading. The dominant heat transfer mechanism was forced air convection to the slipstream, not radiation.)[6]

A typical aircraft radiator of the period consisted of a large number of tubes or cells joined together, forming a honeycomb structure. Air flows through the cells which surround the water passages. Heat in the water is transferred into the metallic cell or tube structure by conduction, and then by convection into the air flowing through cells. Lamblin's design was based upon an annular water flow passage to which were soldered radial copper fins, both on the inside and outside of the annulus. The assembled radiator configuration quickly earned the nicknamed *casier à homards*, for it closely resembled a lobster pot trap. Lamblin built the lobster pot radiator in a variety of sizes depending upon the amount of heat to be dissipated, a function of engine power. They were installed singly and in pairs, and also produced in another configuration designed for installation on a landing gear or wing strut.

These radiators were a decided improvement from the standpoint of both aerodynamics and cooling efficiency. They were quickly adopted for a number of Schneider and Pulitzer racing planes. Even with Lamblin's innovative design, however, these devices still contributed an appreciable amount of drag, though not as much as the flat-faced radiator cores they replaced. Lamblin radiators were fashionable for a few years, but then Curtiss came up with yet a better idea, at least for racing applications.

SURFACE RADIATORS

An even more innovative cooling radiator was publicly introduced in 1922 when the sleek Curtiss Pulitzer and Schneider race planes appeared on the scene. Gone were the familiar bulky radiator appendages jutting from the fuselage as well as the Lamblin-style units. These were replaced by skin radiators mounted on and contoured to the wing airfoil surfaces. Curtiss first conceived of surface radiators in 1920 while designing the Curtiss-Cox *Texas Wildcat* racer for the James Gordon Bennett race. Time did not permit development of the concept, but a pragmatic investigation continued in any event.[7] The product of this development work was demonstrated in time for the 1922 races in the form of the Navy CR-2 racer.[8, 9]

To minimize drag due to large coolant radiators jutting from the fuselage, Curtiss integrated the radiator area with the wing surfaces, top and bottom. When these racers first appeared in the Pulitzer and Schneider races, they elicited a great deal of interest. The absence of a conventional radiator below the engine installation or on the fuselage sides gave the Curtiss machines an exceptionally clean and streamlined appearance.

The Curtiss design consisted of accordion-fold brass sheets of 0.005 inch thickness mechanically clamped and soldered to a second sheet of equal thickness. In cross-section, this assembly formed a series of triangular-shaped water passages with the triangle apex exposed to the air stream.[10] In profile, the thin brass assembly was contoured to duplicate the wing curvature. The assembled radiator formed a sleeve which slipped over the wing structure. Headers fore and aft completed the assembly and facilitated water circulation.

Curtiss refined the surface radiator design over time. When Marine Captain Arthur Page appeared at the 1930 National Air Races, he was flying a highly modified Curtiss F6C-3 Hawk. The modifications were so extensive that the Navy fighter was redesignated XF6C-6: a Conqueror engine replaced the original D-12; the cockpit profile was lowered; streamlined landing gear struts and wheel fairings were added; and, a parasol wing replaced the standard biplane arrangement. Upper and lower wing surface radiator segments replaced the conventional radiator core previously located on the fuselage

Radiators were high-drag components for airplanes equipped with liquid-cooled engines during the early 1920s. A more streamlined unit was developed by A. Lamblin of France. This 1924 advertisement illustrates one Lamblin configuration attached to the landing gear strut of the sketch on the right.

This close-up of the Verville-Packard VCP-R landing gear also shows the radiator installation. In comparison to the 1912 Curtiss radiator, the VCP-R device was considerably smaller, suggesting a significantly more efficient design. The somewhat crude fabric wheel covers have been installed to reduce the drag of the spoked wheels and tires. John Garrett collection

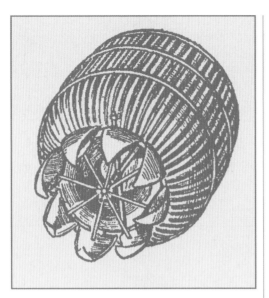

A better-known Lamblin radiator is shown in this sketch. It was popularly called the "lobster pot" because of its shape. It was aerodynamically cleaner than flat-faced radiator cores and more efficient as well. Race planes of the early 1920s typically attached this type of radiator to the landing gear struts or fuselage. Cooling requirements generally necessitated two units for adequate performance.

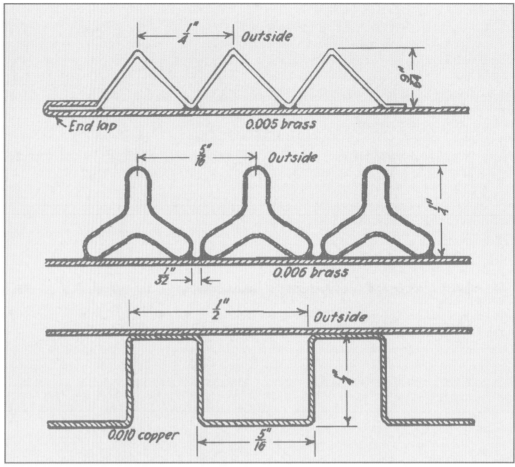

A major advancement in cooling radiators for air racing occurred when Curtiss developed the surface, or skin, radiator. This sketch shows cross-sections of three different radiator tube cross-sections. The upper triangular tube shape was the first used by Curtiss. A later Curtiss design was composed of tubes drawn into a three lobe pattern to increase cooling surface area. The lower cross-section is one used by Supermarine on its Schneider racers. The outer surface was flat copper sheeting, resulting in a significant drag reduction. All tubes on the wing surface were oriented with the chord.

beneath the engine. Water passages in this later Curtiss design consisted of shaped brass tubes having three equidistant radial lobes (120 degrees apart). Tube wall thickness was 0.006 inch, as was the brass sheet onto which the tubes were sweat soldered.

The data in Table 10-2 show moderate but steady improvement in cooling efficiency (with one glaring exception) for Curtiss surface radiators over a six-year period. Even with engines of increasing power and correspondingly greater waste heat loads, the trend in cooling system weight and surface area per horsepower were diminishing. For example, the cooling surface area per horsepower necessary for the Conqueror engine in the 1930 XF6C-6 was 23 percent less than the that required for the 1924 Curtiss XPW-8. Similarly, the system weight in pounds per horsepower was 14 percent less for the XF6C-6 relative to the earlier XPW-8. The one data point that

is anomalous to the general trend in Table 10-2 is found with the 1927 Curtiss XO-13A. The cooling surface area per horsepower was 1.6 times greater than the same figure of merit for the 1930 XF6C-6. It also represented the heaviest system weight at 382 pounds. One explanation may be that the system was simply over designed for the V-1570 Conqueror, this being the first time surface radiators were employed with this engine. Certainly the 1930 Curtiss XF6C-6 skin radiator installation (also for the Conqueror) was a decided improvement.

The British took surface radiator cooling to the ultimate level with their Supermarine Schneider racers. Instead of corrugated surfaces (or variations thereof) as used on the Curtiss racers, Supermarine employed rectangular channels covered with smooth external sheeting. The assembly simultaneously formed the wing exterior surface. Copper was employed in place of brass. Although slightly heavier than brass (about four percent), copper has a thermal conductivity 3.6 times greater than brass. This was a decided advantage from a heat transfer standpoint.

Table 10-2

Wing Surface Radiators for Several Racing Aircraft

Airplane	Year	Engine	Hp	Cooling Surface Area, Ft²	Wt. Of Water* Lb	System Wt. Including Water, Lb	Total Wt. Lb/Hp	Surface Area Ft²/Hp
Curtiss CR-2	1922	CD-12	460	244	73	221	0.48	0.53
Curtiss CR-3	1923	D-12	500	254	45	225	0.45	0.51
Curtiss XPW-8	1924	D-12	460	220	57	226	0.49	0.48
Curtiss R3C-1	1925	V-1400	600	265	57	228	0.38	0.44
Curtiss F6C-3	1926	D-12A	705	266	57	232	0.33	0.38
Curtiss XO-13A	1927	V-1570-1	720	425	90	382	0.53	0.59
Supermarine S.5	1927	Lion VIIA	875	284		481	0.55	0.33
Kirkham-Williams	1927	1A-2750	1,250	292				0.23
Curtiss XF6C-6	1930	V-1570	770	285	128	327	0.42	0.37
Supermarine S.6B	1931	R-R "R"	2,350	380	205	322	0.14	0.16

* Excludes the weight of water in the engine cooling passages.

Data extracted from Table 9:III, p. 260, from Domonoske and Finch, *Aircraft Engines*, John Wiley & Sons, Inc., New York, 1936. See also *Aviation*, July 1931, p. 441. Data for the Kirkham-Williams airplane is a calculated estimate based upon NACA Technical Note No. 318, September 1929, and material presented in *Aero Digest*, September 1927, p. 286-287. Supermarine data from Aeronautical Research and Memoranda Report No. 1575, January 1934, p. 9.

The other pronounced advantage of the Supermarine wing radiator design was its smooth external surface. The radiator installation added weight, but there was little cooling drag penalty.

Although removing conventional radiators from the Curtiss racers lessened airframe drag, using corrugated-type surface radiators in their place was not a free ride. There was still a very distinct drag penalty. This can be illustrated by examining data available for another racer. In 1929 the NACA evaluated radiator-related drag by wind tunnel testing the lower left wing panel from the Kirkham-Williams racer built for the 1927 Schneider Trophy Race. [11]

In spite of its nonparticipation in the 1927 races, the Kirkham-Williams machine is of historical interest because of the NACA test results. [12] Radiator geometry was similar to that used with 1925 Curtiss R3C-1. It was constructed of shaped brass tubing, once again forming a semicorrugated surface. (Corrugations greatly increased radiator surface area for convective heat transfer to the slipstream.) The wing panel was installed in the Propeller Research Tunnel at Langley and drag was evaluated with and without the skin radiators. The difference between wing drag coefficients with and without the radiator was measured to be 0.011. [13] At

an assumed speed of 300 miles per hour and with a total wing radiator surface installation of 292 square feet, associated drag amounted to a husky 370 pounds. [14] To overcome this much drag required 296 horsepower, or about 28 percent of the total thrust horsepower available. A 300-mile per hour top speed may have been more than the Kirkham-Williams racer was capable of, but even at lower speeds the drag penalty of this installation was by no means trivial as shown in Figure 10-1.

POSTSCRIPT

Surface radiators proved to be an interim solution to the problem of adequate heat removal from large liquid-cooled engines in high-speed airplanes. Although surface cooling was tried on one or two pursuit aircraft, it proved impractical. The radiators were subject to damage on the ground as the result of handling and maintenance. Pursuit maneuvering loads in flight strained solder joints, often producing coolant leakage. (Soldering is a method of bonding or connecting two surfaces to form a seal; this type of joint has minimal structural strength.) The massive surface area required for adequate cooling simultaneously exposed the aircraft to a high potential of battle

damage. Although the technique proved highly suitable to racing, it was a nonstarter when applied to combat planes.

Achieving low drag and efficient heat removal systems for powerful liquid-cooled engines was resolved by using a higher boiling point liquid, pressurizing the entire system and in some instances (like the P-51 *Mustang*) recovering a portion of the energy from heated air passing through the radiator. Ethylene glycol, a widely used antifreeze additive for automobile radiators, satisfied the need for a higher boiling point liquid. Air Corps experimentation at Wright Field demonstrated the advantage of this approach. (Pure ethylene glycol was eventually replaced by water-glycol mixtures.) This combined with pressurized coolant systems markedly reduced radiator size (hence drag) and system weight. Drag reduction was also achieved through better radiator duct design. The final touch involved accelerating heated air from the radiator through a nozzle—typically two-dimensional—to realize a measure of thrust. The epitome of this three-pronged approach was realized with the North American P-51 Mustang. Under some high-speed conditions, thrust from the radiator duct offset much of the drag from this installation.

FUEL FOR THOUGHT

From the beginning of powered flight, there has been a voracious demand for more engine power to enable faster speed. Equally demanding has been the search for quality aviation fuels that would permit efficient high power output from compact piston engines. "The incentive for more power from less weight with a low fuel consumption, spurred on considerably by two world wars . . . supported continuous research and development on aviation gasolines."[15] Progress was dramatic through the end of World War II. One author contends that the gasoline used by the Wrights in their Wright *Flyer* engine had an octane rating of about 38![16] This was at a time, of course, when the major product line of most refineries was kerosene for lamps. By the start of World War II octane ratings rose to 100.

Specifications for gasoline were nonexistent at the turn of the century. The first government specification was not issued until 1907. From the horrid fluid available to the Wrights in 1903 to the marginally better gasoline (perhaps 45- or 50-octane) used in World War I, aviation fuels remained deplorable. A major problem with these fuels was detonation, although other complications existed, such as volatility and gum residues. Selection suitable aviation fuels was an empirical process, one of trial and error. Over the battlefields of France it was found that straight run gasoline quality, obtained through simple distillation of crude oil, could vary widely. Crudes from the fields of Borneo, the Dutch East Indies and California proved more satisfactory, due to their higher aromatic content. Gasoline distilled from Pennsylvania and Oklahoma crude oils, on the other hand, caused a great deal of consternation when pumped into the engines of Allied airplanes.[17] The engines overheated almost certainly due to detonation, a phenomenon hardly understood in those early years. Gasolines derived from the fields of these two states was so bad they were eventually banned for military use in Europe.

Detonation has long been a problem lurking in every gasoline piston engine cylinder. The phenomenon is also known as *knock*, due to the sound it makes while the engine is running.

Orderly combustion within the cylinder results in flame front progression of a few feet per second. When detonation occurs, flame propagation rates of

A popular French innovation in radiator design was the Lamblin "lobster pot." Two of these radiators were installed on each of three Verville-Sperry R-3 racers built for the Army in 1922. Reportedly more efficient than conventional flat radiator cores, the Lamblins were also more streamlined. The cooling water passages were generously finned to promote heat transfer. John Garrett collection

Curtiss racers also used Lamblin radiators. This 1921 CR-2 built for the U.S. Navy to enter the Pulitzer contest also utilized the space between the landing gear struts. Note the plumbing installation from the lower portion of the fuselage to the forward end of the radiators. The Navy withdrew from the 1921 race, but Curtiss secured permission to race one of the airplanes in the Pulitzer. Bert Acosta won the race with a speed of 176.7 miles per hour. Peter M. Bowers collection

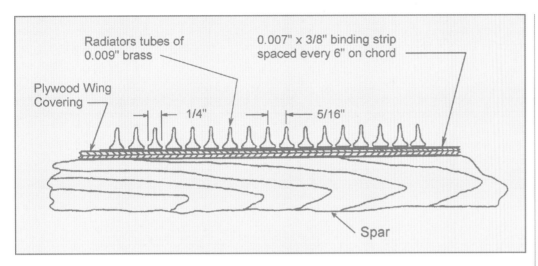

Another variation of the surface cooling tube geometry was employed on the Kirkham-Williams Schneider racer. Similar to the three-lobe Curtiss tube shown in Figure 10-3, this tube geometry was an attempt to expose maximum surface area to the slipstream. Materials of construction for all surface cooling radiators typically consisted of copper tubes sweat-soldered to copper or brass sheeting. The assembly was curved to the airfoil shape.

The mechanically inclined Ricardo was still experimenting in 1914, coincident with the start of World War I. Work in the United States investigating gasoline engine detonation problems during this period was practically nonexistent, in part because the country lagged far behind in the field of aeronautics. The center for aeronautics was truly in Europe with France, Great Britain and Germany in the lead.

After World War I, German chemists actively sought a fuel additive to suppress detonation. Their solution was iron carbonyl, a toxic but reasonably effective compound. It had the annoying disadvantage of fouling spark plugs and rusting cylinder walls, however. Iron carbonyl, an organometallic compound, fell out of favor for political reasons. German state control of alcohol and benzol production forced its citizens to be satisfied with these ingredients in fuel blends. Surpluses had to be used as motor fuel.

Wartime experiences coupled with a postwar growth in automobiles and aircraft operation focused

pressed to a point where it ignites spontaneously. The heat from such a rapid explosive energy release is not easily dissipated, causing the engine to overheat and further aggravating the problem. Engine structural failure can easily result. Detonation, or knock, is different from *preignition*, which occurs before the spark plug is fired. Preignition can occur from hot carbon deposits in the cylinder, for example.

The problem of fuel quality was severe. Finally in 1917 the Bureau of Mines (Petroleum Section) at the behest of the Army Signal Corps began investigating a suitable fuel for what was then called "Fighter Grade" fuel. Their almost immediate recommendation was to use gasoline derived from California crude. The recommendation was turned down for unknown bureaucratic or political reasons. As a consequence, efforts next turned to producing a synthetic fuel composed of 70 percent cyclohexane and 30 percent benzene, with an octane rating thought to have been about 75. An armistice ending the war was signed before this synthetic fuel could be put into production.

TETRAETHYL LEAD

Detonation studies and the search for resolutions began quite early. Noted English engineer Sir Harry Ricardo took an active interest in the phenomenon while studying at Cambridge in 1906.[18]

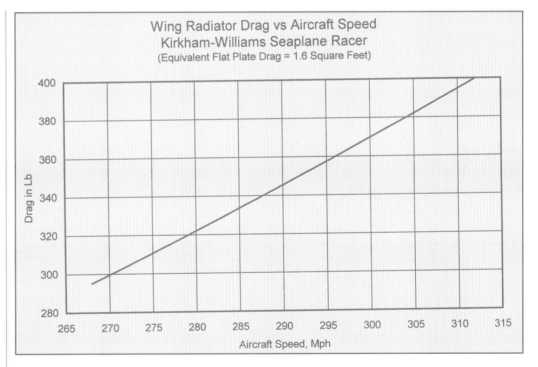

Surface cooling radiators, while an improvement over older types, were not free of drag, as one might assume. NACA wind tunnel measurements with one wing section of the Kirkham-Williams biplane racer documented the drag penalty as shown in this plot. At an assumed speed of 300 miles per hour, parasite drag amounted to a hefty 370 pounds. The Supermarine approach, using a smooth outer surface, was an even better solution.

Curtiss CR-2 racers appeared in 1922 with a new form of engine coolant radiators applied to the wing surfaces. Skin or surface radiators significantly reduced frontal area. Workmen at the Curtiss plant are shown assembling a section of surface radiator to the lower left wing panel. An appreciation for the amount of surface area required to dissipate engine heat by this method is demonstrated by the fact that upper and lower surfaces of both wings were needed. John Garrett collection

thought and research fuel quality problems in the United States. While Ricardo worked and studied the problems associated with engines and fuels in Great Britain, a dynamic impatient American engineer became equally interested. His name was Charles Franklin Kettering, and he quickly became convinced that suppressing detonation could be accomplished through gasoline additives. In 1920 Kettering assigned young 27-year-old Thomas Midgley the task of evaluating fuel additives in a single-cylinder test engine. Midgley was assisted in the experimental work by Thomas Boyd. Ironically, both were mechanical engineers, not chemists or chemical engineers.

What followed was a two-year period of intensive experimentation, at times frustrating, at other times promising. Relatively early in their work, Midgley and Boyd "doped" a test specimen of gasoline with aniline, an organic hydrocarbon compound containing nitrogen. The results were encouraging. Aniline exhibited a decided capability for suppressing detonation. Kettering was working with a new partner at this time, I. E. Du Pont. Although aniline appeared promising, Du Pont representatives pointed out that the price of this compound "was closely tied to the price of dyestuffs, and would soar under pressure from automotive use."[19] This was anathema to

Du Pont interests. Beyond this fiscal consideration, "aniline was costly, smelled horrible in the exhaust, corroded most metals, and gummed up nearly every device used to inject it into the engine."[20] Aniline was eventually set aside because no one was willing to underwrite plant costs for producing the compound in quantities that would be required.

At one point Kettering became enthused with the idea of alcohol fuels, which were inherently detonation resistant. (Coincidentally, Ricardo in England became similarly interested.) Ethyl alcohol, or ethanol, could be produced from vegetable material, a renewable source. Once again, quantity production

Table 10-2

Chemical Compounds

Name	Formula	Density Lb/Gal	Heating Value Btu/Lb	Octane Number	Vapor Press. Lb/In2
Acetone	C_3H_6O	6.6	12,300	100	1.09
Aniline	$C_6H_5NH_2$	8.5			3.57
Benzine	C_6H_6	7.4	17,300	88–110	6.71
Cyclohexane	C_4H_{12}	6.5		75	1.56
Ethyl Alcohol	CH_3CH_2OH	6.6	11,600	99	1.52
Gasoline	Various	6.0	18,500	75–100	7.00
Heptane	$CH_3(CH_2)_5CH_3$	5.5		0	1.90
Isooctane	$(CH_3)_3CCH_2CH(CH_3)_2$	5.8	19,100	100	2.43
Isopentane	$(CH_3)_2CHCH_2CH_3$	5.2		91	0.54
Methyl Alcohol	CH_3OH	6.6	8,600	90–100	1.25
Tetraethyl Lead	$(C_2H_5)_4Pb$	13.8			
Toluene	$C_6H_5.CH_3$	7.2	17,500	98	2.14
Xylene	$C_6H_4(CH_3)_2$	7.3			2.79
Xylidene	$(CH_3)_2C_6H_3NH_2$	8.3			4.21

costs proved a stumbling block. Alcohol fuels are not without their disadvantages either. For one thing they have a great affinity for water. A major drawback, however, is their low heating value compared to gasoline (see Table 10-3). Gasoline has a heating value of between 18,000 and 19,000 Btu per pound, contrasted with 11,600 and 8,600 Btu per pound, respectively, for ethyl and methyl alcohol. Larger fuel tanks, lines, pumps and valves are required to carry the same amount of chemical energy when alcohol is carried in place of gasoline. This may be acceptable in automobiles, but the weight penalty for aircraft is a bit stiff.

The answer to Kettering's quest for a detonation-suppressing additive was found in 1922 when tetraethyl lead (TEL), an organometallic compound, was evaluated by Thomas Boyd in the laboratory test engine. It proved to be 50 times more effective than aniline. Developing an effective cost-efficient process to produce the additive proved almost as difficult as the discovery itself. Nonetheless, commercial leaded automotive gasoline went on sale February 1, 1923, for the first time.

The work of Kettering, Midgley, and Boyd truly altered the future of the internal combustion piston engine. Certainly the automotive industry benefited. The soothing benefits of TEL were even more important in the field of aviation. The way was now open for developing high compression ratio

Various radiator locations were evaluated on both racing and military pursuit aircraft. This Curtiss F6C-3 incorporated a chin radiator beneath the engine. The leading edge of the radiator tunnel cowling was sharply angled in a streamlining gesture. Aside from this and a propeller spinner, this 1927 Navy fighter was not terribly more advanced than its World War I ancestors. Peter M. Bowers collection

This experimental Navy F6C-3 removed the chin radiator and replaced it with a side-mounted fuselage installation. Cooling air was taken in through a scoop just aft of the engine bay. Air was exhausted through a series of louvers. One defect of this installation is the proximity of the engine exhaust stacks, tending to allow hot exhaust gases to enter the cooling duct. Peter M. Bowers collection

Bulky engine cooling radiators were mounted on each side of this Curtiss-Cox Texas Wildcat racer. The otherwise well-streamlined racer, including an enclosed cockpit canopy, is blemished by the radiator installation. This 1920 design was subsequently modified into a biplane configuration prior to the Gordon Bennett race. Peter M. Bowers collection

aircraft engines so vital to good fuel economy. Equally important, increased power was now possible through supercharging.

100 OCTANE

Another critical step in the march toward quality aviation gasoline occurred in 1926 when Dr. Graham Edgar first synthesized iso-octane (2,2,4 trimethylpentane).[21] Edgar's accomplishment was important for two reasons, both related to the detonation phenomenon. One was the use of octane in determining detonation qualities of gasolines, hence the name "octane rating." The other reason is that octane became one of several gasoline blending materials to achieve high detonation resistance.

In the search for better fuels, it became apparent that an orderly methodology was needed in rating fuels by means other than its chemical composition. Test procedures were adopted in 1930 wherein the detonation resistance of mixtures of normal heptane (*n* heptane) and iso-octane were compared to various gasolines. Heptane and iso-octane were arbitrarily assigned values (ratings) of 0 and 100, respectively, indicating the former detonated easily while the latter was quite resistant to the phenomenon. The method utilized an unsupercharged, variable compression ratio test engine.[22] Running test fuel at relatively lean fuel-air mixture ratios, engine compression ratio was increased until the onset of detonation was reached. If a gasoline began to detonate at the same compression ratio as a mixture ratio of 80 percent octane and 20 percent heptane, it was given an 80-octane rating.

Straight run gasolines had an octane rating of about 75 at best. To improve upon this level, it was necessary to blend other compounds with straight run fuel. Blending formulation had also to consider such characteristics as volatility, stability, gum formation and response to tetraethyl lead addition. Several blending materials were used including isopentane, isooctane and the aromatic compounds of benzene, toluene and xylene (refer to Table 10-3).[23]

By the early 1930s commercial aviation gasolines had octane ratings typically between 70 and 80. In 1930, the Air Corps began using 87-octane fuel as its standard or Fighter Grade (referring to other than training airplanes). Within a few years commercial airlines began using 87-octane as well.

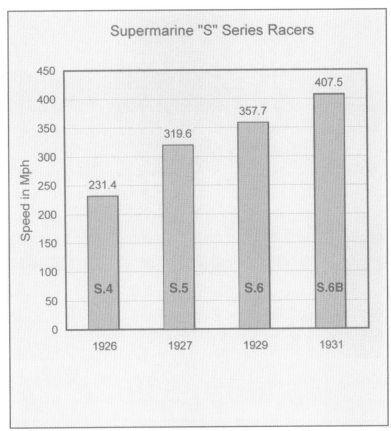

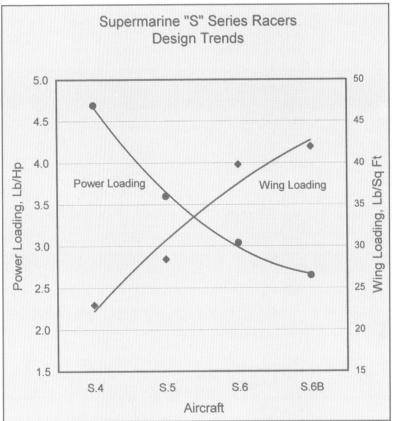

The great Supermarine racers designed by R.J. Mitchell showed a remarkable increase in speed over a five-year period, going from 231 miles per hour to 407 miles per hour. Mitchell and his crew of engineers and technicians diligently refined the basic design and solved cooling problems. With the aid of F.R. Banks, they developed detonation-resistant fuels, while winning the Schneider Trophy and setting world speed records.

Mitchell's Supermarine designs pushed the envelop with respect to the parameters of power loading and wing loading. Magnificent engines by Napier and then Rolls-Royce provided the muscle to complement the clean airframes of Supermarine. Power loading dropped dramatically with each successive design, due to large increases in horsepower. Wing loadings concurrently increased by a factor of two along the way.

As oil companies developed capacity, the cost per gallon of this improved gasoline went down, making it attractive for both commercial and military operations. The push for 100-octane gasoline came about somewhat hesitantly. A few visionaries in this depressed economic era appreciated what 100-octane gasoline promised: more powerful piston engines, increased air transport economy, and greater safety. Imaginative minds, including engineers at Wright Field together with Jimmy Doolittle, appreciated the advantages that 100-octane gasoline offered. Finally in August 1935, the Air Corps requested bids for 300,000 gallons of 100-octane fuel. Standard Oil of New Jersey received the contact. Delivered during December of that year, it was destined for use in engine development and flight test work.[24]

Doolittle was a prime mover in the thrust toward 100-octane gasoline. He had resigned from the Air Corps and taken a job with Shell Oil Company, commencing work in the Aviation Division during February 1930. Even though he was now a civilian, Doolittle was seriously concerned with the deplorable state of American military aviation due to meager appropriations. "The Army Air Corps," he lamented, "was not even a third-rate air force [in the 1930s], compared with the air forces of other nations."[25] He strongly believed that one path to a stronger Air Corps was development of more powerful engines. If this was to happen, however, better fuels were needed.

Doolittle argued, persuaded and cajoled key people at Shell to devote resources for laboratory and pilot plant production of 100-octane fuel. It was not an easy task, nor was it accomplished overnight. He believed with conviction that Shell Oil would in the end profit from the investment. Doolittle did not single handily cause the advanced gasoline to be produced and accepted, but

This view of the Curtiss-Cox *Texas Wildcat well illustrates the size of the fuselage mounted radiators. Engine power was delivered by a Curtiss C-12 engine, developing 427 horsepower at 2,250 rpm. The fixed-pitch racing propeller resulted in excessively long takeoff runs. New biplane wing panels were hastily built in France before the Gordon Bennett race to obtain more lift. Unfortunately, the racer was damaged in a landing accident and did not compete in the 1920 race.* Peter M. Bowers collection

he was certainly highly instrumental. Other key individuals pursuing better fuel were Samuel D. Herron, a noted British engineer who moved across the Atlantic to work for Wright Field; Frank D. Klein, who was then in charge of fuel and oil testing at Wright Field; and Edwin E. Aldrin, another ex-Air Corps pilot working for Standard Oil Development Company. Doolittle was modest about his contributions. "In the ensuing years," he wrote, "I got more credit than was due me for persuading the company to take the risk."[26] Perhaps, but without his enthusiasm and persistence it is quite likely that the United States military would not have standardized on 100-octane fuel until well after 1940. It is not a far stretch to suggest that the Battle of Britain might

have had a different outcome had not America been able to supply this fuel, thus giving the British fighter pilots a valuable competitive edge.

RACING FUELS

Before higher quality aviation gasolines were available as the result of improved refining techniques and the ready availability of tetraethyl lead, race engines were fueled with a number of mixtures, all designed to suppress detonation. Early post-World War I American racers tended to use gasoline distilled from California crude oil, due to its known favorable quality. Increasing sophistication soon led to mixtures of California gasoline and benzene. A popular fuel mixture in the United States utilized benzol 90, a mixture of benzene, toluene

and a small amount of xylene blended with California refined gasoline.[27] Depending upon the gasoline-to-benzol mixture ratio, these fuels probably had an octane rating of perhaps 80 to 85.

Benzine as well as benzol (benzene and toluene) became popular racing fuel constituents, perhaps even more so in Europe than in America. The pinnacle of fuel blending was reached in the Schneider races and world speed record projects between 1929 and 1934. The architect of these fuels was an Englishman, F. R. Banks (Rod). When Banks was asked to consult with Rolls-Royce on the "R" engine for the 1929 Schneider event, he was working for the Technical Sales Department of the Anglo-American Oil Company. Rolls was having difficulty getting the race engine through its test

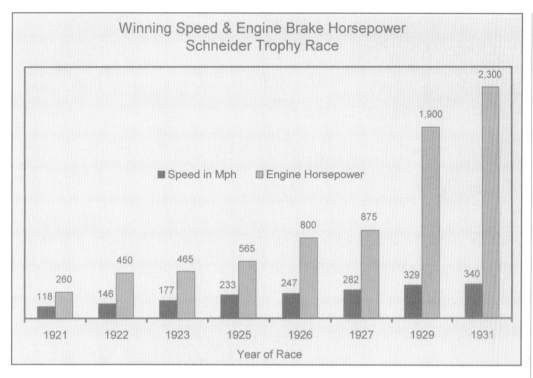

Winning Speed & Engine Brake Horsepower
Schneider Trophy Race

■ Speed in Mph ■ Engine Horsepower

Year	Speed	Horsepower
1921	118	260
1922	146	450
1923	177	465
1925	233	565
1926	247	800
1927	282	875
1929	329	1,900
1931	340	2,300

Year of Race

This bar chart compares winning Schneider Trophy Race speeds with the amount of engine horsepower needed to achieve these velocities. To win the race in 1931 required almost nine times as much horsepower as it did to be victorious in 1921. Over that period of time, the winning speed increased by a factor of slightly less than three. Certainly the 1931 Supermarine S.6B was aerodynamically cleaner than 1921 Macchi M.7 biplane, but brute force power was the dominant factor.

Table 10-4

British Racing Fuels

Event	1929 Schneider Race	1931 Schneider Race	1931 Speed Record
Aircraft	S.6	S.6B	S.6B
Benzol 90	78%	70%	30%
Methanol		10%	60%
Ethanol			
Acetone			10%
Gasoline	22%	20%	
Tetraethyl Lead	3.3 cc/gal	3.3 cc/gal	4.1 cc/gal
Density	6.95 lb/gal	6.91 lb/gal	6.88 lb/gal
Water Tolerance	nil	0.5%	14.3%
Octane No. With TEL	96	95	92
Octane No. Without TEL	91.5	92.5	92
Lower Heating Value	17,600 Btu/lb	16,700 Btu/lb	11,600 Btu/lb

Notes: Tetraethyl lead additions are based on the U.S. gallon. Basic fuel characteristics acquired from Rolls-Royce. Heating values determined by calculation.

program. The tests were being run using straight benzol when Banks arrived on the scene a month before the race. In his autobiography he recalled that "I did not have time to do very much; however, by the simple expedient of diluting the benzol with a 'light cut' Romanian leaded gasoline, it was possible to get the engine through it tests satisfactorily and race-ready."[28] Indeed it was. Flying Officer H. R. D. Waghorn put his Supermarine S.6 racer, one of two built, through the seven-lap, 50kilometer (31.03 miles) course averaging 328.629 miles per hour. Great Britain captured the very prestigious Schneider Trophy for the second time.

The next and final Schneider contest was held two years later in September 1931. The British were uncontested and thus able to fly the course and permanently retire the trophy in London where it resides to this day. There was a certain panache associated with the 1931 event in spite of a dearth in competition. Flight Lieutenant John Boothman, flying a Supermarine S.6B, negotiated the 50-kilometer course in record time with an average speed of 340.08 miles per hour. With the trophy securred, Flight Lieutenant G. H. Stainforth climbed aboard a second S.6B and promptly broke the world absolute speed record over a three-kilometer course. His average speed was a breathtaking 407.001 miles per hour.

Royal Air Force pilots Boothman and Stainforth were but the most visible of a team of men and one woman who made 1931 a glorious year for British aviation. The lone woman was Dame Fanny Lucy Houston, wealthy widow of the late Sir Robert Houston, and outspoken critic of the current Socialist Government for declining to finance a 1931 British entry in the competition. Literally putting her money where her mouth was, Lady Houston donated £100,000 thus assuring an entry in spite of the timorous British cabinet.

Rolls-Royce again built the R engines powering Supermarine's float-equipped racing planes. That Rolls was able to increase brake horsepower from 1,850 in 1929 to an astonishing 2,600 in 1931 was a great technical achievement. It was accomplished in part due to the fuel cocktails again formulated by Rod Banks; one for the Schneider and another for the record speed run. When Boothman ran the triangular Schneider pylon course, the fuel combination (Table 10-4) was heavily weighted with benzol and a dash of

The Curtiss XP-6A was a highly modified airframe built for the 1927 National Air Races. This view shows the surface radiators added to the upper and lower wing panels. Although an improvement over previous radiator arrangements, it was not drag free. Later NACA tests revealed that drag was significant, though less than more traditional radiator installations. Peter M. Bowers collection

Even as aerodynamic refinements were introduced during the 1920s and early 1930s, racing planes such as this Curtiss CR-1, powered by a Curtiss CD-12, engine required special fuels to inhibit detonation or knock. The Curtiss data sheet for this airplane indicates it used a 50–50 mixture of gasoline and benzol, and with this mixture its engine developed 410 horsepower at 2,180 rpm. Peter M. Bowers collection

methyl alcohol blended with 20 percent gasoline. The combination worked well, providing sufficient heating value (16,700 Btu/lb) to ensure that excessive fuel consumption would not be a problem.

Stainforth's speed record run had a different requirement. The British wanted desperately to break the 400-mile per hour barrier; a four-pass speed average of 399.9 miles per hour was just not acceptable. (That the first powered flight occurred just 28 years earlier illustrates the remarkable progress in aviation.) To give the R engine just a bit

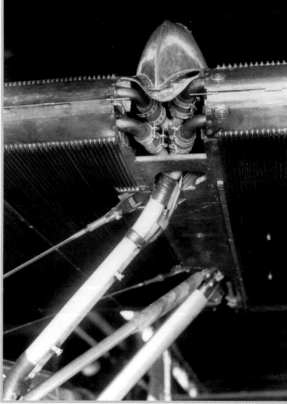

Details of the XF6C-6 wing surface radiator are revealed in this photograph. Seen here is the leading edge of the left wing panel. Headers distribute cooling water to the upper and lower wing surface radiator assemblies via the plumbing and hose connections illustrated. The curved fairing on top of the wing covered a small expansion tank. Wing structural supports and hoses were enclosed in streamline fairings. Peter M. Bowers collection

High-octane gasoline development in the United States surpassed the best efforts of Banks and his colleagues. By the beginning of World War II, the Air Corps routinely used 100-octane aviation gasoline, a product evolved through blending and improved refining techniques. Additional research demonstrated that ratings above 100 octane were feasible and the Performance Number system was adopted resulting in PN values of 100/130 and 115/145. The new rating system recognized that aircraft engines at times run relatively rich (more fuel) mixture ratios during takeoff and climb. Under these conditions, the onset of detonation was delayed.

A final gasoline development occurred toward the end of World War II. A new formulation known as "triptane" (2,2,3 trimethyl butane) was, for all practical purposes, detonation free. Produced in pilot plant quantities, triptane was too late for the war, but did see use in the postwar National Air Races at Cleveland. By this time, turbine engines were recognized as representing the future. A new era was just over the horizon. Triptane was not needed, only kerosene.

Curtiss installed a D-12A high-compression racing engine in the 1923 Navy R2C-1. The 50-50 gasoline-benzol mixture allowed this engine to deliver 500 horsepower at 2,300 rpm. This photograph clearly illustrates the wing radiators. Curtiss was the first to employ this type of radiator. Although it was well suited to racing, it was not practical for military purposes, due to its susceptibility to damage. Peter M. Bowers collection

more power, Banks elected to increase the amount of methyl alcohol in the formula by reducing the benzol content and eliminating all of the gasoline. The final mixture for the "sprint" version of the R engine was 30 percent benzol (benzine and toluene), 60 percent methyl alcohol and 10 percent acetone. This combination produced a relatively low heating value of 11,600 Btu/lb due to the heavy use of methyl alcohol. Fuel consumption rose accordingly. On the other hand, Stainforth had only to make four passes over a three-kilometer course, compared to the 50-kilometer distance of the Schneider race. Fuel capacity was not as critical for the record run. The advantage of the sprint fuel combination is found in the fact that Stainforth was able to run at somewhat higher manifold pressure without detonation. Both sprint and race fuel mixtures used tetraethyl lead as an additive.

Rod Banks brought fuel formulation to a high state on Britain's road to permanent possession of the Schneider Cup. These detonation resistant blends proved excellent for air racing, but were hardly adequate for commercial and military applications.

The last of a decade of Curtiss racers appeared at the 1930 National Air Races in Cleveland, Ohio. The XF6C-6 was modified from a Navy F6C-3 fighter. The most obvious alteration was elimination of the lower wing panels. The stock Curtiss D-12 was replaced by a more powerful Curtiss V-1570 engine. Wing surface radiators occupied about 70 percent of the wing area. The racer crashed while leading the Thompson race, killing its pilot, Marine Captain Arthur Page. Peter M. Bowers collection

Chapter 11

In Conclusion

Things always seem fairer when we look back at them, and it is out of that inaccessible tower of the past that Longing leans and beckons.

James Russell Lowell • *Literary Essays, vol. 1 [1864–1890]*
A Few Bits of Roman Mosaic

The historian's backward glance is antithetical to the oracle's vision. Both can be interesting, even fascinating, but divining the future is filled with risk. Conversely, writing history is greatly benefited greatly by unimpeded hindsight. Consider the less than perceptive prediction of a 1910 sage: "It is in the highest degree unlikely that the expectations of the lay public with regard to the new science [of aeronautics] will be realized."[1] Perhaps the kindest thing that may be said about this prophecy is its lack of equivocation. Note that in 1910 the world speed record was 68 miles per hour. Only two decades later Supermarine's graceful S.6B breached the 400 miles per hour speed barrier! Expectations were not only reached, but exceeded beyond the wildest imagination of anyone in 1910.

Lieutenant Colonel L. F. R. Fell was a little more prescient in a prediction he made in 1930: "Broadly speaking," Fell said, "it may be stated that the limit of power output per unit of [piston engine] cylinder capacity has not yet been reached . . ."[2] Just one year later, probably much sooner than Fell could have imagined, his prediction was confirmed in spades. The 1929 Rolls-Royce R engine developed 0.85 horsepower per cubic inch of displacement, an impressive performance. In 1931 the Rolls Schneider engine was producing 1.05 horsepower for every cubic inch, an astonishing 23 percent increase. Win some, lose some. In any event, the purpose of this writing is not to look ahead, but to look back and draw conclusions about what role, if any, air racing played in the evolution of World War II fighter aircraft.

Pulitzer and Schneider races were dominated by Curtiss biplane racers during the early 1920s. Exemplifying this class of racers were the Curtiss R-6 models built for the Army in 1922. Small, compact and finely detailed, the R-6 racers were capable of over 200 miles per hour. Their Curtiss D-12 engines relied upon wing surface radiators for cooling. John Garrett collection

THE ROLE OF AIR RACING

The role of air racing in promoting high-speed military aircraft design must be dissected into temporal components. United States government interest and financing bolstered air racing from 1920 through 1925. This took the form of contracts with Verville, Thomas-Morse, Loening, and Curtiss for the design and construction of racing airplanes. A case may be made for the United States that government involvement in racing during this era led to improved pursuit aircraft, Curtiss products being the best, though not the only, example. Curtiss aircraft were far and away the most successful, with convincing victories in both the Pulitzer and the Schneider contests. There is little doubt Curtiss pursuit designs benefited from corporate racing experience, both with respect to aerodynamic cleanness and engine development. The racing effort produced a body of knowledge in the form of wind tunnel experiments and flight test results. Designs were analyzed, tests were made and records kept such that when the next design project rolled around, this information was readily available.

Equally important, there was a technical continuity to the Curtiss racing program. Curtiss designer William Wait, Jr., illustrates this fact, as does William Gilmore, Curtiss chief engineer. Wait's tenure at Curtiss began in 1917, and extended well beyond the racing years. His initial race project involvement was with the privately financed Curtiss-Cox machines designed by Gilmore and built for the 1920 Gordon Bennett race. During the ensuing years, Wait gradually assumed greater responsibly, eventually becoming race airplane project engineer. Along the way he helped develop the then-revolutionary wing surface radiator system—he was co-holder of two patents in this regard. Gilmore, in his capacity as chief engineer, was intimately involved in many of the Curtiss racers. Although he eventually departed the company, Gilmore left the racing projects in Bill Wait's capable hands. The continuity of accumulated technical knowledge—corporate memory—was preserved.

During the late 1920s and throughout the 1930s, however, race plane design was the province of private individuals, usually working with meager budgets. Federal government participation in air racing tapered off dramatically after 1925. "The story

Several low-wing monoplanes were built for racing in the decade after World War I. Among them were two Bee-Line BR-1 racers designed by Harry Booth and built during 1922 by a new enterprise, Aerial Engineering Corporation. Race 18, shown here, incorporated wing surface radiators and retractable landing gear. It had a top speed of 177 miles per hour. John Garrett collection

A serious trend toward monoplane designs for American racing planes commenced in 1929 with the successful Travel Air Mystery Ship. It also began a domination of air-cooled radial engines in the Thompson Trophy classic during 8 of the next 10 years. The Travel Air sported a Wright engine, but during the 1930s all winning entries used Pratt & Whitney engines except for the 1936 Caudron and 1937 Folkerts SK-3 racers. Beech via John Garrett collection

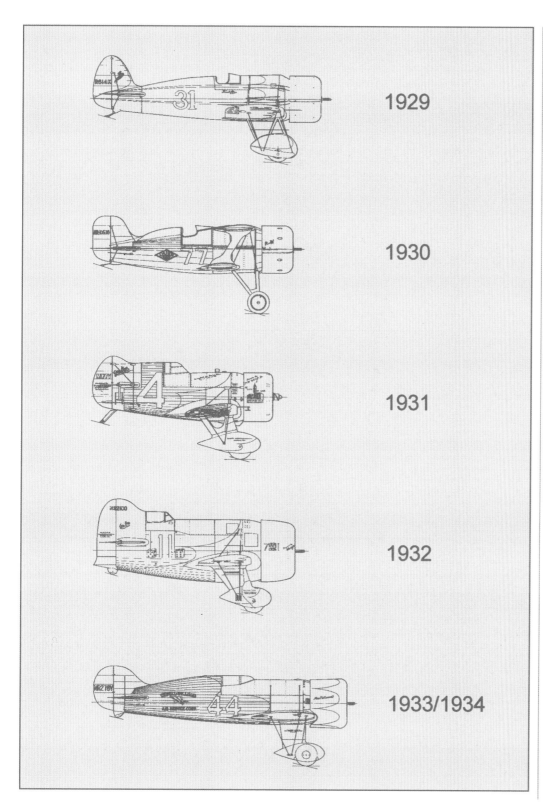

1929

1930

1931

1932

1933/1934

For air racing to have made identifiable technical contributions to American World War II fighter designs, it would have come from racers designed and proven prior to 1935. This was the pivotal year, due to the lead time necessary for design and development of the fighters available when America entered the conflict. Illustrated here are the Thompson Trophy champions from 1929 through 1934. (In 1935, the race was won by a high-wing multi-place cabin airplane, the Howard DGA-6.) Of all the racers illustrated in this figure, only the Wedell-Williams could even be considered for conversion to an Army or Navy fighter plane. By 1935, however, the gallant racer was obsolete and unsuitable by virtually any standard.

the next year [1926] was very different," Bill Wait reported in *Aero Digest*. "The Pulitzer Trophy Race was abandoned, and no new racing planes were built."[3] The United States sought to capture the 1926 Schneider event with three reconstituted 1925 Curtiss biplane racers. It was a futile attempt. Italy's team arrived with the Macchi M.39 racer, a low-wing monoplane harbinger of the future. Major Mario de Bernardi rounded the Schneider course in his M.39 with a 15 miles per hour advantage over second place finisher Lieutenant Christian Frank, flying a Curtiss R3C-2. No biplane would ever again win the Schneider contest.

Quite a few articles appeared in the aviation press touting the advantages bestowed by air racing on contemporary pursuit aircraft design. The first appeared in 1929, four years after the last new Curtiss racer took wing, and coincident with Doug Davis' victory over both the Army and Navy entrants in Event 26 at Cleveland that year. These articles decried, to one degree or another, the expiration of government sponsorship of race aircraft design. Competitive military participation in the National Air Races, although greatly diminished, continued until 1930, when Marine Captain Arthur Page was killed in his Curtiss XF6C-6 during the Thompson Trophy contest.[4] From this point forward until the beginning of World War II, air racing was exclusively a civilian affair.[5]

The British experience was similar. Schneider Cup racing through 1931 seems to have been beneficial to the development of the Rolls-Royce Merlin

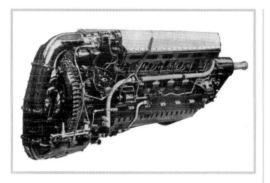

For all out speed, Europeans favored the liquid-cooled engine such as the Rolls-Royce "R" engine, shown here, and used in the Supermarine S6.B. This class of power plant lent itself to smaller frontal areas and greater power outputs, the latter due to the fact that uniform cooling was more easily obtained at that point in time with this medium. Dan Whitney collection

and Supermarine Spitfire. The Merlin had less swept volume and was an entirely new design, but surely lessons learned from the R engine guided Rolls designers in developing the Merlin. Supermarine designer R. J. Mitchell laid down lines for the famous Spitfire in 1935. His experience with the Schneider racers, especially in regard to aerodynamic cleanness, is revealed in the elegant Spitfire lines. The S.6B and the Spitfire were two entirely different airframes, aside from the fact that one was a float plane and the other a land plane. The Spitfire was a blend of later technologies including the wing plan form, cantilever flying surfaces, airfoil selection, retractable landing gear and pressurized tunnel radiator cooling system. The ancestral S.6B contribution to the Spitfire genes is found in the tight packaging of the fuselage and overall attention to drag reduction.

Because United States military racing plane sponsorship virtually evaporated after 1925, correlation between subsequent racing and military pursuit aircraft is impossible. It could be said that any later racing experience contributed in some measure by confirming the general need for clean aerodynamic designs and more powerful engines. This was already apparent as a result of work by the NACA, military investigations and corporate research, often in collaboration with academic institutions. Even this abstraction is untenable if logic is applied. Consider the following tenets:

1. Detail race plane design information and supporting analyses, wind tunnel results and flight test data must be recorded if it is eventually going to be useful in future designs. For example, tests must be conducted such that variables are minimized and controlled. Ideally, one parameter is varied at a time to understand its significance and impact on overall performance.

The last major big-bore American race plane built before World War II was Roscoe Turner's LTR-14 Meteor. Designed around a Pratt & Whitney Twin Wasp R-1830, Turner got off to a slow start in the 1937 Thompson, with a third-place finish. In 1938 and 1939, however, Turner was victorious. Having won the 1934 event, he became the only pilot to win the trophy three times. Emil Strasser photo via Gerry Liang collection

To do this, moreover, requires careful notation be made of indicated air speed, engine operating data, atmospheric conditions and the like. This scenario rarely if ever occurred in context with civilian racing projects.

2. Testing must be conducted in a controlled environment. A major interest with respect to pursuit aircraft is maximum speed under a variety of conditions. Pylon race results produce average speeds, more often than not at or near sea level. This tells little about the absolute maximum speed which can only be inferred. Nor does it indicate expected high speed at any given altitude unless and until the data are reduced to standard conditions and then extrapolated by calculation. Another complicating factor or variable occurs because pylon racing takes place in a three-dimensional arena. There is both lateral and vertical movement as the aircraft rounds the course. The race course is surveyed to determine its length and this can be done quite accurately. The distance any pilot negotiates around the pylons is by definition greater than the measured course length. He must fly outside the pylon markers or be penalized. Nor is the flight path on each lap of a multilap race precisely the same. Pilot skill, race traffic and turbulence alter the actual flight path from one lap to the next. The flight path thus becomes a semicontrolled variable at best, and uncontrolled at worst. A much better indicator of race plane performance is the speed achieved over a measured straight course for record purposes, or in the Shell Speed Dashes used for qualification purposes during the National Air Races for a few years.

3. Race plane design and performance data would have to be disseminated within the aeronautical community. The popular phrase today is "technology transfer." Without this vital step, any benefit air racing might have offered becomes moot. Information transfer rarely happened in the 1930s and then only in a super-ficial way. Real or perceived speed secrets were protected for competitive reasons or because substantive data did not exist in the first place.

4. For air racing to have contributed to World War II fighter designs, the data had to be available in a timely way. There was a substantial time lag between the time a new fighter design was initiated, production began, and the airplane entered service use. As the data in Table 11-2 reveal, this process typically consumed several years. First-line

Although Turner's racer was the best of the American breed, it represented dated technology compared to Air Corps pursuit planes in the design pipeline. Elegantly simple in appearance, the Meteor still employed fixed landing gear, as well as fabric covering on portions of the fuselage. New pursuit designs were of all-metal construction and routinely utilized retractable gear. Emil Strasser photo via Gerry Liang collection

Earl Ortman was a perennial challenger for the Thompson Trophy, flying this Keith Rider R-3 design. The aircraft was designed and built for the 1934 MacRobertson Race. Originally built to use a Pratt & Whitney Wasp Jr. engine, a larger Wasp was installed for the 1936 season, and by 1937 it was modified for a Twin Wasp Jr. Rider used the 1937 design as the basis for a pursuit proposal to the Air Corps. Emil Strasser photo via Gerry Liang collection

The final prewar National Air Race program took place at Cleveland Airport over the Labor Day weekend of 1939. One day before the races began, Germany invaded Poland to launch World War II. Cliff Henderson retired from his post as managing director after the 1939 races. Pearl Harbor was attacked 27 months later. John Garrett collection

Table 11-1

Lead Times From Design Initiation to Production
American Fighters Used In World War II Combat

Type	Design Initiated	First Flight	Production Started	Design to Production	Remarks
P-38	03/36	01/39	08/39	41 Months	
P-39	06/36	04/39	08/39	38 Months	
P-40	03/37	10/38	04/39	25 Months	Derivative of P-36
P-47	06/40	05/41	09/40	3 Months	Derivative of P-44
P-51	04/40	10/40	05/40	1 Month	Emergency order by British
P-63	02/41	12/42	09/42	19 Months	
F2A	11/35	12/37	06/38	31 Months	
F4F	07/36	09/37	08/39	37 Months	
F4U	04/38	05/40	03/41	35 Months	

Source: Francis H. Dean, *America's Hundred Thousand, U.S. Production Fighter Aircraft of World War II*, Schiffer Publishing Ltd, Atglen, Pennsylvania, 1997.

fighters available to our military when hostilities commenced on December 7, 1941, consisted of the Air Corps Bell P-39, Curtiss P-40, and Navy Brewster F2A and Grumman F4F. The design effort for the F2A began at the end of 1935, while the P-39 and F4F designs began in 1936. Curtiss' P-40 design, a derivative of the Curtiss P-36, began in early 1937. The

average length of time between design initiation and start of production for these four aircraft was 33 months, almost three years. For race technology to have had any material impact on our fighter designs in use when the war began, the technology had to come from racers existing in September, 1934, when the races were conducted.

The best of the 1934 racers was the Wedell-Williams Model 44, featuring a fixed main landing gear, tail skid, externally braced wooden wings and welded steel tube fuselage structure having wooden formers and stringers. Part of the airframe structure was fabric covered. Differences between Model 44 and the early World War II American fighters are striking evidence of how newer technology was influencing the design of these aircraft.

Aerodynamically speaking, these mid-1930s fighter designs incorporated retractable landing gear, steerable tail wheels, cantilever flying surfaces, metal construction, flush riveting and newer NACA airfoils with improved lift-to-drag ratios. The NACA four- and five-digit series airfoils were thick enough to accept retractable landing gear as well as to accommodate fuel cells and armament, thereby further reducing parasite drag. The thin NACA M-10 section used for the Wedell wing could not accommodate

these features. The fabled fighter aircraft of Bell, Curtiss, Grumman, Lockheed, North American, and Vought were unique products of their respective design teams.

It is true that a few racing personalities worked for these airframe companies—Art Chester at North American and Bob Hall with Grumman, for instance. Lessons learned in designing and building race planes no doubt added to their overall knowledge and perhaps facilitated problem solving. There was, however, no material racing contribution or influence on World War II fighters in the United States. Indeed, after about 1934, race plane designs did not appreciably advance due, one imagines, to a perennial lack of financing in those Depression years. The creations of Keith Rider, Larry Brown, Harry Crosby and a handful of others merely adopted design features—retractable landing gear, for example—already incorporated in high-performance military pursuit designs. The need for streamlining to reduce drag was well understood both theoretically and in practice.

This Seversky P-35 pursuit from the 1st Pursuit Group, 17th Pursuit Squadron, was one of the new breed of all-metal aircraft coming into service by the mid-1930s. Ironically, the P-35 did not benefit from racing technology, but several examples became race aircraft in the hands of civilian pilots. Emil Strasser photo via Gerry Liang collection

Curtiss was a prime competitor to Seversky. This P-36A was a contemporary to the P-35. The photograph was taken in August 1939, and shows the P-35 in the markings of the 20th Pursuit Group, 79th Pursuit Squadron. The design was a far cry from the wooden biplane racers Curtiss produced for the Pulitzer and Schneider races. Emil Strasser photo via Gerry Liang collection

Late in the decade prior to World War II, the Navy finally abandoned biplane fighters in favor of monoplane configurations. Sturdy Grumman biplanes like this F3F-2 continued in service into 1939, however. Only three concessions to advancing technology are apparent: retractable landing gear, NACA-type engine cowling, and metal fuselage construction. Peter M. Bowers collection

Consider that the last major new racing plane designed and built before the war was not fundamentally different from Jimmy Wedell's Model 44. This was the Laird-Turner *Meteor*, which Roscoe Turner flew to victory in the 1938 and 1939 Thompson Trophy Race. It was the design creation of Howard Barlow at the University of Minnesota.

Turner began exploring the possibility of a new racer with Barlow in November 1934. A year later Barlow's thoughts were down on paper in the form of a preliminary design. Turner approved of what he saw and detail design commenced. Construction of the airplane began in the summer of 1936, but was not completed until March 1937.[6]

Aside from a cantilever wing and more powerful Twin Wasp engine, design and construction techniques were essentially the same as found in the old Wedell racers. Turner's plane retained a fixed landing gear in an age when using retractable gear was becoming *de rigeur*. Contrast this with the state-of-the-art exhibited by a new generation of

Wind Tunnels in the United States

Year	Location	Shape	Throat Size	Remarks
1919	Standford University	Round	6 feet	
1920	Air Corps, Wright Field	Round	5 feet	
1923	Curtiss	Round	7 feet	
1925	University of Michigan	Octagonal	8 feet	
1925	New York University	Square	9 feet	
1927	NACA Langley	Round	20 feet	
1928	NACA Langley	Round	5 feet	
1930	NACA Langley	Rectangular	7 x 10 feet	
1930	Calif. Institute of Technology	Round	10 feet	
1931	NACA Langley	Rectangular		Full scale tunnel
1936	NACA Langley	Round	8 feet	High speed tunnel
1937	Mass. Institute of Technology	Elliptical	10 feet	

Source: Karl D. Wood, *Technical Aerodynamics*, McGraw-Hill, 1947, p. 124.

Grumman Wildcats followed the colorful F3F biplanes into Navy service. This F4F-3 model was at Wright Field when this photo was recorded in 1942. A midwing/fuselage juncture allowed Grumman to retain the retractable landing gear configuration used on the earlier F3F biplane model. The Wildcat was the Navy's first-line fighter when America entered the war. Peter M. Bowers collection

fighter aircraft designed during the *same* 1935–1936 time period as the *Meteor*. Turner's airplane had pleasing lines, was reasonably streamlined, and meticulously constructed. In summary, it was a well-executed but quite dated product, representing early 1930 technology.

The aviation business is highly technical due to the very nature of its product. Outside the aeronautical community, scientific and engineering activities associated with designing and building aircraft are pretty much invisible to the general public. Still they exist. The period between 1920 and 1940 was particularly fertile, marked by increasing aeronautical research, engineering and development. This is perhaps best illustrated by the productivity of the NACA in this period. Augmenting the NACA was research by both the academic community and the aviation industry. One of the primary tools in this research was the wind tunnel, and at least 12 were in operation in the United States before World War II started (Table 11-2). By the end of the war the number of tunnel facilities had grown to about 40.[7]

A FINAL WORD

There is reasonable and credible evidence to conclude that air racing played a role in shaping pursuit aircraft designs in the early 1920s. (Author Thomas Foxworth's seminal book, *The Speed Seekers*, exhaustively treats the beneficial impact racing had on aircraft design progress.) Beyond that point in time, there is no basis to believe air racing advanced pursuit design in any tangible form.

Did air racing provide a grueling aerial laboratory to validate airframe and engine design during

The unconventional Bell P-39 Airacobra was just entering squadron service with the Air Corps when Pearl Harbor was attacked. With the engine amidship and provision for a 37-millimeter cannon in the nose, this Allison-powered fighter had nothing in its heritage even remotely connected to prewar racing designs. Pictured here is a YP-39 service test model, photographed in October 1940. Bell via Birch Matthews collection

Curtiss P-40 fighters were the mainstay of Army Air Corps fighter squadrons when America entered the war. Like the P-39, the Curtiss fighter was on the verge of obsolescence when the war began. Early P-39s and P-40s lacked adequate offensive armament, armor protection, self-sealing fuel tanks, and high-altitude performance. Emil Strasser photo via Gerry Liang collection

Wind tunnel experimental investigations provided a wealth of aerodynamic data for the aviation industry. Government, university, and corporate facilities were active during the decade before World War II. Shown here is a P-36 model being installed in the wind tunnel at Curtiss' Kenmore facility at Buffalo, New York, circa 1938. Hal Andrews collection

North American designed the Mustang for Great Britain, but it was eventually adopted by the Army Air Force. Illustrated here is the Allison-powered XP-51. When equipped with a Rolls-Royce Merlin, the Mustang became one of the best and most versatile fighters of World War II. It soldiered on in Korea and today is king of the closed-course pylon races at Reno, Nevada. North American via Birch Matthews collection

the 1930s? The answer is no. During a 1937 meeting of the Institute of Aeronautical Sciences, Robert Insley of Pratt & Whitney makes the following points:[8]

"American racing engines with few exceptions have been standard commercial or military models. The information resulting from racing service, therefore, simply confirms or supplements that already obtained from other sources. Even the fact that these engines are operated for the greater part of their useful lives at outputs well above normal service ratings is not of great significance, because modern development testing is such a drastic process that few engines reach racing status without having accomplished many hours of testing under conditions equally severe."

The notion that 1930s air racing was an aerial proving ground influencing World War II fighter design is a romantic myth. It just did not happen. Racing was then, as it is now, a tremendously exciting sport enjoyed by tens of thousands. It was a diversion during a time of national economic depression. It was a fascinating spectacle during a time of exceptional public aviation interest. It was a forum in which women could participate, during a time of male domination in virtually all matters outside the home. That was all it was. That was enough . . . .

CHAPTER 1

[1] With the arrival of the jet age, it has become common practice to describe the speed of the airplane in Mach numbers. Mach number is the ratio of the true air speed of the airplane to the speed of sound through the air. The speed of sound varies with air temperature. Considering the standard air temperature at sea level = 59 degrees Fahrenheit, the speed of sound is approximately 761 miles per hour. At higher elevations where the air temperature is lower, the speed of sound diminishes. Thus, at 20,000 feet (-12 degrees Fahrenheit standard temperature) the speed of sound is around 707 miles per hour. The speed of sound (V) relationship between sea level and a given altitude is: $V = V_{s/l} (T/T_{s/l})^{0.5}$.

[2] The terms "fighter" and "pursuit" are used interchangeably in this narrative although when discussing specific Army or Navy airplanes, precise designations will be used. The reason is one of convenience. There were differences between U.S. Army and Navy designations for the same type of combat airplane between 1920 and 1939. Beginning in 1922, the Navy adopted the type designation letter "F" for "fighter," as in Grumman F4F. After using a variety of designation codes for this same type of combat aircraft, the Army standardized on "P" for "pursuit." This occurred in 1926 and remained in use until June 11, 1948. After that date, the letter "F" was used. Thus, the P-51 became the F-51.

[3] Satchel Paige (1909–1982) was a pitching superstar in the old Negro leagues during the years 1924 to 1948. He entered the major leagues with the Cleveland Indians at 42, an age when most athletes had long since retired. His fast ball no longer had blazing speed, but his control was still masterful. This attribute coupled with a comical and disconcerting windup baffled more than one major league batter.

[4] Thomas G. Foxworth, *The Speed Seekers*, Doubleday & Company, Inc., New York, 1974, p. 92.

[5] Historian and author Don Berliner's book, *Victory Over the Wind* (Van Nostrand Reinhold Company, 1983), is an excellent history of the absolute world air speed records.

[6] Wendel's mark stood for 30 years until Darryl Greenamyer pushed his Grumman F8F-2 *Bearcat* to 482.462 miles per hour at Edwards Air Force Base in 1969. Steve Hinton in the *Red Baron* RB-51 raised the record to 499.059 miles per hour 10 years later. Lyle Shelton in another Grumman F8F-2 currently holds the world piston engine speed record of 528.329 miles per hour.

[7] Thompson Products donated a trophy cup that year. It was the forerunner of the famous Thompson Trophy formally instituted in 1930.

[8] The Curtiss XP-3A ("X" indicating experimental) was part of a Wright Field program to improve performance of the standard P-3A model. Engineering Division personnel equipped the first production P-3A with a cowling and propeller spinner during May 1929. By June, top speed was boosted by 24 percent to 190 miles per hour. Curtiss was simultaneously evaluating its own cowling design to improve speed. The aircraft utilized in Event 26, however, was the Wright Field model.

[9] The origins of the Air Force are first found in the Army Signal Corps. The first aviation office was established in 1907 as the Aeronautical Division of the Signal Corps. This became the Signal Corps Aviation Section in 1914. With American involvement in World War I, General John J. Pershing removed air units in France from Signal Corps control in June 1917. The Army Air Service was established as a result. The Air Service became the Army Air Corps on July 2, 1926. The enabling legislation was the Air Corps Act of 1926, based primarily on the Morrow Board report recommendations. The Air Corps became the Army Air Forces on June 20, 1941. On September 18, 1947, the United States Air Force was created as an independent arm of our military forces.

[10] The "DL" designation stood for Detroit-Lockheed. A single DL-2 was built and used as a company demonstrator by Detroit Aircraft Corporation. The DL-2 had a Detroit-built metal fuselage and wooden wing structure from Lockheed in Burbank. It was subsequently equipped with retractable landing gear and denoted as the DL-2A, in reality the prototype Lockheed Altair. At the time Detroit Aircraft submitted a specification to Wright Field, however, the designation was DL-2 Sirius.

[11] The original Detroit Aircraft Corporation specification for the XP-900 called for a supercharged "SV-1550" engine. The as-built configuration did not have a supercharger installation, however.

[12] Navy evaluation of single-wing fighters began in 1932. Prototypes were built by Boeing (XF7B-1), Curtiss (XF13C-1 and -2) and Northrop (XFT-1 and -2). None advanced beyond the experimental stage.

[13] Francis H. Dean, *America's Hundred Thousand*, Schiffer Publishing Ltd., Atglen, Pennsylvania, 1997, p. 7.

CHAPTER 2

[1] Neil Armstrong was the first human being to set foot on the moon. Two famous quotes resulted from that phenomenal journey. The first marked the arrival of Apollo 11 at its destination:

"Houston, Tranquility Base here. The Eagle has landed." Upon disembarking from the Lunar Module, Armstrong radioed his memorable ". . . one giant leap for mankind" message.

2 Reims has also been spelled "Rheims" in some U.S. publications, although this appears to be an older custom no longer observed. It should be noted that on the official program for the races the spelling is Reims.

3 *New York Times*, August 8, 1909, Part 3, p. 4.

4 In English units of measure, each long leg of the course was 2.33 miles. The shorter legs were 0.78 mile giving a total course distance of 6.21 miles.

5 *New York Times*, August 6, 1909, p. 5.

6 *New York Times*, September 26, 1909, Part 6, p. 6. Curtiss gave an extended interview to a *Times* reporter shortly after his return from Europe in 1909. When asked about his Reims *Racer* he stated that it had a 50-horsepower engine. Curtiss repeated the power level in a feature article for *Country Life in America*, November, 1909. At least one source indicates the engine developed 60 horsepower (*Curtiss Aircraft, 1907-1947*, by Peter M. Bowers, Naval Institute Press, Annapolis, 1987, p. 37). All early engine power testimonials should be taken as approximate and based, at best, on calculations rather than accurate test stand results.

7 *New York Times*, July 25, 1909, p. 2.

8 *New York Times*, August 24, 1909, p. 1.

9 The term aeroplanist (pilot) was in vogue for a few years during the 1900s. It gradually fell into disuse.

10 For the history of this land grant, see Robert Cameron Gillingham's *The Rancho San Pedro*, Cole-Holmquist Press, revised edition, 1983. See also *Time and the Terraced Land* by Augusta Fink, Howell-North Books, Berkeley, 1996. Rancho San Pedro borders were irregular. In terms of the present, the northern boundary is represented by Redondo Beach Blvd., Cressey Street and McMillan Street. The western end of the Rancho was the Pacific Ocean in the city of Redondo Beach. To the east, the Rancho bordered the Los Angeles River. The southern boundary ended at what is now the Los Angeles—Long Beach Harbor. Excluded from Rancho San Pedro was the Palos Verdes Peninsula.

11 *New York Times*, December 23, 1909, p. 11.

12 It is historically noteworthy that skirmishes between promoters and regulating bodies are periodically repeated to this day.

13 *New York Times*, January 13, 1910, p. 1.

14 *New York Times*, December 24, 1909, p. 2.

15 Ibid.

16 Ibid.

17 Richard P. Hallion, Editor, *The Wright Brothers, Heirs of Prometheus*, National Air & Space Museum, Washington, D.C., 1978, p. 116.

18 John D. Anderson, Jr., *A History of Aerodynamics*, Cambridge University Press, Cambridge, England, 1997, p. 263. This is an excellent and highly readable book covering the progression of aerodynamics literally from ancient times to contemporary supersonic flight.

19 Reynolds number is defined by the equation $N_R = \$VD \,/\,$, where \$ is the specific weight, V is the fluid velocity, D is a descriptive dimension and is the fluid viscosity. For the specific application of a wing test section in a wind tunnel, V is the air velocity through the tunnel test section, and the representative dimension is the wing chord. The values of specific weight and viscosity represent properties of the air in the tunnel.

20 Anderson, op. cit.

CHAPTER 3

1 The term stress related to materials of construction is defined as the force per unit of area. This is symbolically expressed as $S = P/A$ where P is the applied load in pounds and A is the cross-sectional area in square inches in the English system of measurement. Thus the resulting stress value is given in pounds per square inch (psi).

2 Barbara Tuchman, *The Guns of August*, Random House, Inc., New York, 1994 (paperback edition). The official date for the start of World War I is July 28, 1914.

3 Thomas G. Foxworth, *The Speed Seekers*, Doubleday & Company, Inc., New York, 1974, p. 87.

4 Derek N. James, *Schneider Trophy Aircraft, 1913–1931*, Putnam & Company Ltd., London, 1981, p. xii (preface).

5 Characteristics Sheet, Curtiss Aeorplane & Motor Company, Inc., Garden City, NY.

6 At that point, the military procurement system allowed other companies to bid on the designs of their competition. Boeing simply underbid Thomas-Morse and won the 200-plane contract. The order put Boeing firmly in the military aircraft business.

7 The Lawrence J-1 was the predecessor to the Wright J-4 engine.

8 The S.4 established a new floatplane speed record (and British air speed record) of 226.75 miles per hour prior to being shipped to the United States for the 1925 Schneider contest.

9 Derek James in his excellent book, *Schneider Trophy Aircraft, 1913–1931*, notes that flutter may have been the problem. He suggests that aileron reversal or the failure of a wing flap and aileron interconnection system might also have caused the accident. In any event, pilot Biard survived the accident, thus preventing a complete disaster.

10 C. F. Andrews and E. B. Morgan, *Supermarine Aircraft Since 1914*, Naval Institute Press, Anapolis, Maryland, 1987, p. 180.

11 Italian pilot Francesco Agello set the world speed first in 1933 with a speed of 423.824 miles per hour, breaking the old record held by the British in the S.6B at 407.001 miles per hour. Agello once again broke the record speeding across the course at 440.678 miles per hour in 1934.

12 In reality, water in the engine cooling passages was maintained in liquid state, but under pressure. After passing from the engine, the heated liquid was allowed to flash to steam.

CHAPTER 4

1 Lesley Forden, *Glory Gamblers*, Ballantine Books, New York, 1961, p.21. Jim Dole was born in 1877 and died in 1958.

2 American missionaries from New England arrived in the Hawaiian Islands during 1820. Dole's cousin, Sandford B. Dole, became president of the Republic of Hawaii (formerly known as the Sandwich Islands) after native Queen Liliuokalani was deposed in 1893. Jim Dole moved to the Islands six years later in 1899. He was a typical American entrepreneur who made his fortune by harvesting and then canning pineapple. Canned pineapples could then be exported to the United States. This unique fruit proved

extremely popular with Americans.

3 The Dole $25,000 first place prize money amounts to $521,000 in current day dollars. Second place money is equivalent to $208,000 today. See *The Value of a Dollar*, Scott Derks, editor, Manly, Incorporated, Washington, D.C., 1994.

4 Aviation pioneers Allen and Malcolm Loughead formed their first aviation enterprise in 1913. It was known as the Alco Hydro-Aeroplane Company, and was named after the principal financial investor, Max Mamlock, who ran the Alco Cab Company of San Francisco. The brothers designed and built their first airplane, the Model G. The company was in business only briefly and faded from the scene in 1913. The Loughead Aircraft Manufacturing Company of Santa Barbara (formed in 1916 and liquidated during 1921) was their second aviation venture. The seminal product of this organization was the diminutive S-1 Sport Biplane, which used the molded wooden fuselage concept. A fiscal failure (a ready market did not exist), the design was nonetheless technically sound and certainly innovative.

5 The molding pressure was 15 to 20 pounds per square inch.

6 Gerald F. Vultee, "Fabrication of the Lockheed Vega Airplane Fuselage," paper presented to the Society of Automotive Engineers, Los Angeles Aeronautic Meeting, and reprinted in the S.A.E. *Journal*, November 1928. Jerry Vultee replaced John Northrop as Lockheed chief engineer when the latter departed the company in June 1928.

7 Walter J. Boyne, *Beyond the Horizons, The Lockheed Story*, St. Martin's Press, New York, 1998, p. 29.

8 John D. Anderson, Jr., *A History of Aerodynamics*, Cambridge University Press, Cambridge, England, 1998, p. 331. See also the 1927 NACA annual report.

9 Robert Schlaifer, *Development of Aircraft Engines*, Harvard Graduate School of Business Administration, Harvard University, Boston, 1950, p. 260.

10 Fred E. Weick, *The Drag of a J-5 Radial Air-Cooled Engine*, National Advisory Committee for Aeronautics, Technical Note No. 292, July 1928.

11 Fred E. Weick, *Drag and Cooling With Various Forms of Cowling For a Whirlwind Engine in a Cabin Monoplane*, National Advisory Committee for Aeronautics, Technical Note No. 301, November 1928.

12 Ibid., p. 21.

13 Ibid. See appendix to Technical Note No. 301 prepared by Thomas Carroll.

14 Anderson, op.cit., p. 336.

15 See for example, *Cooling of Airplane Engines at Low Air Speeds*, by Theodore Theodorsen, M. J. Brevoort and George W. Stickle, National Advisory Committee for Aeronautics Report No. 593, June 2, 1936. A subsequent report by Brevoort, Stickle and Herman H. Ellerbrock, Jr., *Cooling Tests of a Single-Row Radial Engine With Several NACA Cowlings*, National Advisory Committee for Aeronautics, Report No. 596, August 20, 1936, is also instructive as to the approach fostered by Theodorsen. A particularly unique cowling experiment was evaluated by Theodorsen, Brevoort, Stickle and M. N. Gough, wherein cooling air was exhausted not from the aft end of the cowl, but discharged through an annular gap at the nose of the cowl form in a region of low pressure. See *Full-Scale Tests of a New Type NACA Nose-Slot Cowling*, National Advisory Committee for Aeronautics Report No. 595, June 5, 1936.

16 Richard Sanders Allen, *Revolution in the Sky*, The Stephen Greene Press, Brattleboro, Vermont, 1967, p. 33.

17 Anderson, op.cit., p. 335. See also *Quest for Performance: The Evolution of Modern Aircraft*, NASA SP-468, National Aeronautics and Space Administration, Washington, D.C., 1985.

18 Lockheed internal memorandum by Richard Von Hake, May 9, 1934.

19 Allen, *op. cit.*

20 Correspondence from Robert E. Gross to Tiffany Carter, August 28, 1934.

21 Joseph P. Juptner, *U.S. Civil Aircraft Series* (Vol. 9), Tab Books, Blue Ridge Summit, Pennsylvania, 1993. P. 176.

22 Certificate of Airworthiness No. 443, issued to Air Commodore Sir Charles Kingsford Smith, Department of Defence, Commonwealth of Australia, September 26, 1934, p. 2. Australian documentation for the Kingsford Smith Altair was kindly provided by Ron Cuskelly.

23 Gross correspondence, *op. cit.*

24 The name "Anzac" is an acronym of the Australian and New Zealand Army Corps, which landed in Gallipoli during World War I. The name was revered and legislation had been passed prohibiting its commercial use. Kingsford Smith was forced to rename the airplane and chose *Lady Southern Cross*. Ironically, he had served at Gallipoli and meant no disrespect.

25 Gross correspondence, *op. cit.*

26 *New York Times*, August 30, 1934, p. 19.

27 Gross correspondence, *op. cit.*

28 Certificate of Airworthiness No. 443, Department of Defense Civil Aviation Branch), Commonwealth of Australia, September 26, 1934.

29 A small fraction of this weight growth was due to the added tanks, associated plumbing, fittings, attachment hardware and valving.

30 Numerous texts on aircraft stress analysis define these terms. See for example, *Fundamentals of Aircraft Structures* by Millard V. Barton, Prentice-Hall, Inc., 1948, pp. 12 and 39. Note that a factor of safety = 1.5 is representative. Under certain anticipated severe operating conditions or for specified components (i.e., castings) this value may be increased.

31 In addition to any of evidence suggesting structural modifications were undertaken in Australia, there would have been an almost total lack of sufficient engineering data, structural drawings, and basic understanding of the Lockheed design to locally alter or reinforce key Altair components. Had such modifications been made, the cognizant Australian authorities would surely have required a complete stress analysis and flight verification as proof that the Altair was still airworthy. In all probability the Australian certificate of airworthiness was issued based upon Lockheed's recommendations and the Group 2 certificate issued by the U.S. Department of Commerce.

32 *New York Times*, *op. cit.*

33 *New York Times*, October 3, 1934, p. 19.

34 New York Times, October 4, 1934, p. 11.

35 The handicap formula was $V = 140 (1 - 0.2 \, L / W - L) (P / A)^{1/3}$, where V = air speed; L = payload; W = gross weight; P = sea level maximum horsepower; and, A = wing area.

36 Terry Gwynn-Jones, *The Air Racers*, Pelham Books, Brisbane, 1983, p. 198.

37 *New York Times*, October 6, 1934, p. 17.

38 *New York Times*, September 22, 1935, Sec. II, p. 12.

CHAPTER 5

1 Phillip S. Meilinger, "The Impact of Technology and Design Choice on the Development of U.S. Fighter Aircraft," *American Aviation Historical Society Journal*, Vol. 36, No. 1, 1991, pp. 67–68.

2 The Event 26 race was advertised as five laps around a 10-mile course for a total of 50 miles. The recorded time for Davis' winning airplane was 14 minutes, 5.9 seconds, which is equivalent to 0.235 hours for an average speed of 194.9 miles/hour. However, 194.9 miles/hour x 0.235 hour yields a total distance of only 45.796 miles, not 50 miles. If the course was truly surveyed to be 10 miles in length, Davis' speed should have been credited at 212.79 miles/hour.

3 Detroit Aircraft Corporation Proposed Specification, Army Two-Seater Pursuit Airplane, XP-900, November 10, 1930.

4 The landing gear failed to extend and the pilot bailed out.

5 Benjamin S. Kelsey, *The Dragon's Teeth*, Smithsonian Institution Press, Washington, D.C., 1982, p. 51.

6 The prototype P-26 was built using Boeing funds and designated its Model 248. Three examples were built. When one of the aircraft was delivered to the Air Corps for further testing it was assigned Wright Field Project Number XP-936. The Air Corps bought the planes, designating them Y1P-26. The production variant, ordered during January 1933 became the P-26A.

7 Francis H. Dean, *America's Hundred-Thousand, U.S. Production Fighters of World War II*, Schiffer Publishing Ltd., Atglen, Pennsylvania, 1997, p.7.

CHAPTER 6

1 The methodology is taken from Laurence K. Loftin, Jr., *Quest for Performance: The Evolution of Modern Aircraft*, National Aeronautics and Space Administration, SP-468, Washington, D.C., 1985. See Appendix C.

2 Ibid. See Appendix A in Loftin's book.

CHAPTER 7

1 Available empty weight values cited (typically 1,500 pounds) for the Wedell-Williams racer are for the racer when equipped with a Pratt & Whitney Wasp Jr. engine. When fitted with the larger Wasp engine, airframe empty weight increased. Therefore, Table 5-6 reflects the removal of the Wasp Jr. and addition of the Wasp based upon Pratt & Whitney engine weight data.

2 The methodology used in determining performance may be ascertained from almost any text on the subject. See, for instance, *Introduction to Flight*, Fourth Edition, by John D. Anderson, Jr.

3 Thrust horsepower is the engine brake horsepower delivered to the propeller shaft multiplied by the propeller efficiency. This efficiency number is always less than 1.0, due to several factors and losses. For example, if an engine delivers 100 horsepower to the propeller shaft and the propeller efficiency is 85 percent, the amount of propulsive thrust horsepower is 100 x 0.85 = 85 horsepower.

4 Benjamin S. Kelsey, *The Dragon's Teeth*, Smithsonian Institution Press, Washington, D.C., 1982, p. 51.

5 Correspondence from H. P. Williams to Major C. W. Howard dated December 19, 1933. Attached to this letter was a one page data sheet describing the Model 44 racer.

6 Pratt & Whitney Aircraft, *Engine Model Designations and Characteristics*, Document PWA- SD 14, January 1, 1945, p. B-4. Turner's engine is identified as Serial Number 4838.

7 Mike Kusenda, Letters to the Editor of the *American Aviation Historical Society Journal*, Vol. 33, No. 4, 1988, p. 320.

8 World War II vintage R-1340 Wasps were rated at 600 horsepower using 92-octane fuel.

9 E. F. Bruhn, *Analysis and Design of Airplane Structures*, Tri-State Offset Company, Cincinnati, Ohio, 1943, p. D1.2. The Army and Navy determined load factors for each of the different types of aircraft in service use.

10 Uncertainties can arise due to variations in material strength properties and limitations in the analysis model for complex structures. The advent of computer modeling via finite element analysis has greatly enhanced the ability of stress analysts to accurately predict what loads a structure can withstand. Even so, a factor of safety is still applied to the design load requirement.

11 Correspondence from Captain A. J. Lyons to Wedell-Williams Air Service Corporation, February 8, 1934.

12 Don Berliner, *Victory Over the Wind*, Van Nostrand Reinhold Company, Incorporated, New York, 1983, p. 134. Wedell's record of 304.522 miles per hour was still considerably below the absolute air speed record of 423.824 miles per hour, set by Francesco Agello of Italy flying a Macchi-Castoldi MC.72 float plane.

13 Correspondence to Chief of the Air Corps, Major General Benjamin Foulois, from Captain Claire L. Chennault, February 14, 1934.

14 Ibid.

15 Ibid.

16 Wedell had earlier devised a "quick change" setup so that he could interchange the Wasp and Wasp Jr. on both the Model 44 and Model 45. When Jimmy Wedell was killed in an airplane accident in June 1934, Doug Davis was selected to fly the Model 44 in the National Air Races. He won the Bendix race using the Wasp Jr. engine. John Worthen placed second in the new Wasp-powered Model 45 in the cross-country classic. Davis next turned his attention to the Thompson Trophy Race after swapping engines with the Model 45. He was leading this race when he inadvertently cut a pylon. While attempting to circle the cut pylon, a requirement in the Thompson to avoid disqualification, the airplane stalled and crashed. Davis was killed and the racer demolished. Worthen, also entered in the Thompson, placed a slow third at 208 miles per hour.

17 Irving Brinton Holley, Jr., *Buying Aircraft: Matériel Procurement for the Army Air Forces*, U.S. Government Printing Office, Washington, D.C.,1964, p. 139. See also: Robert Hirsch, "Wedell-Williams Air Service Corp. and Air Racing," *American Aviation Historical Society Journal*, Vol. 33, No. 2, 1988, p. 116;

Lloyd S. Jones, *U.S. Fighters*, Aero Publishers, Incorporated, Fallbrook, California, 1975, p.80; and, Ray Wagner, *American Combat Planes*, Third Edition, Doubleday & Company, Incorporated, Garden City, New York, 1982, p. 237.

[18] Ibid.

[19] Employing competitive procurement in contracting for experimental airplanes posed real difficulties. Most manufacturers during these Depression years did not have the financial resources to compete if a sample aircraft was required. In the absence of sample aircraft for evaluation, the Air Corps could write an extremely tight specification to ensure a high degree of equity in the proposal responses. The risk with this approach was that one or more contractors might have worthy designs innovations or concepts that would not meet the specification or be overlooked. Conversely, if loose specifications were used the Air Corps might not get the desired product. And finally, creative new designs emanated not from the understaffed engineering group at Wright Field, but from individual designers and manufacturers.

[20] Ibid.

[21] For a discussion of the evolution of interceptor aircraft and the Bell XFM-1, see Chapter 1 in the book authored by Birch Matthews entitled *Cobra! Bell Aircraft Corporation 1934–1946*, Schiffer Publishing Ltd., Atglen, Pennsylvania, 1996.

[22] It is believed the designation stood for "Crosby Interceptor Pursuit." The number five was apparently indicative of his fifth model design.

CHAPTER 8

[1] William H. Severns and Howard E. Degler, *Steam, Air, and Gas Power*, John Wiley & Sons, Inc., New York, 1948, p. 409.

[2] Takashi Suzuki, *The Romance of Engines*, Society of Automotive Engineers, Inc., Warrendale, Pennsylvania, 1997, p. 21.

[3] Richard P. Hallion, *The Wright Brothers, Heirs of Prometheus*, Smithsonian Institution Press, Washington D.C., 1978, p. 128.

[4] *Development of Aeronautical Engines by the Army and Navy*, National Advisory Committee for Aeronautics, Technical Memorandum No. 9, March, 1921. Material presented by the NACA was taken from the *Air Service Newsletter*, Vol. 5, No. 9, March 3, 1921.

[5] C. S. Fliedner, *Condensed Data on the Aircraft Engines of the World*, National Advisory Committee for Aeronautics, Report No. 303, April, 1929, pp. 2–6.

[6] An excellent summary of the little-known and unusual Allison X-4520 engine may be found in Daniel D. Whitney's *Vees for Victory*, Schiffer Publishing Ltd., Atglen, Pennsylvania, 1998, pp. 20–21.

[7] The Wright-Martin Company was formed in 1915 when Wright & Company acquired the Glen L. Martin Company, thus forming the Wright-Martin Company. Wright had previously acquired the Simplex Automobile Company of Brunswick, New Jersey, giving it the infrastructure to manufacture internal combustion engines. Another acquisition was the General Aeronautic Company of America. The amalgamation was renamed the Wright-Martin Company. The firm was dissolved two years later (1919). The surviving organization was renamed Wright Aeronautical Corporation. It retained the Hispano-Suiza manufacturing license and commenced engine manufacturing operations in Brunswick.

[8] Although aluminum has excellent heat transfer properties, steel does not. In addition, dead air trapped in the threaded joint (between the steel cylinder liner and the aluminum casting) resulted in an effective partial heat transfer barrier. Storm windows and double glass pane windows in a house utilize this principle to minimize heat loss in the winter and heat gain in the summer. Temperatures resulting from combustion in a piston engine are discussed in *Aircraft Power Plants*, by Arthur P. Fraas, McGraw-Hill Company, Inc., New York, 1943, pp. 157–159. See also, Arthur B. Domonoske and Volney C. Finch, *Aircraft Engines*, John Wiley & Sons, Inc., New York, 1936, p. 178.

[9] Larry M. Rinek, "Menasco Aircraft Engines and Their Air Racing Heritage," Part 2, *Skyways*, January 1998, p. 32. Most if not all Menasco racing engines were factory modified. Greater horsepower output was obtained by increasing the blower drive gear ratio on the C4S ("S" signifying supercharged) engine. This resulted in higher manifold pressure operation. Other modifications typically included higher lift and longer duration racing camshafts, special low friction piston rings, and higher compression ratio pistons.

[10] Hugo T. Byttebier, *the Curtiss D-12 Aero Engine*, Smithsonian Institution Press, Washington, D.C., 1972, p. 82.

[11] The chemical formula for ethylene glycol is CH_2OH-CH_2OH.

[12] Public acknowledgment of the Wright Field work with glycol coolant was first mentioned in *The New York Times*, April 12, 1929, p. 29. Research with high temperature engine coolants in the United States actually began much earlier at McCook Field in March 1923. See note Number 129 on page 50 in *Vees for Victory* by Daniel D. Whitney, Schiffer Publishing, Atglen, Pennsylvania, 1998.

[13] Byttebier, op.cit., p. 83.

[14] S. J. DeFrance, *Drag of Prestone and Oil Radiators on the YO-31A Airplane*, National Advisory Committee for Aeronautics, Technical Note No. 549, December 1935, p. 2.

[15] Jacqueline Cochran entered the 1934 MacRobertson Race, but not with the Northrop Gamma. Instead she flew a Gee Bee design called the *Q.E.D.*, powered by a 675 horsepower Pratt & Whitney Model SD Hornet. Unfortunately, Jackie was forced out this race with mechanical problems

[16] This Conqueror was built up from two different military engines according to George Washburn, "The Brief Saga of *Mr. Smoothie*," *The Golden Age of Air Racing*, edited by S. H. Schmid and Truman C. Weaver, EAA Aviation Foundation, 1991, p. 496. Parts for the Conqueror, according to the author, were ostensibly acquired from Navy Curtiss Hawk fighters. This is unlikely, although they might have been experimental engines under evaluation. The Navy had settled on air-cooled radial engines in 1928, and no liquid-cooled powerplants, including the Curtiss Conqueror, were used in Navy fighters until a contract was awarded in November 1938, for the experimental Allison V-1710-powered Bell XFL-1.

17 Ibid.

18 Robert Schlaifer, Development of Aircraft Engines, Graduate School of Business Administration, Harvard University, Boston, 1950, p. 259.

CHAPTER 9

1 Thomas G. Foxworth, *The Speed Seekers*, Doubleday & Company, Inc., New York, 1974, p. 67–67.

2 Bill Gunston, *The Development of Piston Aero Engines*, Patrick Stephens Limited, England, 1993, p. 110.

3 Reportedly the instrument panels on World War I Nieuport pursuits carried a warning placard stating that the "Maximum speed of revolution must not exceed 1,400 rpm." See *Wings Over the World, The Life of George Jackson Mead*, The Swannet Press, Wauwatosa, Wisconsin, 1971, p. 17.

4 *The New York Times*, October 14, 1915, p. 8.

5 Anon., *The Pratt & Whitney Aircraft Story*, Pratt & Whitney Aircraft Division of United Aircraft Corporation, August 1950, p. 29.

6 Lou Eltscher, "Curtiss-Wright: Greatness and Decline," *American Aviation Historical Society Journal*, Vol. 39, No. 4, p. 273. There was a strong tendency on the part of management to adhere to and continually modify one design. Examples of this philosophy are seen with the overlong perpetuation of the Hawk biplane fighters of the 1920s and the P-36/P-40 designs of the 1930s. The company was not a technology leader. For a while this strategy paid off, but in the end it spelled trouble. Following a long string of Army and Navy airplanes dating to the 1920s, Curtiss-Wright suspended further development in December 1965, of a vertical takeoff and landing (VTOL) aircraft designated the X-19. It was the last airframe the company would ever build.

7 Correspondence from Harvey H. Lippincott to the author dated June, 23, 1961. Lippincott was at the time an installation engineer for Pratt & Whitney. With a lifelong interest in aviation history, he later became corporate historian for United Technologies. The R-1535-11 was purchased for the Northrop A-17A by the Army.

8 *Skyways: The Journal of the Airplane 1920–1940*. See the July 1997 and January 1998 issues.

9 *New York Times*, November 13, 1935.

10 The name Menasco Motors, Inc., came into usage some time after Harry Tucker died in the Vega accident. Available records make it unclear just what time period this name was used. It may have been a defacto corporation probably circa 1929–1930.

11 Correspondence from John Underwood to the author, March 5, 1998.

12 Robert H. Gross correspondence to Courtlandt Gross, 27 April 1935.

13 The concept is mentioned by Courtlandt Gross to his brother Robert Gross in correspondence dated 23 May 1935. Courtlandt wondered if the Commerce Department would accept this concept if and when a government sponsored twin-engine small passenger liner request for proposal was issued.

14 This is a cam and roller coupling assembly driving a gear engaged with the propeller reduction gear mechanism. It had been used in automobiles and power machinery for a number of years. The concept was described in the Society of Automotive Engineers *Journal* by A. M. Wolf in July, 1932.

15 There is some dispute as to whether these two *Gipsys* should be called Wright or American Cirrus engines. A photograph of the two engine combination clearly shows a Wright Aeronautical nameplate; however, the engines were acquired by Al Menasco from the American Cirrus bankruptcy auction.

16 Correspondence from Cyril Chappellet to Robert E. Gross dated June 13, 1935.

17 Purchase agreement between Lockheed and Menasco Manufacturing dated July 1, 1935. Chappellet was not referring to a *Unitwin* engine in this instance; rather the use of individual C6S-4 engines, one in each wing.

18 Ibid.

19 The C6S-4 was eventually rated at 290 horsepower for takeoff.

20 Correspondence from Robert Gross to Courtlandt Gross dated September 3, 1935. Available references circa 1935 suggest that the C6S-4 was then delivering about 250 horsepower. The 1938 Federal Government ATC rated the engine at 260 horsepower, 290 horsepower available for takeoff.

21 Ibid. The horsepower quoted is for each engine.

22 Ibid.

23 Bob Gross tried to get the Bureau of Air Commerce to ante up $15,000 in lieu of an airplane order in recognition of Lockheed's winning design in the competition. It is doubtful that this ever happened.

24 Correspondence from Robert E. Gross to Jack Frye, dated April 15, 1936.

25 As of November 1939, Gross and Chappellet owned 12,550 shares and 12,700 shares, respectively.

26 Report of the President, Menasco Manufacturing Company, for the fiscal year ended June 30, 1938.

27 Correspondence from Robert E. Gross to his father, Robert H. Gross, June 20, 1938.

28 Correspondence from Robert E. Gross to J. H. Geisse, Civil Aeronautics Authority, Washington, D.C., March 10,1939. Gross revealed some of the history of his connection with Menasco in this letter to Geisse.

29 Ibid.

30 Ibid.

31 *Aviation*, September 1938, p. 64.

32 Underwood correspondence, *op.cit.*

33 Using the same fuel, liquid-cooled engines typically produce more power per cubic inch than air-cooled engines, due to more uniform and effective cooling.

34 Ralph J. Schmidt, The Menasco Story, Coltec Industries, 1994, p. 11.

CHAPTER 10

1 These are but two of the many factors contributing to the development of aircraft and engines. Other components are equally important, such as improvement in spark plugs, flight instrumentation, the evolution of wind tunnels, and so forth. Space does not allow these to be historically evaluated. The development of quality fuels and rating standards, as well as managing waste heat removal are among the most important factors, however.

2 The rating of 460 horsepower for the 1922 Curtiss CD-12 racing engine is given by G. A. Luburg, "Wing Radiator Development," *American Society of Mechanical Engineers Transactions*, Vol. 54, No. 1, p. 39. Luburg was assistant chief engineer at Curtiss and presented design data on Curtiss

surface radiator designs for various race planes designed and built by the company. Another source states the power output at 410 horsepower: Curtiss Aeorplane & Motor Company, Inc., Characteristics Sheet for the CR-1 racer. Because Luburg was directly involved with engine cooling, his number appears creditable as it relates to this particular racing application. Note that in 1925 Curtiss listed its D-12 High Compression Ratio engine at 460 horsepower at 2,300 rpm.

[3] In this example, a surface radiator was used on the racer with a heat dissipation rate of 48 Btu/ft^2 per minute. See Domonoske and Finch, op.cit., p. 259.

[4] Lionel S. Marks, Editor, *Mechanical Engineers' Handbook*, McGraw-Hill Book Company, Inc., New York, 1924, p. 1267.

[5] Thomas Foxworth, *The Speed Seekers*, Doubleday & Company, Inc., New York, 1974, p. 75.

[6] In fairness to the author, it should be pointed out that contemporary literature for the Lamblin radiators used the term radiation.

[7] G. A. Luburg, "Wing Radiator Development," *American Society of Mechanical Engineers Transactions*, Vol. 54, No. 1, p. 37.

[8] Initial flight testing was carried out using a Curtiss Oriole biplane during 1921 and early 1922. This aircraft was powered by a Curtiss C-6 water-cooled engine. This combination proved adequate for gathering basic design information and heat transfer data. See Luburg, op.cit., and Thomas G. Foxworth, *The Speed Seekers*, Doubleday & Company, Inc., New York, 1974, pp. 76–78.

[9] Peter M. Bowers, *Curtiss Aircraft 1907–1947*, Naval Institute Press, Annapolis, Maryland, 1987, p. 228.

[10] Total height of the structure was 0.145 inches and the triangle peaks were 0.25 inches apart.

[11] This was a privately financed racing endeavor. The U.S. government decided against further financial support for an American entry in the Schneider Trophy Race. Ironically, one more victory would have permanently retired the trophy to the United States. In the end, development problems forced withdrawal of the racer, and permanent possession of the trophy went to Great Britain in 1931.

[12] Fred E. Weick, *Full Scale Investigation of the Drag of a Wing Radiator*, National Advisory Committee for Aeronautics Technical Note No. 318, September 1929.

[13] Ibid, p. 3.

[14] Drag, $D = C_d q S$ where C_d is the drag coefficient, q is the dynamic pressure or _ V^2 (V= velocity), and S is the plan form area of the radiators.

[15] G. D. Hobson, editor, *Modern Petroleum Technology*, John Wiley & Sons, New York, p. 527.

[16] Alexander R. Ogston, "A Short History of Aviation Gasoline Development, 1903–1980," *Aeronautical Journal*, December 1981, p 441.

[17] Distillation involves heating the crude oil sufficiently to vaporize hydrocarbon fractions (compounds) based upon their boiling points. Once segregated, a given compound is cooled until condensed into a liquid. Lighter fractions are used for gasoline.

[18] Sir Harry Ricardo, *The Ricardo Story*, Society of Automotive Engineers, Inc., Warrendale, Pennsylvania, 1990, p. 93.

[19] Stuart W. Leslie, *Boss Kettering*, Columbia University Press, New York, 1983, p. 153.

[20] Ibid., p. 154.

[21] Dr. Graham Edgar would go on to be a vice president of the Ethyl Gasoline Corporation during the 1930s

[22] Actually, there were four similar test methods in use during the 1930s, one by the Army identified as the U.S. Army Air Corps Method; another by A.S.T.M., the American Society for Testing Materials; a third known as the C. F. R. from the Cooperative Fuel Research Council; and, a fourth version called the British Air Ministry Method, adopted by Great Britain. All give similar ratings although there is variation.

[23] See William H. Hubner's "Prospects of Fuels of Higher Octane Number in the Transport Field," *Journal of the Aeronautical Sciences*, Vol. 7, No. 8, June 1940, pp. 319–331; and, Arthur P. Fraas, *Aircraft Power Plants*, McGraw-Hill Book Company, Inc., New York, 1943, pp. 203–208.

[24] Ogston, op.cit., p. 446.

[25] James H. Doolittle, *I Could Never Be So Lucky Again*, Bantam Books, New York, 1991, p. 188.

[26] Ibid., p. 190.

[27] Benzol 90 Percent consisted of 80 to 85 percent benzene, 13 to 15 percent toluene, and 2 to 3 percent xylene. It was called 90 percent because in its distillation 90 percent distills over at below at 100 degrees Centigrade(212 degrees Fahrenheit).

[28] F. R. Banks, *I Kept No Diary*, Airlife Publishing Ltd., England, 1983, p. 89.

CHAPTER 11

[1] Anon., "Is Aviation A Failure?" *Science and Discovery*, December 1910, p. 633.

[2] L. F. R. Fell, "Limit of Racing Power Plant Performance," *Aviation*, September 1930, p. 145.

[3] William Wait, Jr., "The Value of Air Races," *Aero Digest*, May 1931, p. 48.

[4] The parasol-winged XF6C-6 was a highly modified Navy F6C-3 biplane fighter. The basic design originated in 1925.

[5] Government aircraft design sponsorship in Europe was sporadic in the 1930s. Had not Lady Houston stepped forward in 1931, the Schneider Trophy would not have found a permanent home in Great Britain. The most notable government-sponsored racing plane designs emanated thereafter from Italy and then Germany. These appeared more matters of nationalistic pride and propaganda, although technically nonetheless impressive.

[6] Construction of the racer was started by Larry Brown; however, a disagreement developed over changes Brown unilaterally instituted, and Turner obtained the services of Matty Laird to complete the job. See Kenneth D. Wilson's "The Story of Roscoe Turner—Someone and Something Special," *The Golden Age of Air Racing*, edited by S. H. Schmid and Truman C. Weaver, EAA Foundation, Inc., revised 1991, pp. 466–481.

[7] Alan Pope, *Wind-Tunnel Testing*, John Wiley & Sons, Inc., New York, 1954, pp. 23–25.

[8] Robert Insley, "Institute Meeting at the National Air Races," *Journal of the Aeronautical Sciences*, Vol. 4, No. 11, September 1937, p. 479.

Appendix A
List of Airplane Entries
1909 Grande Semaine d'Aviation de la Champagne, Reims, France

Race No.	Country	Pilot	Aircraft	Engine	Owner
1	France	Robert Esnault Pelterie	R.E.P. Monoplane	R.E.P., 30 hp, 7 cyl.	R.E.P.
2	France	Laurens	R.E.P. Monoplane	R.E.P., 30 hp, 7 cyl.	R.E.P.
3	France	Maurice Guffroy	R.E.P. Monoplane	R.E.P., 30 hp, 7 cyl.	R.E.P.
4	France	Paul Tissandier	Wright Biplane	Wright 30 hp, 4 cyl.	Paul Tissandier
5	France	Jean Gobron	Voisin Biplane	Gobron 50 hp, 8 cyl.	Jean Gobron
6	France	Roger Sommer	Biplan à Queue	60 hp, 4 cyl.	Roger Sommer
7	France	Compte De Lambert	Wright Biplane	Wright 30 hp, 4 cyl.	Compte De Lambert
8	U.S.A.	Glenn Curtiss	Reims Racer	Curtiss 50 hp, 8 cyl.	Glenn Curtiss
9	U.S.A.	Glenn Curtiss	Second entry that did not arrive.		
10	France	Maurice Guffroy	R.E.P. Monoplane	R.E.P. 30 hp, 7 cyl.	R.E.P.
11	France	Hubert Latham	Antoinette Monoplane	Antoinette 50 hp, 8 cyl.	Société Antoinette
12	France	René Demanest	Antoinette Monoplane	Antoinette 50 hp, 8 cyl.	Société Antoinette
13	France	Hubert Latham	Antoinette Monoplane	Antoinette 50 hp, 8 cyl.	Société Antoinette
14	France	Alberto Santos Dumont	Dumont and his monoplane did not arrive		
15	France	Paul Tissandier	Wright Biplane	Wright 30 hp, 4 cyl.	Paul Tissandier
16	France	Léon Delagrange	Blériot Monoplane	Anzani 20 hp, 3 cyl.	Léon Delagrange
17	France	De Rue	Voisin Biplane	Antoinette 50 hp, 8 cyl.	De Rue
18		Klüytmans	Biplane	50 hp, 8 cyl.	Klüytmans
19	France	Louis Bréguet	Biplane	50 hp	Louis Bréguet
20	France	Louis Paulhan	Voisin Biplane	Gnome	Société L'Aviation
21	France	Louis Blériot	Blériot Monoplane		Louis Blériot
22	France	Louis Blériot	Blériot Monoplane	E.N.V. 50 hp	Louis Blériot
23	France	Alfred Leblanc	Blériot Monoplane	Anzani	Louis Blériot
24	France	Alfred Leblanc	Blériot Monoplane	Anzani	Louis Blériot
25	France	Eugène Lefebrve	Wright Biplane	Wright 30 hp, 4 cyl.	Société Ariel

Race No.	Country	Pilot	Aircraft	Engine	Owner
26	France	Paul Tissandier	Wright Biplane	Wright 30 hp, 4 cyl.	Société Ariel
27	France	Étienne Bunau-Varilla	Voisin Biplane	50 hp	Étienne Bunau-Varilla
28	France	Henry Rougier	Voisin	60 hp, 4 cyl.	Henry Rougier
29	France	Hubert Latham	Antoinette Monoplane	Antoinette 50 hp, 8 cyl.	Capitaine Burgeat
30	France	Henry Farman	Farman Biplane		Henry Farman
31	France	Roger Sommer	Farman Biplane		Henry Farman
32	England	Georges Cockburn	Farman Biplane		Georges Cockburn
33	France	Henry Fournier	Voisin Biplane	Itala 50 hp	Henry Fournier
34	France	Louis Shreck	Wright Biplane	Wright 30 hp, 4 cyl.	Louis Schreck
35		Antonio Fernandez	Fernandez Biplane	Antoinette 24 hp	Antonio Fernandez
36	France	Comte De Lambert	Wright Biplane	Wright 30 hp, 4 cyl.	Comte De Lambert
37		Sanchez-Besa	Voisin Biplane	E.N.V. 60 hp	Sanchez-Besa
38	France	Georges Legagneux	Voisin Biplane		Voisin
39	England	Reserved for English entry in Gordon Bennett Trophy Race (did not arrive)			
40	England	Reserved for English entry in Gordon Bennett Trophy Race (did not arrive)			
41	Italy	Lt. Mario Calderara	Wright Biplane	Wright 30 hp, 4 cyl.	Did not arrive
42	Italy	Reserved for Italian entry in Gordon Bennett Trophy Race (did not arrive)			
43	Italy	Reserved for Italian entry in Gordon Bennett Trophy Race (did not arrive)			
44	Austria	Reserved for Austrian entry in Gordon Bennett Trophy Race (did not arrive)			

Source: Official program for 1909 Reims Race

Appendix B List of Entries
1910 Domínguez Aviation Meet Entries

Airplanes

Race No.	Pilot	City	Aircraft
1	Louis Paulhan	Paris, France	Farman Biplane
2	Louis Paulhan	Paris, France	Blériot Monoplane
3	Didier Masson	Paris, France	Blériot Monoplane
4	Charles F. Miscarol	Paris, France	Blériot Monoplane
5	Charles K. Hamilton	Hammondsport, NY	Curtiss Biplane
6	Glenn H. Curtiss	Hammondsport, NY	Curtiss Biplane
7	J.C. Klassen	Los Angeles, CA	California Monoplane
8	Roy Knabenshue	Toledo, OH	Wright Biplane (modified)
9	Charles F. Willard	New York, NY	Curtiss Biplane
10	H.W. Gill		Gill-Dash
11	Clifford B. Harmon	New York, NY	Curtiss Biplane
	Baroness de la Roche	Paris, France	(Blériot Monoplane) see Paulhan
DNA	Aero Navigation Co. of America	Girard, KS	Monoplane
DNA	H.P. Warner	Beloit, WI	Curtis Biplane
DNA	J.C. Klassen	Los Angeles, CA	Gyroplane
DNA	H.LaV. Twinning	Los Angeles, CA	Ornithopter
DNA	William Stevens	Los Angeles, CA	Monoplane
DNA	A.L. Smith	Los Angeles, CA	Biplane
DNA	A.G. Gonzales	Los Angeles, CA	Biplane
DNA	H.L. Heimer	Los Angeles, CA	Ornithopter

Airplanes Race No.	Pilot	City	Aircraft
DNA	E.S. Smith	Tropico, CA	Monoplane
DNA	Pacific Aero Club	San Francisco, CA	Biplane
DNA	Pacific Aero Club	San Francisco, CA	Monoplane
DNF	Grant M. Fowler	Phoenix, AZ	Desert Eagle Biplane
DNA	Charles Borok	New York, NY	Monoplane
DNA	Louis J. Bergdoll	Philadelphia, PA	Blériot Monoplane
DNA	Ralph Soulnier	New York, NY	Monoplane
DNA	Donald H. Gordon	Bostonia, CA	Unknown
DNA	J.W. Curzon	Cincinnati, OH	Farman Biplane
DNA	Dana P. Goodwin	San Francisco, CA	Monoplane
DNA	San Diego Airplane Co.	San Diego, CA	Monoplane
DNA	A.M. Williams	Douglas, AZ	Monoplane
DNA	La Batt Brothers	Yuma, AZ	Ornithopter
DNA	James A. Liston	San Diego, CA	Monoplane
DNA	S.Y. Beach	New York, NY	Unknown
DNA	H.W. Gale	New York, NY	Unknown
DNA	B.F. Rochig	San Diego, CA	Monoplane
DNA	G.H. Loose	San Francisco, CA	Monoplane
DNA	W.D. "Waldo" Waterman	San Diego, CA	Biplane
DNA	E.J. Campbell	Los Angeles, CA	Biplane
DNA	W.G. Davis	Los Angeles, CA	Double Biplane
DNA	D.H. Johnson	Los Angeles, CA	"Aerofoll"
DNA	R.G.V. Milton	Los Angeles, CA	Biplane
DNA	Charles Scoglund	Los Angeles, CA	Monoplane
DNF	Prof. H. LaVern Twining		Monoplane
DNA	Prof. J.S. Zerbe	Los Angeles, CA	Multiplane

Dirigibles			
11	Roy Knabenshue	Toledo, OH	5,500 Cu Ft
2	Lincoln Beachy	Toledo, OH	5,500 Cu Ft
3	Lt. Beck	California A.N.G.	20,000 Cu Ft
DNA	Thomas S. Baldwin	New York, NY	
DNA	J.C. Classen	Los Angeles, CA	
DNA	A. Carter	San Jose, CA	

Balloons			
1	Roy Knabenshue	Toledo, OH	The Dick Ferris
2	George B. Harrison	Los Angeles, CA	City of Los Angeles
3	Clifford B. Harmon	New York, NY	City of New York
4	Frank J. Kanne	Peoria, IL	City of Peoria
5	J.C. Mars	Oakland, CA	City of Oakland
6	Charles D. Colby	Calif. National Guard	Co. A, Signal Corps
7	A.C. Pillsbury		The Fairy
DNA	G.T. Bumbaugh	Indianapolis, IN	
DNA	H.E. Honeywell	St. Louis, MO	
DNA	J. Bettis	St. Louis, MO	
DNA	A. Leo Stevens	New York, NY	
DNA	Richard Ferris	Los Angeles, CA	America

DNA = Did Not Arrive
Sources: Official program and *New York Times*, December 25, 1909, p. 8.

BACKGROUND

Published physical characteristics of the racers vary somewhat, depending upon the source. This was particularly true for the Wedell-Williams Model 44 racer. Part of the problem was that modifications were made over time, so dimensions were altered accordingly. Data presented in the following table represent a synthesis of available information, and were used in the sample performance calculations for Number 44 which follow.

Perhaps the most difficult parameter to select in several instances was maximum horsepower. Race pilots and crews at times extracted more power than the man-

ufacturer's rating. This was accomplished by increasing the rpm and over boosting manifold pressure. In the final analysis, a judgment was made where available information strongly indicated that engine output exceeded rated power. At best, contemporary claims of increased horsepower were extrapolated from a curve, and almost certainly did not represent test stand measurements. In all other instances, the manufacturer's maximum rated horsepower was used in the calculations.

Propeller efficiency (h) was assumed to be 0.8 for the initial zero lift drag coefficient calculation. This was

adjusted as needed later when a propeller characteristics curve was consulted while determining thrust available. In other words, the propeller efficiency number was iterated until the zero lift drag coefficient calculation was consistent with the efficiency used in determining thrust available.

Airframe efficiency (Œ) values were selected based upon a review of the literature and consultation of Professor Hubert Smith (Skip), Pennsylvania State University. For low-wing aircraft, a value of 0.6 to 0.7 was used.

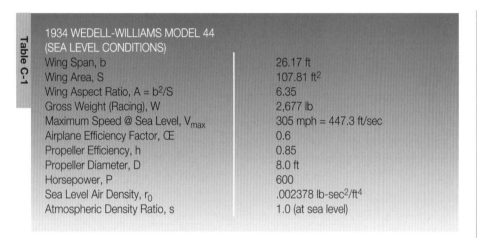

Table C-1

1934 WEDELL-WILLIAMS MODEL 44 (SEA LEVEL CONDITIONS)	
Wing Span, b	26.17 ft
Wing Area, S	107.81 ft^2
Wing Aspect Ratio, A = b^2/S	6.35
Gross Weight (Racing), W	2,677 lb
Maximum Speed @ Sea Level, V_{max}	305 mph = 447.3 ft/sec
Airplane Efficiency Factor, Œ	0.6
Propeller Efficiency, h	0.85
Propeller Diameter, D	8.0 ft
Horsepower, P	600
Sea Level Air Density, r_0	.002378 lb-sec^2/ft^4
Atmospheric Density Ratio, s	1.0 (at sea level)

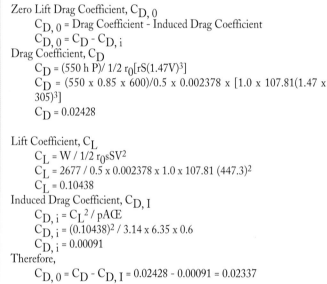

Zero Lift Drag Coefficient, $C_{D,0}$
$$C_{D,0} = \text{Drag Coefficient - Induced Drag Coefficient}$$
$$C_{D,0} = C_D - C_{D,i}$$
Drag Coefficient, C_D
$$C_D = (550 \, h \, P)/ \, 1/2 \, r_0 [rS(1.47V)^3]$$
$$C_D = (550 \times 0.85 \times 600)/0.5 \times 0.002378 \times [1.0 \times 107.81(1.47 \times 305)^3]$$
$$C_D = 0.02428$$

Lift Coefficient, C_L
$$C_L = W / 1/2 \, r_0 sSV^2$$
$$C_L = 2677 / 0.5 \times 0.002378 \times 1.0 \times 107.81 (447.3)^2$$
$$C_L = 0.10438$$
Induced Drag Coefficient, $C_{D,I}$
$$C_{D,i} = C_L^2 / pA\text{Œ}$$
$$C_{D,i} = (0.10438)^2 / 3.14 \times 6.35 \times 0.6$$
$$C_{D,i} = 0.00091$$
Therefore,
$$C_{D,0} = C_D - C_{D,I} = 0.02428 - 0.00091 = 0.02337$$

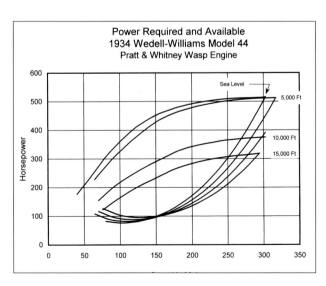

Power Required and Available
1934 Wedell-Williams Model 44
Pratt & Whitney Wasp Engine

Figure C-2 *Power required and available for the Wedell-Williams Model 44 is shown here for sea level as well as altitudes of 5,000 feet, 10,000 feet and 15,000 feet. The sea level and 5,000 feet power available curves are very close because the engine supercharger is rated to 5,000 feet. A maximum speed of 317 miles per hour is reached at 5,000 feet, due to the lower air density at this altitude. Beyond 5,000 feet, speed drops off because of reduced engine power output, offset to some extent by decreasing air density.*

The foregoing calculations are based upon *wing surface area*, because the total wetted surface area of the airframe is unknown. To compensate, the (airframe wetted area) zero lift drag coefficients calculated by Loftin were recalculated using wing area only.[1] The resulting values are shown in Table C-2 together with the original $C_{D,0}$ values. A comparison of these data show that the wetted area zero lift drag coefficients were on average about four percent greater than those determined using wing area only. Therefore, all zero lift drag coefficients calculated using only wing area were increased by that amount, except where the airframe wetted area was known.

**Comparison of Zero Lift Drag Coefficients
Computed Using Wing Area & Airframe Wetted Area**

Aircraft	Wing Area $C_{D,0}$	Wetted Area $C_{D,0}$	Difference	Ratio Wetted/Wing
Seversky P-35	0.0244	0.0251	0.0007	1.03
Boeing P-26	0.0421	0.0448	0.0027	1.06
Lockheed Vega 5C	0.0260	0.0278	0.0018	1.07
Lockheed Orion 9D	0.0201	0.0210	0.0009	1.04
Northrop Alpha	0.0256	0.0274	0.0018	1.07
Supermarine S.4	0.0267	0.0274	0.0007	1.03
Curtiss R2C-1	0.0212	0.0206	<0.0006>	0.97
Boeing 247D	0.0208	0.0212	0.0004	1.02
Douglas DC-3	0.0233	0.0249	0.0016	1.07
Average =	1.04			

Note: Wetted airframe values of $C_{D,0}$ taken from Laurence K. Loftin, Jr., *Quest for Performance: The Evolution of Modern Aircraft*, National Aeronautics and Space Administration, SP-468, Washington, D.C., 1985.

For the Wedell-Williams Model 44 racer, the corrected zero lift drag coefficient is:
$$C_{D,0} = 0.02337 \times 1.04 = 0.02430$$
To construct a drag polar, a range of lift coefficients was assumed and corresponding drag coefficients determined from $C_D = C_{D,0} + C_{D,i}$ as shown in Table C-3. These data are plotted in Figure C-1.

**Drag Polar Data
Wedell-Williams Model 44**

Assumed Lift Coef.	Zero Lift Drag Coef.	Induced Drag Coef.	Drag Coef.
-0.40	0.02430	0.01337	0.03767
-0.30	0.02430	0.00752	0.03182
-0.20	0.02430	0.00334	0.02764
-0.10	0.02430	0.00084	0.02514
0	0.02430	0	0.02430
0.10	0.02430	0.00084	0.02514
0.20	0.02430	0.00334	0.02764
0.30	0.02430	0.00752	0.03182
0.40	0.02430	0.01337	0.03767
0.50	0.02430	0.02089	0.04519
0.60	0.02430	0.03008	0.05438
0.70	0.02430	0.04094	0.06524
0.80	0.02430	0.05347	0.07777
0.90	0.02430	0.06767	0.09197
1.00	0.02430	0.08355	0.10785

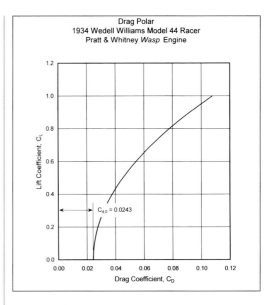

Figure C-1 *The drag polar shown here was plotted from data presented in Table C-3. The zero lift drag coefficient for the Wedell-Williams Model 44 racer is 0.0243, as shown on the plot.*

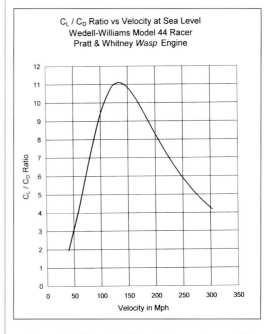

Figure C-3 *The ratio of lift coefficient to drag coefficient as a function of aircraft velocity for the Model 44 racer is shown here. This ratio peaks at about 125 miles per hour. At maximum sea level velocity (calculated to be 303 miles per hour) the ratio is just over 4 to 1.*

THRUST AND POWER REQUIRED

The thrust required, T_R, is the gross weight of the aircraft divided by the ratio of C_L to C_D. For maximum speed:

$$T_R = W/(C_L/C_D) = 2{,}677/(0.1058/0.0252) = 637.6 \text{ lb}$$

Horsepower required (Hp_R) is determined by multiplying the velocity of the aircraft by the thrust required, and that quantity divided by 550 ft-lb/sec. At a maximum sea level speed (V_{max}) of 303 mph or 444.4 ft/sec,

$$Hp_R = (637.6 \times 444.4)/550 = 515 \text{ horsepower}$$

HORSEPOWER AVAILABLE

Power available (Hp_A) is the product of propeller efficiency and engine brake horsepower, that amount of power delivered to the propeller shaft. In this example calculation considering the case of maximum velocity, the maximum brake horsepower number is used.

Propeller efficiency (hp) is a number less than 1.0 and read from a propeller characteristics curve depicting the propeller advance ratio, J, and the propeller power coefficient, C_P.

$$J = V/nD \text{ where } V = \text{velocity; } n = \text{propeller rpm, and } D = \text{propeller diameter.}$$

For the Wedell-Williams racer at maximum sea level velocity, a direct drive Wasp engine developing 600 brake horsepower at 2,200 rpm and a propeller diameter of 8.0 feet,

$$J = 444.4/(2{,}200 \times 8 \times 1/60) = 1.515$$

The propeller power coefficient (C_P) is determined from the engine brake horsepower (P), number of propeller blades(B), engine speed (n), propeller diameter (D), and the altitude density ratio (&). At sea level where & = 1.0. The relationship is:

$$C_P = P \times 10^{11}/Bn^3D^5 \text{&}$$
$$C_P = (600 \times 10^{11})/[2 \times (2{,}200)^3 \times (8)^5 \times 1.0] = 0.086$$

At these conditions, propeller efficiency is approximately 0.85 as read from the propeller characteristics chart in reference 2.[2]

Thrust horsepower available is then:

$$Hp_A = 600 \times 0.858 = 515 \text{ horsepower}$$

This is exactly equal to the horsepower required, and therefore defines the maximum speed of the racer. Shell speed trial results give a speed of 306 miles per hour for Jimmy Wedell's racer. The calculations are in remarkably good agreement at 303 miles per hour, within one percent of the measured speed.

The same procedure was used for a range of aircraft speeds to facilitate plots of power required and available as shown in Figure C-2. It was repeated for altitudes up to 15,000 feet in 5,000 feet increments. A sample of calculated sea level performance for the Wedell-Williams Model 44 is given in Table C-3.

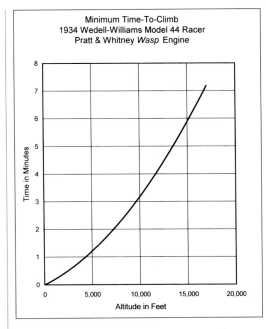

Figure C-5 *Sheer speed in level flight is not the only parameter of interest when considering whether a 1930s era race plane might have been a suitable basis for a pursuit airplane. Time to climb is another important performance factor, and this chart illustrates the calculated minimum climb time for the Wedell-Williams Model 44. With the Wasp engine used in 1934, the racer was capable of reaching 10,000 feet in just over three minutes. Climbing to 15,000 feet would have taken about six minutes.*

Figure C-6 *The minimum time to climb and maximum rate of climb presented in Figures 7-3 and 7-4, respectively, in Chapter 7 were based upon maximum excess horsepower. This number was obtained by plotting power available versus aircraft speed, as shown in this illustration. At sea level, maximum excess power is around 353 horsepower at a speed of 160 miles per hour in level flight. The same plots were made for 5,000 feet, 10,000 feet and 15,000 feet, where excess power amounted respectively to 338, 198 and 142 horsepower.*

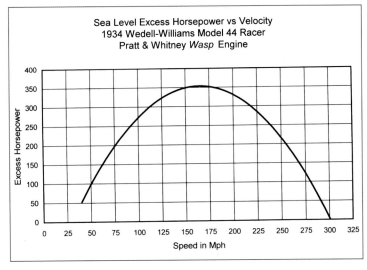

Table C-4

Wedell-Williams Model 44 Racer Performance at Sea Level
Gross Weight = 2,677 Pounds

Speed Mph	C_L	C_D	C_L/C_D	Hp Reqd	Prop Eff, h_p	Hp Avail.	Excess Hp
40	6.0677	3.1002	2.0	146	0.295	177	31
60	2.6968	0.6319	4.3	100	0.400	240	140
80	1.5169	0.2165	7.0	82	0.510	306	224
100	0.9708	0.1030	9.4	76	0.600	360	284
120	0.6742	0.0623	10.8	79	0.675	405	326
130	0.5745	0.0519	11.1	84	0.710	426	342
140	0.4953	0.0448	11.1	90	0.732	439	349
150	0.4315	0.0399	10.8	99	0.752	451	352
160	0.3792	0.0363	10.4	109	0.770	462	353
170	0.3359	0.0337	10.0	122	0.783	470	348
180	0.2996	0.0318	9.4	136	0.795	477	341
200	0.2427	0.0292	8.3	172	0.817	490	318
220	0.2006	0.0277	7.3	217	0.832	499	283
240	0.1685	0.0267	6.3	271	0.843	506	235
260	0.1436	0.0260	5.5	336	0.851	511	174
280	0.1238	0.0256	4.8	413	0.854	512	99
300	0.1079	0.0253	4.3	502	0.857	514	12
303	0.1058	0.0252	4.2	516	0.860	516	0

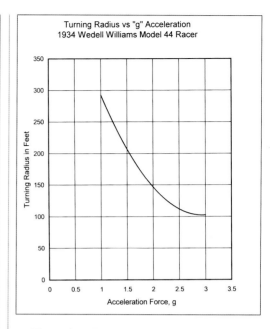

Figure C-7 *The Wedell-Williams 44 had a greater turning radius than the 1929 Travel Air Mystery Ship. For instance, as seen in this curve, a "two-G" minimum turning radius required about 150 feet. A comparable turn with the Travel Air (see Figure 6-3 in Chapter 6) needed only 125 feet. Minimum turning radius is a function of wing loading. The Travel Air was lighter and had a larger wing area than the Wedell racer, and this gave it a shorter turning radius.*

OTHER PERFORMANCE PARAMETERS

In addition to maximum speed, other parameters were estimated through calculation for selected racing planes and hypothetically converted pursuit versions of these aircraft. Sample results are presented in Figures C-3 through C-7. All of these examples represent the 1934 Wedell-Williams racing plane re-engined with a Pratt & Whitney Wasp. Figure C-3 shows the ratio of lift and drag coefficients obtained over a range of speeds from about 50 miles per hour to its maximum sea level speed of just over 300 miles per hour. Maximum climb rate and time-to-climb are shown in Figures C-4 and C-5. These were calculated using maximum excess horsepower at each of the four altitudes under consideration (sea level, 5,000, 10,000, and 15,000 feet). Maximum excess horsepower was determined graphically for each altitude of interest as shown by the example curve in Figure C-6. Minimum turning radius (R_{min}) as a function of acceleration (g) for the racer is shown in Figure C- 7. This was calculated using the equation given by Anderson:[3]

$$R_{min} = 2/r\, C_{L,\,max}\,(W/S)$$

Maximum lift coefficient ($C_{L,\,max}$) was determined using an estimated stall speed based upon landing speed. Landing speed was assumed to be 20 percent above stall speed.

NOTES

[1] Laurence K. Loftin, Jr., *Quest for Performance: The Evolution of Modern Aircraft*, National Aeronautics and Space Administration, SP-468, Washington, D.C., 1985. See Appendix A, Table II.

[2] U.S. Army Air Corps, *Handbook of Instructions for Airplane Designers*, Vol. I, p. 249.

[3] John D. Anderson, Jr., *Introduction to Flight*, McGaw-Hill, New York, 2000, p. 435.

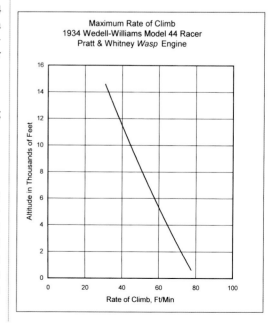

Figure C-4 *Another perspective of the climbing ability of the Wedell-Williams 44 is obtained by assessing the maximum "rate of climb." As shown in this curve, the rate of climb near sea level is about 80 feet per minute. Rate of climb diminishes with increasing altitude. In this instance, by the time the racer reaches 11,000 feet the rate of climb is cut in half.*

Model	Year	No. Cyl	Bore In	Stroke In	Displ. In^3	Comp Ratio	Hp	Rpm	Dry. Wt Lb	Lb/ Hp	Remarks
Liberty		12	5.000	7.000	1,649.3		225	1,950			Max. Hp = 240 @ 2,000 rpm
1A- 744	1920	8	4.750	5.250	7,44.3	5.56	162	1,600			60deg V-8, Direct Drive
1A- 825	1922	8	1.000	1.000	6.3						60deg V-8,Direct Drive
1A-1116	1919	12	4.750	5.250	1,116.4	5.56	313	1,800	733	2.34	Direct Drive
1A-1116	1919	12	4.750	5.250	1,116.4	5.56	330	2,000	733	2.22	Direct Drive
1A-1116	1919	12	4.750	5.250	1,116.4	6.50	333	1,800	733	2.20	Direct Drive
1A-1116	1919	12	4.750	5.250	1,116.4	5.56	350	2,200	733	2.09	Direct Drive
1A-1237	1920	12	5.000	5.250	1,237.0	5.50	300	1,800	738	2.46	Direct Drive
2A-1237	1922	12	5.000	5.250	1,237.0	5.50	300	1,800	NA		Direct Drive
1A-1500	1925	12	5.375	5.500	1,497.6	5.50	500	2,000			Crankcase failed high-speed endurance test
2A-1500	1928	12	5.375	5.500	1,497.6	5.1, 5.5 or 6.0	525	2,100	760	1.45	Direct Drive-Improved crankcase, articulated rods
2A-1500	1928	12	5.375	5.500	1,497.6	5.1, 5.5 or 6.0	525	2,100	880	1.68	Geared
2A-1500	1928	12	5.375	5.500	1,497.6	5.1, 5.5 or 6.0	525	2,100	780	1.49	Inverted Direct Drive
2A-1500	1927	12	5.375	5.500	1,497.6	5.1, 5.5 or 6.0	600	2,500	760	1.27	Direct Drive
2A-1500	1927	12	5.375	5.500	1,497.6		600	2,500	880	1.47	Geared
2A-1500	1928	12	5.375	5.500	1,497.6		600	2,500	915	1.53	Geared
3A-1500	1929	12	5.375	5.500	1,497.6		525	2,100			Direct Drive
1A-2025	1920	12	5.750	6.500	2,025.4	5.08	550	1,800	1,146	2.08	60deg V-12, Direct Drive
1A-2500	1925	12	6.375	6.500	2,489.7	5.7 or 5.3	800	2,000			Direct Drive-Articulated Rods
2A-2500	1928	12	6.375	6.500	2,489.7	5.1 or 5.7	800	2,000	1,160	1.45	Direct Drive
2A-2500	1928	12	6.375	6.500	2,489.7	5.1 or 5.7	800	2,000	1,380	1.73	Geared
2A-2500	1927	12	6.375	6.500	2,489.7		800	2,000	1,150	1.44	Direct Drive
2A-2500	1927	12	6.375	6.500	2,489.7		800	2,000	1,370	1.71	Geared
3A-2500	1928	12	6.375	6.500	2,489.7		800	2,000	1,220	1.53	Direct Drive
3A-2500	1928	12	6.375	6.500	2,489.7		800	2,000	1,435	1.79	Geared
4A-2500	1928	12	6.375	6.500	2,489.7	NA	950	2,180	1,640	1.73	Allison Reduction Gears and S/C w/10.08:1 stepup
1A-2775	1928	24	5.375	5.000	2,722.9	6.00	1,250	2,750	1,400	1.12	X-24
1A-2775	1928	24	5.375	5.000	2,722.9	6.00	1,250	2,750	1,625	1.30	X-24, with S/C, Direct Drive

Appendix E
Wright Liquid-Cooled Engines

Model	Year	No. of Cyl	Bore In	Stroke In	Piston Area In^2	Cyl Vol In^3	Displ. In^3	Comp Ratio	Hp	Rpm	Dry Wt. Lb	Lb/Hp	Remarks
Wright T-3 Tornado	1923	12	5.75	6.25	26.0	162.3	1947.5		650		1,160	1.78	Direct Drive
Wright T-3 Tornado		12	5.75	6.25	26.0	162.3	1947.5	6.50	675	2,000	1,160	1.72	Direct or 5:3
Wright T-3 Tornado	1923	12	5.75	6.25	26.0	162.3	1947.5		800	2,000	1,166	1.46	
Wright T-3B Tornado	1925	12	5.75	6.25	26.0	162.3	1947.5		575	1,160		2.02	Direct Drive
Wright T-4 Tornado	1923	12	5.75	6.25	26.0	162.3	1947.5		675				

Appendix F
Curtiss Liquid-Cooled Vee-Type Aircraft Engines

Curtiss Model	Military Model	Year	No. of Cyl.	Bore In	Stroke In	Articul. Stroke In	Displ. Volume In3	Comp Ratio	Hp	RPM	Weight Lbs	Lb/ Hp	Propeller Drive & Remarks
Silver Dart		1908	8	3.750	4.000		353.4		50	1,600	97	1.94	Direct
Reims Racer		1909	8	4.250	4.437		503.6		63	1,475	225	3.57	Direct
		1910	8	3.750	4.000		353.4		50		175	3.50	Direct
		1910	8	4.500	4.000		508.9		65	1,150			Direct
		1911	8	4.000	4.000		402.1		50	1,200	202	4.04	Direct
L		1911	8	5.020	4.000		633.4		70	1,500	275	3.93	Direct
O		1912	8	4.000	5.000		502.7		75	1,100	285	3.80	Direct
OX		1913	8	4.000	5.000		502.7						Direct
OX-2		1914	8	4.000	5.000		502.7						Direct
OX-3			8	4.000	5.000		502.7						Direct
OX-4			8	4.000	5.000		502.7						Direct
OX-5	OX-5	1917	8	4.000	5.000		502.7	4.92	90	1,400	400	4.44	Direct
OXX		1914	8	4.300	5.000		580.9		100	1,400	401		
OXX-6		1914	8	4.300	5.000		580.9		100		401	4.01	Direct
C		1914	8	4.500	5.500		699.8		110				
V		1914	8	5.000	7.000		1,099.6		160	1,100	700	4.38	
V-2		1916	8	5.000	7.000		1,099.6		200	1,400			Direct
V-4	V-4	1916	12	5.000	7.000		1,649.3		250	1,400	1,125	4.50	Direct
VX													
AB	AB	1916	8	4.000	5.500		552.9		300	2,250	725	2.42	Geared
D-1200	D-1200	1917	12	4.500	6.000		1,145.1	5.50	375	2,250	625	1.67	Geared
K-12	K-12	1917	12	4.500	6.000		1,145.1	6.00	400	2,350	665/680	1.66/1.70	Geared 5:3
C-12	C-12	1919	12	4.500	6.000		1,145.1	5.50	400	2,250	675/712	1.69/1.78	Geared 5:3
CD-12	CD-12	1920	12	4.500	6.000		1,145.1	5.23	325	1,800	700	2.15	Direct
CD-12A	CD-12A	1921	12	4.500	6.000		1,145.1	6.09	375	2,000	700	1.87	Direct
D-12, Hi CR	D-12, Hi CR	1925	12	4.500	6.000		1,145.1	6.00	460	2,300	694	1.51	Direct
D-12, Lo-CR	D-12, Lo-CR	1922	12	4.500	6.000		1,145.1	5.30	435	2,300	694	1.60	Direct
D-12A	D-12A	1923	12	4.500	6.000		1,145.1		500				Direct
D-12C	V-1150-1	1925	12	4.500	6.000		1,145.1	5.30	435	2,300	672	1.54	Direct
D-12D Hi-CR	D-12D Hi-CR	1928	12	4.500	6.000		1,145.1	6.00	475	2,300	680	1.43	Direct
D-12D Lo-CR	V-1150-3	1926	12	4.500	6.000		1,145.1	5.30	435	2,300	680	1.56	Direct

No. Curtiss Model	Military Model	Year	Articul. of Cyl.	Bore In	Displ. Stroke In	Stroke In	Volume In3	Comp Ratio	Hp	RPM	Propeller Weight Lbs	Lb/ Hp	Drive & Remarks
D-12E	V-1150-5	1927	12	4.500	6.000		1,145.1	5.30	435	2,300	700	1.61	Direct
D-12F	V-1150-7	1925	12	4.500	6.000		1,145.1	5.30	552	2,800	700	1.27	Direct
D-12G	V-1150-9	1929	12	4.500	6.000		1,145.1	5.30	435	2,300	626	1.44	Direct
D-12M	D-12M	1922	12	4.500	6.000		1,145.1	5.30	435	2,300	680	1.56	Direct, "M" for "Modernized"
V-1400	V-1400	1924	12	4.875	6.250	6.429	1,420.0	5.50	510/620	2,100	660/685	1.29/1.10	Direct, articulated con rod
V-1550	V-1550	1927	12	5.125	6.250	6.426	1,569.0	5.50	625	2,400	725-755	1.16/1.21	Direct, articulated con rod
GV-1550	GV-1550	1927	12	5.125	6.250	6.426	1,569.0	5.50	600	2,400	845	1.41	Geared 2:1, articulated con rod
GIV-1570	V-1570- 5/-7		12	5.125	6.250	6.426	1,569.0	5.80	600	2,450			Geared 7:5, articulated con rod
GIV-1570A1/A2	V-1570-11/-13		12	5.125	6.250	6.426	1,569.0	5.80	600	2,450	965	1.61	Geared 7:5, articulated con rod
GIV-1570-B	V-1570-21		12	5.125	6.250	6.426	1,569.0	6.10	600	2,450	965	1.61	Geared 7:5, articulated con rod
GIV-1570C1/C2	V-1570-27/-29	1931	12	5.125	6.250	6.426	1,569.0	6.10	600	2,450	925/935	1.54/1.56	Geared 7:5, articulated con rod
GIV-1570-E2	V-1570-33/-37		12	5.125	6.250	6.426	1,569.0	6.10	600	2,450	980/1020	1.63/1.70	Geared 7:5, articulated con rod
GIV-1570-EX	V-1570-45		12	5.125	6.250	6.426	1,569.0						Geared, Inverted
GIV-1570-EX	V-1570-49		12	5.125	6.250	6.426	1,569.0						Geared, Inverted
GIV-1570-F	V-1570-53	1932	12	5.125	6.250	6.588	1,589.0	6.25	600	2,450	980/1,020	1.63/1.70	Geared 7:5, articulated con rod
GIV-1570-F	V-1570-57	1933	12	5.125	6.250	6.588	1,589.0	6.25	675	2,450	980/1,020	1.45/1.51	Geared 7:5, articulated con rod
GIV-1570-F	V-1570-59	1933	12	5.125	6.250	6.588	1,589.0	7.25	675	2,450	980/1,020	1.45/1.51	Geared 7:5, articulated con rod
GIV-1570-F-2	V-1570	1935	12	5.125	6.250	6.588	1,589.0	7.25	675	2,450	996	1.48	Geared 7:5, articulated con rod
GIV-1570-TS	V-1570-61	1935	12	5.125	6.250	6.426	1,569.0	7.25	700	2,450	1,040	1.49	Geared 7:5, articulated con rod
GV-1570	V-1570- 3	1928	12	5.125	6.250	6.426	1,569.0	5.80	600	2,450	845	1.41	Geared 2:1, articulated con rod
GV-1570-B	V-1570-19	1931	12	5.125	6.250	6.426	1,569.0	6.10	600	2,450	965	1.61	Geared 2:1, articulated con rod
GV-1570-C	GV-1570C	1931	12	5.125	6.250	6.426	1,569.0	6.00	600	2,450			Geared, articulated con rod
GV-1570-F	GV-1570F	1932	12	5.125	6.250	6.588	1,589.0	6.25	600	2,450	970/985	1.62/1.64	Geared 2:1, articulated con rod
SGV-1570-F	SGV-1570F	1932	12	5.125	6.250	6.588	1,589.0	6.25	750	2,400	1,110	1.48	Geared 2:1, articulated con rod
SGV-1570F-4	V-1570	1935	12	5.125	6.250	6.588	1,589.0	6.50	705	2,450	1,080	1.53	Geared 2:1, articulated con rod
SV-1570-A	V-1570-15		12	5.125	6.250	6.426	1,569.0						Direct, articulated con rod
SV-1570-F	SV-1570F	1932	12	5.125	6.250	6.588	1,589.0	6.25	700	2,400	975	1.39	Direct, articulated con rod
V-1570	V-1570- 1	1928	12	5.125	6.250	6.426	1,569.0	5.80	625	2,400	755	1.21	Direct, articulated con rod
V-1570-A	V-1570- 9		12	5.125	6.250	6.426	1,569.0	6.10	600	2,400	885	1.48	Direct, articulated con rod
V-1570-B	V-1570-17		12	5.125	6.250	6.426	1,569.0	5.80	600	2,400	885	1.48	Direct, articulated con rod
V-1570-C1/C2	V-1570-23/25		12	5.125	6.250	6.426	1,569.0	6.10	600	2,400	850	1.42	Direct, articulated con rod
V-1570-CM	V-1570-39		12	5.125	6.250	6.426	1,569.0						Direct, "M" for "Modernized"
V-1570-CM	V-1570-41		12	5.125	6.250	6.426	1,569.0						Direct, "M" for "Modernized"
V-1570-E1/E2	V-1570-31/35		12	5.125	6.250	6.426	1,569.0	6.10	600	2,400	900	1.50	Direct, articulated con rod
V-1570-EN	V-1570-47		12	5.125	6.250	6.426	1,569.0						Direct, articulated con rod
V-1570-F	V-1570-51/55	1932	12	5.125	6.250	6.588	1,589.0	6.25	600	2,400	900	1.50	Direct, articulated con rod
	V-1570-54		12	5.125	6.250	6.588	1,589.0		600				
GV-1570F1		1936	12	5.125	6.250	6.588	1,589.0	6.50	625	2,450	995	1.59	Geared 2:1 or 7:5, articulated con rod
GV-1570F2		1936	12	5.125	6.250	6.588	1,589.0	7.25	675	2,450	1,000	1.48	Geared 7:5, articulated con rod

Bibliography

BOOKS

Anderson, John D. Jr., *A History of Aerodynamics*, Cambridge University Press, Cambridge, England, 1997.

Anderson, John D. Jr., *Introduction to Flight*, Fourth Edition, McGraw-Hill, Boston, 2000.

Andrews, C. F. and E. B. Morgan, *Supermarine Aircraft Since 1914*, Naval Institute Press, Annapolis, 1981.

Banks, F.R., *I Kept No Diary*, Airlife Publishing Limited, Shrewsbury, England, 1983.

Berliner, Don, *Victory Over the Wind*, Van Nostrand Reinhold Company, New York, 1983.

Biddle, Wayne, *Barons of the Sky*, Simon & Schuster, New York, 1991.

Bonney, Walter T., *The Heritage of Kitty Hawk*, W. W. Norton & Company, Inc., New York, 1962.

Bowers, Peter M., *Curtiss Aircraft—1907–1947*, Naval Institute Press, Annapolis, 1987.

Bruhn, E.F., *Analysis and Design of Airplane Structures*, Offset Publishing Company, Cincinnati, Ohio, 1945.

Byttebier, Hugo T., *The Curtiss D-12 Aero Engine*, Smithsonian Institution Press, Washington, D.C., 1972.

Chatfield, Charles Hugh and Charles Fayette Taylor, *The Airplane and Its Engine*, McGraw-Hill Book Company, New York, 1932.

Combs, Harry with Martin Caidin, *Kill Devil Hill*, Houghton Mifflin Company, Boston, 1979.

Dean, Francis H., *America's Hundred Thousand*, Schiffer Publishing Ltd., Atglen, Pennsylvania, 1997.

Doolittle, James H. with Carroll V. Glines, *I Could Never Be So Lucky Again*, Bantam Books, New York, 1991.

Domonoske, Arthur B. and Volney C. Finch, *Aircraft Engines*, John Wiley & Sons, Inc., New York, 1936.

Dyke, A.L., *Dyke's Aircraft Engine Instructor*, The Goodheart-Willcox Company, Inc., Chicago, 1928.

Emme, Eugene M., Editor, *Two Hundred Years of Flight in America*, American Astronautical Society, San Diego, California, 1997.

Emme, Eugene M., *Aeronautics and Astronautics*, National Aeronautics and Space Administration, U.S. Government Printing Office, Washington, D.C., 1961.

Faulconer, Thomas P., *Introduction to Aircraft Design*, McGraw-Hill Book Company, New York, 1942.

Forden, Lesley, *Glory Gamblers*, Ballantine Books, New York, 1961.

Fink, Augusta, *Time and the Terraced Land*, Howell–North Books, Berkeley, 1966.

Foxworth, Thomas G., *The Speed Seekers*, Doubleday & Company, Inc., New York, 1974.

Fraas, Arthur P., *Aircraft Power Plants*, McGraw-Hill Book Company, Inc., New York, 1943.

Friedman, Norman, *U.S. Aircraft Carriers*, Naval Institute Press, Annapolis, Maryland, 1983.

Gibbs-Smith, Charles H., *The Invention of the Aeroplane (1799–1909)*, Taplinger Publishing Co., Inc., New York, 1966.

Gillingham, Robert Cameron, *The Rancho San Pedro*, Cole–Holmquist Press, 1983.

Goodstein, Judith R., *Millikan's School*, W. W. Norton & Company, New York, 1991.

Gruse, William A. and Donald R. Stevens, *Chemical Technology of Petroleum*, McGraw-Hill Book Company, Inc., New York, 1960.

Gunston, Bill, *The Development of Piston Aero Engines*, Patrick Stephens Limited, England, 1993.

Hallion, Richard, editor, *The Wright Brothers, Heirs of Prometheus*, Smithsonian Institution Press, Washington, D.C., 1978.

Hanle, Paul A., *Bringing Aerodynamics to America*, The MIT Press, Cambridge, Massachusetts, 1982.

Harris, Sherwood, *The First to Fly*, Simon and Schuster, New York, 1970.

Hemke, Paul E., *Elementary Applied Aerodynamics*, Prentice-Hall, Inc., New York, 1946.

Hirsch, Robert S., *Schneider Trophy Racers*, MBI Publishing Company, Osceola, Wisconsin, 1993.

Hobson, editor, *Modern Petroleum Technology*, Fourth edition, John Wiley & Sons, New York, 1973.

Hoerner, Sighard F., *Fluid-Dynamic Drag*, Revised, Published by Author, Brick Town, New Jersey, 1965.

Howard, Fred, *Wilbur and Orville*, Alfred A. Knopf, New York, 1987.

James, Derek N., *Schneider Trophy Aircraft, 1913–1931*, Putnam & Company, Limited, London, 1981.

Juptner, Joseph P., *U.S. Civil Aircraft Series*, (various volumes) Tab Aero Division of McGraw-Hill, Inc., Blue Ridge Summit, Pennsylvania.

Käsmann, Ferdinand, *World Speed Record Aircraft*, Putnam Aeronautical Books, London, 1990.

Kerley, Robert, *Military Aviation Fuel Characteristics, 1917–1945*, Society of Automotive Engineers, Inc., Warrendale, Pennsylvania, 1993.

Kimes, Beverly Rae, Editor, *Packard, A History of the Motor Car and the Company*, Princeton Publishing Inc., Princeton, New Jersey, 1978.

Leslie, Stuart W., *Boss Kettering*, Columbia University Press, New York, 1983.

Lieberg, Owen S., *The First Air Race*, Doubleday & Company, Inc., Garden City, New York, 1974.

Loftin, Laurence K., Jr., *Quest for Performance: The Evolution of Modern Aircraft*, National Aeronautics and Space Administration, SP-468, Washington, D.C., 1985.

Matthews, Birch, *Wet Wings & Drop Tanks*, Schiffer Publishing Ltd., Atglen, Pennsylvania, 1993.

Mead, Cary Hoge, *Wings Over the World, the Life of George Jackson Mead*, The Swannet Press, Wauwatosa, Wisconsin, 1971.

Miller, Ronald and David Sawers, *The Technical Development of Modern Aviation*, Praeger Publishers, New York, 1970.

Millikan, Clark B., *Aerodynamics of the Airplane*, John Wiley & Sons, Inc., New York, 1941.

Nelson, W. L., *Petroleum Refinery Engineering*, McGraw-Hill Book Company, Inc., New York, 1941.

Nelson, Wilbur C., *Airplane Propeller Principles*, John Wiley & Sons, Inc., New York, 1944.

Niles, Alfred S. and Joseph S. Newell, *Airplane Structures*, John Wiley & Sons, Incorporated, New York, 1938.

Otis, Arthur S., *Elements of Aeronautics*, World Book Company, New York, 1941.

Pagé, Victor W., *Modern Aircraft*, The Norman W. Henley Publishing Company, New York, 1928.

Ricardo, Sir Harry, *The Ricardo Story*, Society of Automotive Engineers, Inc., Warrendale, Pennsylvania, 1992.

Shanley, F., *Weight-Strength Analysis of Aircraft Structures*, McGraw-Hill Book Company, Incorporated, New York, 1952.

Shiner, John F., *Foulois and the U.S. Army Air Corps, 1931–1935*, U.S. Government Printing Office, Washington, D.C., 1983.

Suzuki, Takashi, *The Romance of Engines*, Society of Automotive Engineers, Inc., Warrendale, Pennsylvania, 1997.

Sweetman, Bill, *High Speed Flight*, Jane's Publishing Company, Limited, London, 1985.

Teichmann, Frederick K., *Airplane Design Manual*, Pitman Publishing Corporation, New York, 1939.

U.S. Navy, *Dictionary of American Naval Fighting Ships*, Vol. II, Government Printing Office, Washington, D.C., 1963.

U.S. Navy, *United States Naval Aviation, 1910–1970*, NAVAIR 00-80P-1 U.S. Government Printing Office, Washington, D.C., 1970

Villard, Henry Serrano, *Contact! The Story of the Early Birds*, Bonanza Books, New York, 1968.

Wagner, Ray, *American Combat Planes*, Third Edition, Doubleday & Company, Inc., Garden City, New York, 1982.

Whitney, Daniel D., *Vees for Victory*, Schiffer Publishing Ltd., Atglen, Pennsylvania, 1998.

Wohl, Robert, *A Passion for Wings*, Yale University Press, New Haven, 1994.

Wolko, Howard S. (editor), *The Wright Flyer, An Engineering Perspective*, Smithsonian Institution, Washington, D.C. 1987.

Wood, Karl D., *Technical Aerodynamics*, McGraw-Hill Book Company, Inc., 1947.

von Kármán, Theodore, *The Wind and Beyond*, Little, Brown and Company, Boston, 1967.

JOURNALS

Ackroyd, J. A. D. and P. J. Lamont, *The Aeronautical Journal* (Paper No. 2486), February 2000, pp. 53–58.

Cole, Martin and H. L. (Herm) Schreiner, "Charles Willard, The Exhibition Years," *American Aviation Historical Society Journal*, Vol. 19, No. 3, 1974, pp. 177–191.

Eltscher, Lou, "Curtiss-Wright: Greatness and Decline," *American Aviation Historical Society Journal*, Vol. 39, No. 4, 1994, pp. 260–274.

Forden, Lesley N., "The Dole Race, Part I," *American Aviation Historical Society Journal*, Vol. 20, No. 3, 1975, pp. 151–160.

Forden, Lesley N., "The Dole Race, Part II," *American Aviation Historical Society Journal*, Vol. 20, No. 4, 1975, pp. 260–267.

Heron, S. D. and Harold A. Beatty, "Aircraft Fuels," *Journal of the Aeronautical Sciences*, Vol. 5, No. 12, pp. 463–479.

Hubner, William H., "Prospects of fuels of Higher Octane Number in the Transport Field," *Journal of the Aeronautical Sciences*, Vol. 7, No. 8, June 1940, pp. 319–331.

Kavelaars, H.C., "The DC-2, the Dutch, and the 1934 Melbourne Race," *American Aviation Historical Society Journal*, 1984, Vol. 29, No. 4, pp. 256–274.

Kettering, C.F., "Fuels and Engines for High Power and Greater Efficiency," *Society of Automotive Engineers Journal* (Transactions), Vol. 53, No. 6, pp. 352–357.

Luburg, G.A., "Wing Radiator Development," *American Society of Mechanical Engineers Transactions*, Vol. 54, No. 1, AER-54-5, pp. 37–40.

Meilinger, Phillip S., "The Impact of Technology and Design Choice on the Development of U.S. Fighter Aircraft," *American Aviation Historical Society Journal*, 1991, Vol. 36, No. 1, pp. 60–69.

Molson, K.M., "Early Curtiss Aircraft Engines," *American Aviation Historical Society Journal*, Vol. 11, No. 2, 1966, pp. 133–137.

Molson, K.M., "The JN-4 (Can)," *American Aviation Historical Society Journal*, Vol. 17, No. 4, 1972, pp. 225–241.

Ogston, Alexander, "A Short History of Aviation Gasoline Development, 1903–1980," *Aeronautical Journal*, December 1981, pp. 441–450.

Phillips, Ed, "Mystery Ship," *American Aviation Historical Society Journal*, 1982, Vol. 27, No. 4, pp. 286–295.

Phillips, Ed, "Woolaroc!" *American Aviation Historical Society Journal*, 1985, Vol. 30, No. 1, pp. 24–31.

Phillips, William H., "Recollections of the Langley Memorial Aero Lab," *American Aviation Historical Society Journal*, 1992, Vol. 37, No. 2, pp. 117–127.

Rossano, Geoffrey, "When Curtiss Racers Ruled the Roost," *American Aviation Historical Society Journal*, 1985, Vol. 30, No. 2, pp. 109–113.

Thornton, Earl A., "MIT, Jerome C. Hunsaker and the Origins of Aeronautical Engineering—1913–1916," *American Aviation Historical Society Journal*, 1998, Vol. 43, No. 4, pp. 306–315.

Townend, H.C.H., "The Townend Ring," *The Journal of the Royal Aeronautical Society*, Vol. XXXIV, 1930, pp. 813–848.

Weeks, E.D., "Curtiss Reims Racer," *American Aviation Historical Society Journal*, 1965, Vol. 10, No. 3, pp. 186–189.

PERIODICALS

Anon., "Modern Radiators for Aeronautical Engines: The New Lamblin Radiator Described," *Aviation*, May 19, 1924, pp. 536–537.

Army Air Service News Letter, *Development of Aeronautical Engines by the Army and Navy*, Vol. 5, No. 9, 1921. See also National Advisory Committee for Aeronautics Technical Memorandum No. 9, March 3, 1921.

Berliner, Don, "Engines That Made History," *Model Aviation*, February 1978, pp. 8–15, passim.

Chatfield, Charles Hugh, "Controllable Pitch Propellers in Transport Service," *Aviation*, June 1933, pp. 180–181.

Curtiss, Glenn H., "Winning the International Cup for America," *Country Life in America*, Vol. 17, No. 1, November 1909, pp. 27–31.

Fanshier, Keith J., "The New Aviation Gasolines," *Aviation*, May 1935, pp. 295–296.

Lombard, A. E. and T. P. Wright, "Pitch Control," *Aviation*, December 1933, pp. 376–378.

McLaughlin, George F., "Lieut. Williams' Racing Seaplane," *Aero Digest*, September 1927, pp. 286–288.

Mock, Richard M., "Retractable Landing Gears," *Aviation*, February 1933, pp. 33–37.

Neville, Leslie E., "The S.A.E. Discusses Fuel," *Aviation*, November 1930, pp. 273–277.

North, J.D., "Air-Cooled Engine Cowling, A Historical Survey With an Account of the Latest Work on the Townend Ring" *Aircraft Engineering*, April 1934, pp. 100–110.

Rankin, Robert H., "The Gordon Bennett Racers," *Popular Aviation*, February 1937, pp. 23–24, 62.

Theodorsen, Theodore, "The Fundamental Principles of the NACA Cowling," *Journal of the Aeronautical Sciences*, Vol. 5, No. 5, March 1938, pp. 169–174.

Vultee, Gerard F., "Fabrication of the Lockheed Vega Airplane Fuselage," *S.A.E. Journal*, November 1928.

MISCELLANEOUS

New York Times, various years and editions

Official Program, Grande Semaine d'Aviation de la Champagne, 1909.

TECHNICAL REPORTS & PAPERS

Abbott, Ira H., *Airfoils, Significance and Early Development*, American Institute of Aeronautics and Astronautics Paper No. 80-3033, presented at the Wing Design Symposium, Dayton, Ohio, March 1980.

Anon., *Summary of NACA Technical Memo No. 925 (Effect of Wing Loading, Aspect Ratio and Span Loading on Flight Performance)*, Vega Airplane Company, Report No. R-116, March 1940.

Army Air Corps, *Handbook of Instructions for Airplane Designers*, Vol. I, Part II, Aerodynamics, Revision 3, July 1, 1939.

Army Air Corps Materiel Division, *Performance Test of Boeing XP-936 Airplane Equipped With Pratt & Whitney SR-1340-G Engine*, Wright Field, May 10, 1932. (The XP-936 was a prototype of the P-26 series aircraft.)

Army Air Corps Materiel Division, *Performance Test of Seversky P-35 Airplane Equipped With Pratt & Whitney R-1830-9 Engine*, Wright Field, November 18, 1937.

Bobbitt, Percy J., "Langley Airfoil–Research Program," *Advanced Technology Airfoil Research*, National Aeronautics & Space Administration Conference Publication No. 2045, Part I, Airfoil Research, Vol. 1, 1978, pp. 11–37.

Bona, C.F., *Italian High-Speed Airplane Engines*, National Advisory Committee for Aeronautics Report No. 944, June 1940.

Brevoort, M.J., George W. Stickle and Herman H. Ellerbrock, Jr., *Cooling Tests of a Single-Row Radial Engine With Several NACA Cowlings*, National Advisory Committee for Aeronautics Report No. 596, August 20, 1936.

Biermann, David and William H. Herrnstein, Jr., *The Drag of airplane wheels, Wheel Fairings and Landing Gears—Nonretractable and Partly Retractable Landing Gears*, National Advisory Committee for Aeronautics Report No. 518, June 21, 1934.

Collected Reports on British High Speed Aircraft for the 1931 Schneider Trophy Contest, Aeronautical Research Committee Report and Memoranda No. 1575, January 1934.

Dearborn, C. H. and Abe Silverstein, *Drag Analysis of Single-Engine Military Airplanes Tested in the NACA Full-Scale Wind Tunnel*, National Advisory Committee for Aeronautics, Wartime Report L-489, October 1940.

Dearborn, C.H., Abe Silverstein and J. P. Reeder, *Tests of XP-40 Airplane in N.A.C.A. Full-Scale Tunnel*, National Advisory Committee for Aeronautics Memorandum Report (for the Army Air Corps Materiel Division), May 16, 1939.

DeFrance, Smith J., *Aerodynamic Characteristics of P-26A Airplane With and Without Split Trailing-Edge Flaps*, National Advisory Committee for Aeronautics Memorandum Report (for the Army Air Corps Materiel Division), June 23, 1934.

DeFrance, Smith J., *The Aerodynamic Effect of a Retractable Landing Gear*, National Advisory Committee for Aeronautics Technical Note No. 456, March 16, 1933.

Dickinson, H.O., W. S. James and R. V. Kleinschmidt, *General Analysis of Airplane Radiator Problems*, National Advisory Committee for Aeronautics Report No. 59, 1919.

Dickinson, H. O. and R. V. Kleinschmidt, *Synopsis of Aeronautic Radiator Investigations for Years 1917 and 1918*, National Advisory Committee for Aeronautics Report No. 43, 1920.

Diehl, Walter S., *The Calculation of Take-Off Run*, National Advisory Committee for Aeronautics Report No. 450, September, 1932.

Fliedner, C.S., *Condensed Data on the Aircraft Engines of the World*, National Advisory Committee for Aeronautics Report No. 303. April, 1929.

Herrnstein, William H., Jr., and David Biermann, *The Drag of Airplane Wheels, Wheel Fairings, and Landing Gears—III*, National Advisory Committee for Aeronautics Report No. 522, November 21, 1934.

Lednicer, David A., *Aerodynamics of the Bell P-39 Airacobra and P-63 Kingcobra*, Society of Automotive Engineers Paper No. 00GATC-55, 2000.

Margoulis, W., *Notes on Specifications for French Airplane Competitions*, National Advisory Committee for Aeronautics Report No. 20, October 1920.

Margoulis, W., *The Gordon Bennett Airplane Cup*, National Advisory Committee for Aeronautics Report No. 50, April 1921.

Ober, Shatswell, *Estimation of the Variation of Thrust Horsepower With Air Speed*, National Advisory Committee for Aeronautics Report No. 446, February 1933.

Paris, Auguste Jean, Jr., *A New Process for the Production of Aircraft Engine Fuels*, National Advisory Committee for Aeronautics Report No. 42, circa 1920.

Pinkel, Benjamin, *Heat-Transfer Processes in Air-Cooled Engine Cylinders*, National Advisory Committee for Aeronautics Report No. 612, June 11, 1937.

Pratt & Whitney Aircraft, *Engine Models & Characteristics*, Report No. PWA-SD14, January 1, 1945.

Pratt & Whitney Aircraft, *The Aircraft Engine and its Operation*, Report No. PWA 01.100, December 1952.

Schey, Oscar W., Vern G. Rollin and Herman H. Ellenbrock, Jr., *The Effect of Increased Cooling Surface on Performance of Aircraft Engine Cylinders as Shown by Tests of the NACA Cylinder*, National Advisory Committee for Aeronautics Report No. 779, July 1, 1944.

Silverstein, Abe, and F. R. Nickle, *Test of the XP-39 Airplane in the N.A.C.A. Full-Scale Wind Tunnel*, National Advisory Committee for Aeronautics Memorandum Report, September 27, 1939.

Smith, R.H., *Resistance and Cooling Power of Various Radiators*, National Advisory Committee for Aeronautics Report No. 261, 1928.

Theodorsen, Theodore, M. J. Brevoort and George W. Stickle, *Cooling of Airplane Engines at Low Air Speeds*, National Advisory Committee for Aeronautics Report No. 593, June 2, 1936.

Theodorsen, Theodore, M.J. Brevoort, George W. Stickle and M. N. Gough, *Full-Scale Tests of a New Type NACA Nose-Slot Cowling*, National Advisory Committee for Aeronautics Report No. 595, June 5, 1936.

Weick, Fred E., *Drag and Cooling With Various Forms of Cowling for a Whirlwind Engine in a Cabin Fuselage*, National Advisory Committee for Aeronautics Report No. 301, November 1928.

Weick, Fred E., *Full Scale Investigation of the Drag of a Wing Radiator*, National Advisory Committee for Aeronautics Report No. 318, September, 1929.

Weick, Fred E., *Full Scale Wind Tunnel Tests on Several Metal Propellers Having Different Blade Forms*, National Advisory Committee for Aeronautics Report No. 340, March 18, 1929.

Weick, Fred E., *Tests of Four Racing Type Airfoils in the Twenty-Foot Propeller Research Tunnel*, National Advisory Committee for Aeronautics Report No. 317, September 1929.

Weick, Fred E., *The Drag of a J-5 Radial Air-Cooled Engine*, National Advisory Committee for Aeronautics Report No. 292, July 1928.

Wetmore, J.W., *The Rolling Friction of Several Airplane Wheels and Tires and the Effect of Rolling Friction on Take-Off*, National Advisory Committee for Aeronautics Report No. 583, undated.

Wood, Donald H., *Full Scale Wind Tunnel Test of a Propeller With the Diameter Changed by Cutting Off the Blade Tips*, National Advisory Committee for Aeronautics Report No. 351, December 10, 1929.

Ziembinski, S., *Possible Improvements in Gasoline Engines*, Premier Congres International de la Navigation Aerienne, Paris, November, 1921, Vol. IV. Republished by the National Advisory Committee for Aeronautics in Technical Memorandum No. 182, January, 1923.

Index